THE ULTIMATE CHRISTMAS

Over 240 projects to help you make, bake and decorate everything for Christmas!

Reader's Digest

The Reader's Digest Association, Inc.

Montreal • Pleasantville, New York • London • Sydney • Singapore

Contents

Christmas Craft

Common household items such as scissors, pencil, ruler, white paper and water, are not listed under what you will need for each project; specific or unusual items will be found in the "You Will Need" lists.
For recipes, salt and pepper are not listed where they are only required for seasoning to taste.

❗ *Always make sure candles stand inside a glass container, and never leave burning candles unattended.*

Chapter 2
Joy of Giving

Christmas Cheer

❶ *Several of the projects in this book are ideal for children to
do. Always make sure children are supervised and have adult
help when cutting out items, or cooking.*

Christmas Cooking

Chapter 5

Appetizers and Brunch

Chapter 6

Main Meals

Introduction

It has been said that Christmas is not just a date but a state of mind, an outpouring of love and good fellowship that is anticipated in delicious excitement. Now is the time to revel in the sights, the sounds, the aromas, and the joy of Christmas and spend time with family and friends. Let this delightful treasury guide you through the hectic holiday season and show you hundreds of ways to add your own personal touch.

The Ultimate Christmas book promises you your best Christmas ever—a celebration that lives up to your most cherished dreams and does not overwhelm you in the process. Each section of this beautifully illustrated book sets out a host of fabulous ideas and explains, step by step, exactly how to achieve them with a minimum of fuss.

Festive Home helps you set the mood for the holidays. Starting with color schemes and ornaments for your tree, it also shows how to use natural materials for wreaths and table decorations. And you'll get a chance to indulge your sewing skills with some stunning but simple table linens that are truly heirlooms-in-the-making.

Continue your enjoyment of crafts by making your own gifts—in **Joy of Giving** you'll find lots of inspiring ideas for everyone on your gift list, using all kinds of fun techniques including knitting, patchwork, embroidery, beading, and tin work. We'll even show you how to wrap up and present everything in style.

Because children love to be creative, we've included **Just for Kids** to ensure that their lively minds and busy hands feel included in holiday preparations and activities. You'll find cards and decorations to make, cakes to bake, and a special "Rudolph the Red-Nosed Reindeer" puppet show to put on, complete with patterns for easy-to-make puppets, props, and scenery.

Christmas Cooking rounds up all those wonderful traditional recipes without which no Christmas would be complete. From mouth-watering snacks and appetizers, through Christmas dinner with all the trimmings, to sumptuous desserts, seasonal baking, and tasty treats for giving, the emphasis is on clever ideas and making ahead, so you can enjoy the best of both worlds—the unrivaled pleasures of Christmas cooking…and then getting out of the kitchen in time to enjoy the festivities with your guests.

All your efforts will culminate in **Holiday Entertaining,** where we show you how to put together six different parties with food and craft ideas including easy-to-prepare menus, planning advice, and enchanting layouts for table settings, including professional-looking floral decorations, atmospheric candles, napkin folding, place cards, invitations, and favors. Your parties are sure to be the memorable occasions that will carry you and your loved ones through to next year—and another wonderful Christmas!

> *"I wish we could put up some Christmas spirit in jars and open a jar of it every month"*
>
> Harlan Miller

Christmas Crafts

★ have a merry christmas ★

CHAPTER ONE

FESTIVE HOME

Set an impressive scene for the holidays by
decorating your home with your own beautiful
creations—from clever handmade tree ornaments
to wreaths and table decorations featuring candles
and natural materials.

Christmas Tree Gallery

The centerpiece of the home during the holidays is the Christmas tree and for many people, the festive season doesn't truly begin until its branches are beautifully decorated with brilliant lights, dazzling ornaments, and treasured family mementos.

For a Monochromatic Tree

Using only one color with a white complement creates an elegant effect. Gold, for example, is eternally elegant, and reflective white lights make the ornaments sparkle. Stand a tree close to a mirror for increased impact, but make sure your tree is decorated all around. Simple lengths of satin-edged ribbon embellish the sophisticated effect.

For a Traditional Tree

For a stunning look, make sure your tree is laden with ornaments. The traditional colors of red and gold, mixed with green, shown left, suits every home and welcomes your guests.

For Special Focus Ornaments

To provide an eye-catching feature, include some larger and more detailed ornaments such as the stained glass ball below. Plain balls can have designs applied with glass outliner, which is available in many colors. Once dry, the area within the outliner can be painted with glass paint.

Styrofoam shapes are sold in many sizes: brush them with white (PVA) glue, then roll in glitter or wrap in shiny ribbon yarn. Add flat-backed jewels applied with glue, or sequins with glass-headed pins pushed through the central holes.

For Dough Ornaments

This dough is a quick way to make new decorations such as this angel, painted cream with a flat (matte) varnish.

1 Take 2 cups (8 oz./230 g) all-purpose flour, 1 cup (7 oz./200 g) salt and 1 cup (8 fl oz./250 ml) water. Mix the dry ingredients with half the water and knead in the bowl to a smooth dough. Gradually add more water until the dough is firm, but do not allow the dough to become sticky.

2 Continue to knead the dough for about 10 minutes, then roll it out on baking parchment and use cookie cutters or a small knife and a template to cut shapes. Pierce a hole for a hanging loop with a toothpick, making it ⅛ in. (3 mm) larger than it needs to be, because it will close up while baking. Bake at 250°F (120°C/Gas Mark ½) until the dough has hardened.

3 Paint with an undercoat of flat latex (matte emulsion) and allow to dry, then use any acrylic or craft paint to decorate, and finish with a gloss or flat (matte) varnish.

tip

Look out for the way Christmas trees are styled in malls, hotels and restaurants. Colors and ornaments change year by year—don't be afraid of adopting new ideas.

For a Country-Style Tree

Dress your tree with simple-shaped, plain ornaments and feature hearts made from plain and gingham fabrics. Use imitation candle lights for a cozy Christmas in the country appeal.

Continue your theme through to the tree's container or surrounding objects, such as a wooden nativity scene, or adapt the tree skirt shown on page 28.

For a Blend of Pretty Foliage

Red poinsettias and gold-sprayed weeping fig leaves are surrounded by clear lights to make a sumptuous tree. Potted poinsettias can be placed around the foot of the tree to echo the decorations. Holly, ivy, and cinnamon sticks can all be colored with gold spray paint, and tied to the tree with gold cord.

For Ribbon Decorations

These large, colorful paper bows measure 8 in. (20 cm) across. Make two large loops, each from a strip measuring 16 in. (45 cm) in length. Then cut one 18 in. (46 cm) length for tails and trim each end to a "V" to prevent fraying. Pinch or gather the loops and tails at the center and bind with a separate piece of ribbon. Secure at the back with sticky tape. Fix to the tree with a piece of wire through the binding.

Layer two ribbons of different widths and type, such as wide satin and narrow tartan. Experiment with wire-edged ribbon, which works well for large bows and is available in many dramatic finishes.

Ribbon decorations fill the tree and can act as a quick and economical way to change the tone of your decorations: A bright red will be cheery whereas a deep burgundy will give a more sophisticated result.

For a Tree Topper

Soft loops and long tails of satin ribbon, with a cluster of shiny ball ornaments in toning colors make a striking and unusual topping to a modern-style tree.

For a Snow-Covered Tree

For a stylish look, discard bright colors and decorate your tree with swathes of white marabou feathers or loops of fancy "eyelash" yarn. Choose pale-colored ornaments to a few basic shapes. Top the tree with a whimsical star and carry the look through to the tree stand—use a plain silver bucket or pail.

For a Tree with a Theme

Amuse your visitors by trimming your tree with surprising motifs—gorgeous jeweled butterflies, tiny toys, miniature dolls, or fine china cups. Plan your theme early so you will have lots of time to collect or create ornaments in the theme you choose.

Pretty Pink Angel

You will need:

- tracing paper
- double-sided tape
- used-up ball-point pen or embossing tool
- superglue

For the Standing Angel

- 2 sheets heavy-duty silver foil, 7 1/4 in. x 11 1/2 in. (185 mm x 295 mm)
- pink glass paint
- 110 small pink metallic beads
- 1 sheet heavy-duty copper foil, 11 1/2 in. x 8 1/4 in. (279 mm x 432 mm/A4)
- 6 pieces fine-gauge metallic pink wire, 4 in. (10 cm) long

For the Hanging Angel

- 6 in. (15 cm) square heavy-duty silver foil,
- 5 in. (13 cm) square heavy-duty copper foil
- 1 small piece of heavy-duty copper foil for face
- 2 pieces fine gauge brass wire 6 in. (15 cm) long, and 3 pieces 8 in. (20cm) long
- 2 medium pearl beads
- 46 small gold beads
- 44 copper seed beads
- 5 in. (13 cm) gold metallic thread

Perk up a small side table or seasonal display with this sweet smiling angel, or go crazy and add a host of sparkling angels to shine against rich green foliage.

For the Standing Angel

1 Trace off the templates from page 264 and enlarge them by 150 percent. Secure the body and head templates to the back of one piece of silver foil with double-sided tape. Working on a soft surface, take a used-up ball-point pen, or embossing tool, to trace over the star shape, scalloped line and facial features to create an embossed effect on the other side.

2 Do not trace the outer line. Instead use sharp scissors to cut out the body, following the line of the template edge.

3 Pour a little glass paint onto an old saucer. Test the color on a scrap of silver foil and dilute according to the manufacturers' instructions until you can achieve a translucent effect. Work on the side of the foil with embossed lines raised. Flood the top section of the body with the paint, keeping the raised star area free of color. Leave to dry.

4 Secure the wing template onto the second sheet of silver foil and cut around the edge. Using superglue, affix pink beads around the edges, leaving a gap at the bottom where the wings will be attached to the body.

5 Secure the star border template to the piece of brass foil, and emboss as in Step 1. Cut out the border. Using the photograph as a guide, affix the raised surface to the bottom of angel's body with double-sided tape to create an imprinted effect.

6 Bend the body into a cone shape, with an overlap on the back edge, and secure with double-sided tape. Use tape to secure the neck inside the cone. Add the wings with a center strip of tape. Fill any gaps where the wings meet the body with pink beads.

7 Take the six lengths of pink wire and create a spiral at one end. Gently twist three lengths together and tidy any excess wire into curls at the forehead. Affix to the top of the angel's head with a small piece of double-sided tape. Repeat for the other side.

For the Hanging Angel

Trace the templates on page 265 and use to cut out and emboss the foil pieces as for the Standing Angel, using the photograph as a guide. Glue the layers together. Use brass wire for the legs, bend over the end of the wire and add one pearl for each foot. Thread 20 small gold beads onto each wire leg, secure by bending over the end of the wire. For the hair and halo, thread six gold beads onto an 8-in. (20-cm) length of wire and position them centrally. Bend ends of the wire down and curl ends into spirals for hair. Add a second piece of curled wire to each side by inserting into the last bead. Use superglue to affix embellishments. Glue copper seed beads evenly to wings. Add a hanging loop using the gold metallic thread.

Beaded Decorations

Add a personal touch to seasonal decorations using simple beading techniques to make these eye-catching ornaments. They are lovely on the tree or use them as embellishments on gifts.

You will need:

For the Beaded Star

- 27 1/2 in. (70 cm) of 24-gauge (0.6–0.8mm) silver wire
- iridescent 1/4 in. (5 mm) seed beads
- 2 blue round beads
- 2 glass beads
- 1 droplet bead

For the Festive Spiral

- 47 in. (120 cm) of red 24-gauge wire
- iridescent 1/4 in. (5 mm) seed beads
- 1 larger glass bead
- 2 rounded disk beads
- pearly sequins
- wooden spoon

For the Beaded Star

1 Tape one end of the wire 5 in. (12 cm) from the end, to prevent the beads sliding off as you work. About 1 1/4 in. (3 cm) from one end, bend the wire to make an angle, then bend the wire again to form a zig-zag shape. Make a total of ten bends at 1 1/4-in. (3-cm) intervals along the wire.

2 Thread on enough iridescent beads to fill the zig-zag area of the wire. Once complete, twist the wire from the end of the zig-zags around the taped end of the wire.

3 Remove the tape, form a loop and twist the wire around itself to secure it. Onto the free end of the wire, which hangs down into the middle of the star, thread one iridescent bead and a sequence of the larger beads to take up 1 3/4 in. (4.5 cm) of wire. Trim the end of the wire and bend it over.

4 Finally, gently shape the wire into the star, making sure the angles are more or less even.

For the Festive Spiral

1 Thread an iridescent bead onto the wire then fold the wire in half making sure the bead is positioned at the bottom fold of the wire. Thread both strands of the wire through a glass bead and two disk beads.

2 Thread iridescent beads and sequins alternately onto the double strand of wire for about 16 in. (40 cm). Twist the wires together at the top for 2 1/2 in. (6 cm) and bend it into a loop. Twist the wire back around itself to secure it and trim the excess.

3 Bend the beaded wire around the handle of a wooden spoon to shape it into a coil. Carefully remove the handle, leaving a spiral shape.

Lace-Trimmed Cones

Give your tree an elegant green, gold and white theme this Christmas with these dainty paper cones trimmed with ribbon, lace and a pretty doily. Perfect for popping in some popcorn.

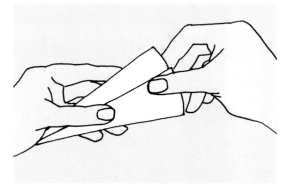

You will need:

For each Cone

• sheet of firm white paper

• a compass

• double-sided tape

• white paper doily

• 6 in. (15 cm) green organdy ribbon, 2-in. (5-cm) wide

• paper (white PVA) glue

• 6 in. (15 cm) gold lace trim, ¹/₂-in. (1-cm) wide

• 1 blue and 1 green feather

• 10 in. (25 cm) fine gold cord

1 Cut a square 5 in. x 5 in. (13 cm x 13 cm) from a sheet of firm white paper. Place the point of a compass at one corner of the square and draw a quarter circle with a radius of 5 in. (13 cm), joining the adjacent corners. Cut out.

2 Roll the quarter circle of paper into a cone shape and secure the straight edges with double-sided tape. Cut a 1¹/₂-in. (4-cm) strip from the doily to fit around the top of the cone. Stick the strip to the cone with double-sided tape, so that its lacy border protrudes about ¹/₄ in. (5 mm) above the edge.

3 Stick double-sided tape along one edge of the green organdy ribbon and attach it just below the doily. Trim to fit at the back. Glue the gold lace along the seam between the ribbon and doily, tucking a blue and a green feather underneath. Make a small hole on either side of the cone and thread through gold cord for hanging.

tip

To speed up the marking and cutting of the cones, cut out all the paper squares first and mark the quarter-circle on one of them. Place one or more squares neatly underneath it and cut the curved edges of them all at once.

Hanging Tree Sachets

Hand-stitched sachets add another dimension to Christmas tree decorations and can be filled with delicious Christmas aromas, chocolates or small gifts. There's a style to suit every tree.

Country-Style Heart

You will need:

- tracing paper
- 5½ in. x 11 in. (14 cm x 28 cm) burlap (hessian cloth)
- scrap of red-and-white gingham
- 6-strand cotton embroidery floss, one skein of red
- crewel needle
- handful cloves

1 Trace the large and small heart templates given on page 266 and enlarge by 150 percent. Use these tracings as pattern pieces to cut out two large heart shapes from the burlap and one small heart shape from red-and-white gingham.

2 Using all six strands of the red embroidery floss and a crewel needle, stitch the gingham heart centrally to one of the burlap hearts with running stitch.

3 Lightly crush the cloves to release their scent and place them in the center of the second burlap heart. Place the first heart on top and pin together around the edge. Beginning at the center top, use the red embroidery floss to stitch around the edge with running stitch.

4 Before you cut the thread, make a hanging loop and secure at the back of the heart with a few back stitches.

Organdy Gift Bag

You will need:

- 4½ in. x 13 in. (11 cm x 32 cm) organdy
- 12 in. (30 cm) matching cord

1 Fold the organdy in half and machine-stitch the sides taking a ½ in. (1 cm) seam.

2 Turn the top 1½ in. (4 cm) of fabric to the wrong side and make two rows of stitching ½ in. (1 cm) apart, the top one ¾ in. (2 cm.) from the top edge. Turn bag right side out, thread cord through the channel, knot the ends and fill bag with gifts.

Christmas Cross-Stitch

You will need:

For the Heart Sachet

- 14½ in. x 4 in. (37 cm x 10 cm) 26-count white evenweave cotton or linen
- 6-strand cotton embroidery floss, in red
- crewel needle
- 8 in. (20 cm) narrow colored cord

For the Christmas Tree Sachet

- 16 in. x 4 in. (40 cm x 10 cm) 26-count white evenweave cotton or linen
- 6-strand cotton embroidery floss, in green and red
- crewel needle
- 8 in. (20 cm) narrow colored cord

1 Lay the linen flat and, using contrast colored thread, sew a row of stitches across the fabric from the middle of a long and a short side.

2 The shorter row of stitches marks the base fold of the sachet. Measure ¾ in. (2 cm) from this row along the longer row of tacking for the starting point of the stitching.

3 Starting at the base of the motif and following the chart, stitch the cross-stitches over two threads of fabric in each direction, using two strands of the appropriate color embroidery floss and a crewel needle.

4 Once the embroidery is complete, iron from the wrong side on a padded surface. Fold the fabric in half along the short row of tacking with the right side inside. Hand- or machine-stitch along the side edges, taking a ½ in. (1 cm) seam allowance.

5 Fold 1½ in.(4 cm) to the wrong side along the top edge and hand-sew in place. Iron and then turn the sachet through to the right side.

6 Fill the sachet with a Christmas potpourri, cloves or a small present. Tie with the cord and hang from the tree.

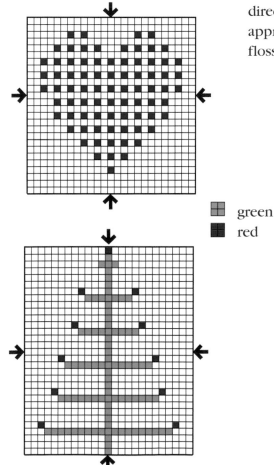

green
red

Banister Bunches

You will need:

- red ornaments with a diameter of about 3 in. (8 cm)
- eucalyptus foliage with small, delicate leaves
- fine (24-gauge) florist's wire
- thick (18-gauge) florist's wire
- wire cutters
- 2-in. (5-cm) wide red organza or soft, wire-edged ribbon: allow 1 yd. (1 m) for each decoration
- panel pins or fine nylon wire

Delicate gray-green foliage and bold scarlet-ribbon-tied ornaments make a striking decoration for a stairway. The technique is simple and you can vary the foliage and colors to suit your interior.

1 Decide how many decorations you need, depending on the banisters, and buy the appropriate number of ornaments, ribbon and foliage. Cut pieces of eucalyptus foliage about 8 in. (20 cm) long and group into the same number of equal-sized bunches.

2 Wind fine florists' wire firmly around the stems of each bunch, ensuring that the foliage is secure. Make all the bunches match in size and shape.

4 Attach the ornament decorations to the staircase by tying them with the narrow red ribbon looped through the wire loop.

5 Complete each decoration by adding a ribbon bow. Take a long length of wide organza or soft, wire-edged ribbon, loop it around the baluster and tie in a double knot, then tie a soft bow behind the ornament to cover the wires completely.

Did you know?

The earliest decorations on trees associated with Christmas are detailed in the Medieval plays that tell the story of Adam and Eve. The trees in the Garden of Eden were, according to these legends, adorned with apples and cookies.

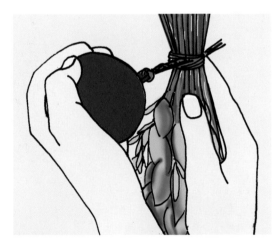

3 Wire an ornament onto each bunch of foliage using a piece of thick florists' wire pushed through the wire already holding the stems together. Twist the ends at the back of the bunch to create a small hanging loop to be hidden by the stems. Cut off the excess wire with wire cutters.

tip

Vary your decoration from year to year by choosing a different foliage, such as rosemary, spruce or pine, butcher's broom (Ruscus aculeatus), yew or cypress, smilax, or protea. You'll create a very different mood by changing the color of the ornaments and ribbon: silver is cool and sophisticated, gold is warm and opulent.

Tin Tree Decorations

Mounting embossed foil onto foam core board makes these bright tree decorations a little more substantial so you can use them year after year.

You will need:

- tracing paper
- 6 in. x 4 in. (15 cm x 10 cm) of heavy-duty aluminum foil
- blunt pencil or used-up ball-point pen
- craft knife
- spray adhesive
- foam core board
- acrylic paints in pale blue, green, orange, yellow, and purple
- 3 pieces of ⅛ in. (3 mm) blue ribbon, 12 in. (30 cm) long

1 Trace the star design from page 266 onto a piece of tracing paper. Position the tracing paper centrally over the foil and, working on a soft surface, trace over the lines of the star using a blunt pencil. As you draw, the design will be pressed into the foil.

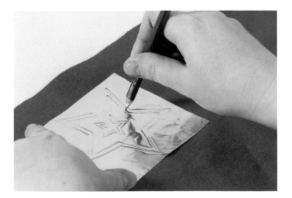

2 Remove the tracing paper and press a series of dots between the two outside lines to create a border. Repeat with the central star.

3 Cut out the star leaving a ⅛ in. (3 mm) border all around the outer line. Stick the star onto a piece of foam core board. Trim around the decoration with a craft knife.

4 Paint the borders of the stars in pale blue, allowing the raised tin dots to show through the paint. Next paint the sides orange, including the sides of the foam core board. Paint the purple center last.

5 Attach the ribbon to the reverse of the decoration with a piece of sticky tape, so that you can hang it from your tree. Repeat steps 1–5 for the tree (see above) and candy cane (see right) using the photograph as a guide to the paint colors.

tip

If you would like more of the foil to show, leave the pale blue border areas unpainted.

Gingerbread Cookies

These pretty iced cookies will give your Christmas tree an extra-festive sparkle. Use star-shaped cookie cutters and create some simple snowflake patterns with piped icing. If you've never done any piping before, test your skills on a board first. You'll soon find practice makes perfect!

You will need:

- one portion of ginger-bread cookie mixture, see page 241
- star-shaped cookie cutter

To decorate

- confectioners' sugar icing and fine nozzle pastry bag or tube of piping icing (see page 245 for royal icing recipe)
- edible silver balls
- fine silver ribbon or cord

MAKES ABOUT 50

1 Knead the dough until smooth, roll it out ¼-in. (6-mm) thick on a floured surface, and cut out the cookies using a star-shaped cutter. Pierce a hole in one point of each star and lift onto baking sheets with a spatula.

2 Bake the cookies at 350°F (180°C/ Gas Mark 4) until firm, about 15 minutes. Cool them on the baking sheets for 5 minutes before lifting off with a spatula and transferring them to a wire rack to cool.

3 Decorate the cookies with snowflake patterns using piped icing. Use a fine nozzle pastry bag or a tube of piping icing.

4 To cover the tops of the cookies completely with icing, pipe a thin line around the edge of each cookie, leave it to set, then fill the center with icing thinned with a few drops of water so it can be spread easily to fill the shape. Referring to the photograph, pipe geometric patterns on top once the icing is set. Add silver balls at the star tips and centers.

5 Allow the completed decoration to set thoroughly. Thread fine ribbon or silver cord through the holes and hang the cookies on the tree.

tip

If you prefer, the cookies can be decorated with colored icing and gold ribbon.

Reindeer Fun

This jolly tree skirt becomes three dimensional due to the padded reindeer heads and the puffy paint used for the antlers and snow. Only simple sewing skills are required, so go ahead and create!

❄ **Did you know?**
Reindeer are resourceful animals. They not only pull sleighs, but are also raised for their milk. In the town of Wales in Alaska, the mail used to be delivered by reindeer-drawn sleigh.

You will need:

- 45 in. (115 cm) square of red felt
- 12 in. x 40 in. (30 cm x 100 cm) piece of beige fleece
- small amount of polyester batting
- 10 large black oval beads for eyes
- 5 large brown buttons
- 1 slightly smaller red button
- 6-strand embroidery floss in dark green
- 14 in. (35 cm) of 36-in. (90-cm)-wide dark green printed cotton
- 10 in. (25 cm) of 36-in. (90-cm) wide green-and-white printed cotton
- 10 in. (25 cm) of 36-in. (90-cm) wide gold cotton
- tube black puffy paint
- tube white puffy paint

1 Fold the square of red felt in half, then half again to find the middle. Leave folded. Tie a knot in a piece of string and tie the other end of the string around a pencil, making sure the distance between the pin and the pencil is 22$^{1}/_{2}$ in. (55 cm). Pin the knot into the folded corner of the square (the center). Draw an arc around the square.

2 Now draw a smaller arc with a radius of 4 in. (10 cm). Cut through all four layers of felt along the pencil lines. Cut straight down one of the folds to make the back opening.

3 Using the template on page 267, cut five reindeer heads from the beige fleece. Pin one directly opposite the opening, about 1 in. (2 cm) from the outside edge. Pin the other four equally spaced around the skirt.

4 Starting at the nose, sew around the edge of the first head, turning under $^{1}/_{4}$ in. (6 mm) as you go. At the ears, do not sew down but pinch slightly at the base and sew across, leaving the ears free to give a 3D effect.

5 Leave a 2-in. (5-cm) gap in the stitching and push a piece of batting into the head. Using the end of a pencil, arrange the batting evenly then sew up the opening. Referring to the diagram, sew the eyes in place and then the button nose. Complete the other four reindeer, sewing a red button on top of the brown button on the middle reindeer.

6 Transfer the diagram of the branch onto the spaces between the reindeer. Lay all six strands of dark green embroidery floss over the line and couch in place with two strands in your needle. Using the leaf pattern, cut out 15 dark green printed leaves and 15 green-and-white printed leaves. Cut out 30 berries from gold cotton. Using the diagram as a guide, appliqué the leaves and berries in place.

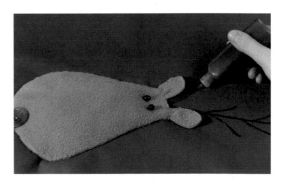

7 Using black puffy paint, hold the tube nozzle against the skirt and squeeze out the antler outlines (use the diagram as a guide). Then carefully dot white puffy paint randomly over the skirt for snow. Leave to dry for 24 hours. To make the paint puff up, press the skirt, wrong side up, with a steam iron, section by section over a padded surface.

Beaded Crystal Star

Transform your Christmas tree with a sparkling decoration that catches the light when it moves. This crystal star can also be used to embellish candles and gifts for a coordinated theme.

You will need:

- 12 clear crystal faceted beads, 12 mm in size
- 3 silver eye pins, ¼-in. (5-mm) thick
- 6 clear round glass beads, 8 mm in diameter
- wire cutters
- round-nose pliers
- lengths of beaded wire, about 2½-in. (6-cm) long

For the Candles

- candles to decorate
- wide voile ribbon
- glue gun
- white feather

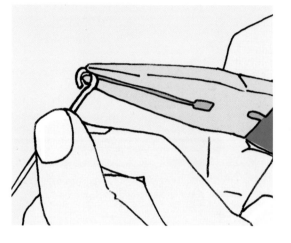 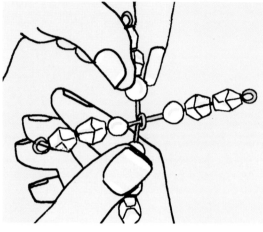

1 Thread two faceted beads onto each eye pin, then two round beads, and then another two faceted beads. Shorten the pins to size, leaving a 1¼-in. (3-cm) length of wire at the ends. Using round-nose pliers, curl over the tips of the pins to match the opposite ends.

2 Lay out the pins in a star shape. Separate each pair of round beads, forming a ⅞-in. (2-cm) gap in the middle of each pin. Using pliers, twist both diagonal pins around the vertical one. Bend the beaded wire to form a hook and attach to an eye pin.

tip

Instead of using both pliers and a wire cutter, look for pliers with a wire cutter in the center of the jaws. These are available in your craft or hardware store.

For the Candles

To decorate a candle, first measure the circumference and cut a length of ribbon to fit, allowing a ½-in. (1-cm) overlap. Wrap the ribbon around the candle and glue the overlapping ends securely. Attach a beaded crystal star and/or a feather with glue. Alternatively, tie a bow around the candle and glue a star just beneath.

"*At the sight of the star they were overjoyed.***"**

Matthew 2, v.10

Glowing Candle Bags

Cut out star motifs add a festive touch illuminated by twinkling votive candles set inside elegant white and gold paper bags. Place in groups for maximum effect.

You will need:

- tracing paper
- white and gold paper
- craft knife and cutting mat, or sharp, pointed scissors
- paper glue
- thin cardboard
- glass votive candle holders and candles

1 Trace the template on page 267, and mark the lines in pencil. Trace either the stars or the shooting stars onto one face of the bag. Enlarge by 350 percent and transfer onto white or gold paper. Cut around the outer lines.

2 Using a craft knife and cutting mat, or sharp, pointed scissors, carefully cut out around the outlines of the stars and shooting stars on the template (do not cut out the ones which are black). Put these to one side.

3 Crease all the fold lines, either as "mountains" or as "valleys" (refer to the template). Fold up the long fold at the foot of the bag first, then fold the corners, tucking the base in place. Glue the long edge on one side with paper glue, then apply dots of glue to secure the corner folds in the base of the bag.

4 Cut a piece of cardboard 3 in. x 4 in. (7.5 cm x 10 cm). Apply a line of glue around the edges on one face, and place in the base of the bag so that the glue adheres to the folded-in strip on the inside of the bag.

5 Glue the cut-out motifs to the right side of the bag front, to match the marked motifs remaining. Erase any pencil marks that are not covered. The combination of the cut-out motif and the glued-on motif will give an effect of light and shadow once the candle is placed in the bag.

6 Insert a votive candle into a votive candle holder or small glass jar, and carefully lower the candle holder inside the bag. Light the candle carefully with a long taper. Arrange the bags on a windowsill or mantelpiece.

tip

You could substitute brightly colored craft paper for the white and gold if this would suit your Christmas décor better. Try some bags in red and some in green.
If you cannot find glass votive candle holders, you could use any small, glass dish or container that will sit safely inside the bags.

Did you know?

Candles are an important part of Christmas for many and they play a crucial part in Christmas Eve celebrations in Gouda, Holland. Gouda is the center of the Dutch candle-making industry. On Christmas Eve all of the electrical lights are turned off while the mayor reads the story of the Nativity to an audience by candlelight in the town square.

❝ *Star of wonder, star of night,*
Star with royal beauty bright **❞**

John Henry Hopkins, Jr.

Rose Wreath

Sophisticated red roses combined with silver eucalyptus, deep red berries and trailing ivy create a very special celebration wreath. Hang it on your gate to give a festive welcome, or use it flat with candles as a sumptuous table centerpiece.

tip

Because this wreath is made on a plastic base with florist's foam, it is quite heavy. For a lighter version, cover a wire wreath base with sphagnum moss by wrapping wire around the base and the moss. Spray the moss base to keep it damp and fresh. For a less expensive, but still colorful wreath, use carnations instead of the roses, and for a permanent wreath, use good quality silk flowers and artificial evergreen foliage.

You will need:

- 12 in. (30cm) circular plastic wreath base, plus florist's wet-style foam to fit
- fine reel wire
- eucalyptus foliage
- skimmia or other foliage with dark red berries
- trails of ivy
- red roses
- florist's scissors
- thick (18-gauge) florist's wire

1 Press the florist's foam into the wreath base. Secure the end of the reel wire and wrap the wire around the entire wreath securing the foam. Thoroughly soak the florist's foam.

2 Cut eucalyptus foliage into about 4 in. (10 cm) pieces. Begin inserting the pieces into the foam, making sure each piece is secure. Continue adding eucalyptus pieces all facing roughly the same way, working around the frame until the whole surface is covered in foliage.

3 Now cut pieces of skimmia and push them in among the eucalyptus, aiming to create more concentrated areas of deep red berries among the gray-green eucalyptus. Keep turning the wreath to ensure you achieve a balance of color. Make sure there is no wire showing.

firmly into the foam and wind the trails around the foliage, securing the other end by pushing it into the foam again. Continue until the wreath is full, and looks natural and luxurious.

5 Cut the stems of the red roses about 3 in. (7 cm) long, at an angle, with florist's scissors. Push the stems into the foam base so you create natural groups of blooms. Aim for a balanced but not too symmetrical distribution of flowers. Hold the wreath up, as it will hang, and shake gently to check the roses are secure.

6 Make a small loop at the back of the wreath with thick florist's wire twisted around the plastic base, and twist in any excess wire. Spray the wreath with water before hanging on your gate. Keep the foam damp by spraying each day, and replace any roses that fade as necessary.

4 When the top of the foam is completely covered with foliage, take long strands of ivy, push one end

Mantel Garland

Candlelight and a crackling fire add to the spirit of the season. Here, candles, glossy fruits, graceful flowers and aromatic foliage create a dramatic display to dress up your mantel for the holidays.

You will need:

- one or more plastic florist's trays to fit the width of the mantelpiece
- florist's wet-style foam blocks to fit the trays
- waterproof florist's tape
- chicken wire
- sphagnum moss
- thick string
- 9 white or cream pillar candles of varying diameters and 10 in.– 12 in. (25 cm–30 cm) in height
- pine branches
- trails of green and variegated ivy
- thick (18-gauge) florist's wire
- 8 green apples
- 12 green chilies
- 18 large cinnamon sticks
- raffia
- 6–8 large white trumpet lilies

1 Tape wet-style foam blocks into the trays with waterproof florist's tape, wrapping the tape over the foam and underneath the trays to secure it in place. The trays allow the display to be watered to keep it fresh.

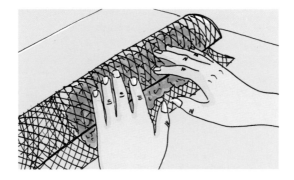

2 Cut a length of chicken wire long enough to span the mantelpiece and hang down at each side, and wide enough to curl into a wide roll. Fill the ends of the wire with damp sphagnum moss, and roll and flatten the wire to hold it in place. Position the wire over the foam blocks, folding down the ends to create the hanging sections.

3 To secure the structure to the mantelpiece, pass a length of string underneath the mantel ledge, up through the chicken wire at each end, and over the top, tying firmly. Cut holes into the wire, and push the candles into the foam in a balanced but asymmetrical arrangement. For thick

pillar candles, hollow out a little of the foam to make this easier. Ensure the candles will stand safely, and sit well above the foliage.

4 Water the foam blocks until they are completely soaked. Begin by inserting pieces of pine foliage into the moss-filled hanging sections, and build up the central part of the display by pushing larger pieces of foliage into the foam blocks. When all the foam and wire is hidden, insert long trails of ivy.

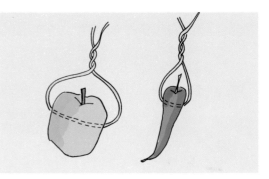

5 Push lengths of thick florist's wire through the apples and chilies, twist the ends together, and secure them to the chicken wire. Tie bundles of six large cinnamon sticks with raffia, and affix them into the chicken wire. Insert large white trumpet lilies into the foam along the top of the garland. Keep the foam blocks watered daily and spray the hanging ends to keep the moss damp.

tips

This garland can be made from a range of evergreen foliage. Blue spruce has attractive curving growth and is richly aromatic. Other pines or holly, yew or laurel, bay or boxwood, eucalyptus or rosemary all provide a rich evergreen background.

Fruits such as green apples, clove-studded oranges, and chilies provide a pleasing contrast. Cut the stamens from the lilies to avoid the pollen staining clothes. Replace the fresh lilies with silk ones for a display that will last throughout the holiday season.

❝ *Now nature hangs her mantle green...* ❞

Robert Burns

Light Up Your Table

This stunning candle, hydrangea and artichoke centerpiece will put the finishing touch to a festive table. It is simple and elegant and will complement your Yuletide décor.

tip

To prolong the life of your fresh centerpiece, keep it in a cool place for as long as possible before using. Keep it damp by placing it on moist paper towels and spray with water to prevent it wilting.

You will need:

- fresh boxwood or other evergreen foliage to give about 15 sprigs
- pruning shears
- straw base (from florist or craft shop)
- 2 yd. (2 m) medium (20-gauge) florist's wire
- 3 artichoke heads
- 3 hydrangea heads
- 6 sprigs of artificial red berry sprigs
- display dish
- candle and candle holder

1 Take some fresh boxwood and cut sprigs roughly 3 in. (7.5 cm) in length. Bind each sprig around the base lengthwise by winding it with a length of florist's wire.

2 Place alternating artichoke and hydrangea heads around the base, at equal distances. Each head requires a 2 in. (5 cm) stem to fix to the base securely. Carefully bind each stem with florist's wire. Fill in any spaces that are left with more boxwood.

3 For a luscious green look, add more boxwood to the base. Bind the last sprigs in the opposite direction to the rest, to create a fuller look. Add artificial red berries to complete the wreath. Place the finished wreath onto a suitable display dish and finish by standing a candle in a candleholder in the center.

"*Remembrance, like a candle, burns brightest at Christmas time.***"**

Charles Dickens

Gilded Pendant

Christmas is the perfect time to spend a little extra on top-quality, realistic-looking artificial foliage. Gold adds an extra shimmer to this display that will last all through the holiday season, right through to New Year's Day.

You will need:

- protective gloves
- 2 florist's wet-style foam blocks
- chicken wire
- thick (18-gauge) florist's wire
- gold spray paint
- gold 3D outliner paint
- 3 sprays artificial poinsettia bracts
- 2 gilded artificial apples
- 1 branch artificial eucalyptus
- 3 sprays artificial oak leaves
- 3 sprays artificial ivy, preferably with berries
- 15-in. (38-cm) thick gold braid

" The holly and the ivy,
When they are both full grown,
Of all the trees in the wood,
The holly bears the crown."

Traditional

festive home

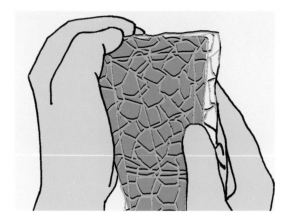

1 Wearing protective gloves, lay the foam blocks end to end on the chicken wire. Cover the blocks with the wire, securing the sharp ends, and mold the wire around the foam until you have a long rectangle. Attach a loop of thick florist's wire at one end, as a hanging hook.

2 Using spray paint, spray the poinsettia bracts and berries gold. Leave to dry. Turn the chicken wire shape over and lay it on a flat surface.

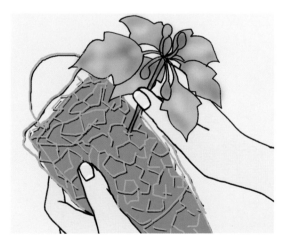

3 Push the stems of the poinsettia into the foam and wire, placing one at the top, one halfway down, and one pointing downward, at the base to help create the trailing form.

4 Hang up the pendant so that you can assess the display as you add foliage. Push the apple into the foam. Thread the eucalyptus vertically down the center of the pendant, and insert the oak leaves and ivy in between, to conceal the wire base.

5 Remove the wire hanging hook and tie the thick gold braid securely to each side of the top of the chicken wire and hang in position.

tip

To gild the foliage and berries, lay each piece individually on newsprint and spray evenly with gold paint. Add texture with gold three-dimensional outliner on the tips of the leaves. Highlight some of the oak leaves by applying dabs of three-dimensional outliner with a paintbrush.

Gift Box Wreath

This modern alternative to a traditional foliage wreath features shiny and metallic gift-wrapped boxes. An eye-catching decoration for your front door, it also makes an original gift for a friend or a neighbor.

❄ *Did you know?*

In many European countries, gifts are traditionally given to children by St. Nicholas, who arrives on December 6th with his mischievous servant Black Peter. If the children are good, St. Nicholas gives them nuts, sweets, or small presents. However, if the children are bad, they will be threatened with sticks by Black Peter.

You will need:

- wooden wreath, measuring 12 in. (30 cm) in diameter
- 12½ in. (32 cm) square thick batting
- red metallic gift wrap
- glue gun
- assortment of small pieces of gift wrap, preferably with metallic finishes in at least five different colors
- 86 mini boxes (available at craft stores)
- red and blue knitting yarn
- metallic elastic thread
- red bow
- D-ring hook

1 Place the wooden wreath on top of the batting and draw around it with a pen. Cut out the circle and place it on top of the wreath. Wrap red metallic gift wrap all round the batting and wooden base, securing it at the back with dabs of glue.

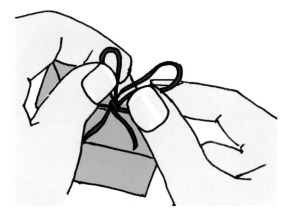

2 Cut the assortment of gift wrap into small pieces. Place the boxes on the gift wrap and wrap individually, cutting off any excess paper so the presents don't become misshapen. Secure with glue.

3 Embellish each gift by tying a small strand of knitting yarn or metallic elastic thread around it. Secure with a knot and a bow.

4 Position the presents over the front of the wreath base. Make sure that there are as few gaps between the boxes as possible. Secure each present in place with a dab of glue. Leave to dry for 30 minutes.

5 Attach the red bow using a dab of glue. Leave for 30 minutes for the glue to dry. Attach a D-ring hook to the back of the wooden base. Secure the hook in place with glue or a small metal tack, and hang on front door.

tip

To make your wreath more dazzling, use shiny and metallic gift wrap for the presents. This will catch the light and make the finished project vibrant. If you are short on time, you can use store-bought mini gift boxes.

Gift-Laden Coronet

This stunning wreath embodies the colors and aromas of Christmas. Hang it from a hook in the ceiling and impress one and all.

You will need:

- tracing paper
- plain cardboard
- craft knife
- white craft (PVA) glue
- red shiny giftwrap
- glue dots
- 39 in. (1 m) heavy (18-gauge) wire
- pine branches
- reel wire
- 19½ ft. (6 m) red ribbon, ¼-in. (5-mm) wide, cut into 20 lengths
- 6½ ft. (2 m) shiny red ribbon, about 4-in. (10-cm) wide
- 4 straight pins

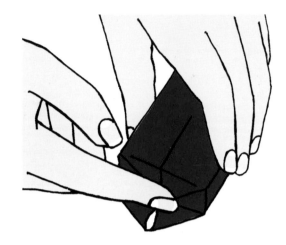

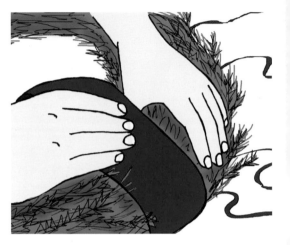

1 Trace the outlines for the boxes from the template on page 268 and transfer onto cardboard to make 20 boxes. Cut around the solid lines and lightly score the dotted lines. Crease the folds, place a thin layer of glue on the tabs and assemble the boxes. Wrap in giftwrap and secure with a glue dot.

2 Bend the heavy wire into a circle, twisting the ends together to secure. Wrap and layer the pine branches around the wire, tucking in the ends to conceal them and to make the wreath firm. Once the wire is covered, wrap reel wire around the foliage to secure the branches in place.

3 Tie the thin ribbon around each present, finishing with a bow but leaving one short and one very long end. Tie the long end to the wreath. Tuck one end of the wide ribbon into the wreath and wrap it around five times. Secure with two pins. Wrap the other end around the opposite side of the wreath. Secure with pins and suspend from the ceiling.

tip

Conceal the pins used to secure the hanging loop with star decorations. Use a glue gun to place a dab of glue on the ribbon. Hold each star in place until it is set.

festive home

"The pine tree seems to listen,
the fir tree to wait. "
Friedrich Nietzsche

Swag of Gift Bags

A far cry from the traditional stocking, this row of gift bags doubles as a decorative swag for your mantelpiece. Each bag is trimmed with beautiful poinsettias made from felt and beads.

You will need:

For five bags

- 1½ yd. (1.4 m) pink velvet, 36-in. (90-cm) wide
- tracing paper
- ¾ yd. (0.7 m) white felt, 36-in. (90-cm) wide
- approx. 220 round iridescent glass beads in pinks and blues
- sewing thread matching beads
- 1½ yd. (1.40 m) fine cord for hanging

"At Christmas play and make good cheer, for Christmas comes but once a year."

Thomas Tusser

tip

Don't be tempted to press your bag as the iron will mark it. Velvet should be only minimally pressed from the wrong side after placing it on a scrap piece of velvet so that you don't crush the pile.

1 From the pink velvet, cut out ten rectangles 8 in. x 16 in. (20 cm x 40 cm). With right sides facing and taking a ½ in. (1 cm) seam allowance, stitch together in pairs around the sides and base to make five bags. Cut across each corner to within ½ in. (3 mm) of stitching to remove the excess seam allowance.

2 On each bag, fold the top edge under ½ in. (1 cm), then 3 in. (7.5 cm) more to make a deep hem. Secure with slip stitch.

3 Trace the petal template on page 268. Cut out and use as a pattern piece to cut 120 petals from the white felt. To make a flower, take six petals and run a gathering thread through the base of each in sequence to form a circle of petals. Gather up the petals and hand sew the flower to the front of one of the bags, about 2½ in. (6.5 cm) down from the top, starting at a side edge. Repeat to complete four flowers for each bag, stitching them in a row near the top of the bag.

4 Stitch enough round beads in a tight cluster at the center of each flower to hide the gathering stitches. Cut the cord into five 10 in. (25 cm) lengths. Hand sew a length of cord to each bag to hang them.

festive home

Rose and Ivy Panel

Here, on this cross-stitch panel, the beautiful hellebore, or Christmas rose, complements a trailing stem of ivy. A tartan ribbon adds the finishing touch. Hang the panel in your entrance hall to welcome visitors in style.

You will need:

- 26 in. x 9 in. (65 cm x 23 cm) 14-count red Aida fabric for cross-stitch

- contrast sewing thread

- 6-strand cotton embroidery floss, one skein each in cream, rose pink, light green, mid green, lime green, bright green, and dark green

- 6-strand metallic embroidery floss, one skein in gold

- tapestry needle

- 3⅓ yd. (3 m) tartan ribbon 1-in. (2.5-cm) wide

- 1 wooden dowel rod, at least 10-in. (25-cm) long and ½ in. (1 cm) in diameter

- wood stain (optional)

Finished size

22 in. x 5 in.
(55 cm x 13 cm)

1 Begin by folding the aida fabric in half lengthwise and mark the crease line with tacking stitches through a row of holes, using a contrasting sewing thread. Repeat widthwise; the point where the two lines of tacking cross marks the center of the design.

2 The chart given on page 268 shows one half of the design. This section should be worked twice, once above and once below the horizontal center line, as marked on the fabric.

3 Each colored square on the chart equals one cross-stitch worked over one square of the aida fabric. The colors of embroidery floss are given in the key. For easy reference, tape a small piece of each color next to its corresponding number in the key. Note: some cream areas are worked with two strands and some with four.

4 Begin stitching the design at the marked center on the fabric, making sure that all the top threads of your cross stitches slant in the same direction. Use two strands of the 6-strand embroidery floss in your needle for most of the cross-stitching.

The only exceptions are indicated on the key; these are the outer tips of the flower petals, where four strands of cream are used, and the metallic gold floss, which is worked with six strands. When you have completed the top half of the design, repeat it once more underneath.

5 When the embroidery is finished, press it from the wrong side over a padded surface. On the long sides, fold the excess fabric to the wrong side, three squares from the outside of the embroidery and press. Trim to ½ in. (1 cm).

Did you know?

Ivy has been a popular plant to use as a Christmas decoration in houses for centuries. The custom of decorating homes with ivy and other evergreens dates back to pre-Christian times when ivy was believed to be linked with the power of eternity. Ivy represented life continuing through the cold months of winter.

6 Fold the lower edge to form a point. Fold the top edge under twice to form a 1 in. (2.5 cm) channel. Tack all around the edges about ³⁄₈ in. (8 mm) in from the folded edges.

7 Run a gathering thread along one edge of the tartan ribbon and gather it up to fit all around the panel. Tack in position just under the folded edges of the Aida fabric, with the ribbon ends meeting at the lowest point. Machine stitch or back stitch the two long sides and the lower pointed edge close to the edge of the Aida fabric.

8 At the top edge, hand stitch the ribbon to the underside of the main piece at each side of the channel, and slip-stitch under the fold at the top of the channel so that the wooden dowel rod can be threaded through the channel behind the ribbon.

9 If a dark wooden dowel would suit your decor better, stain the dowel rod with an appropriate wood stain. Allow to dry completely before threading it through the channel and hanging on your wall.

tip

This classic Christmas rose and ivy design is perfect for decorating festive table linen. Repeat the pattern along the center of a table runner, and use a single Christmas rose motif at the corner of matching napkins.

Holly Berry Base

Celebrate Christmas in style by making this versatile circular table centerpiece. Smaller versions are ideal for offering your guests some snacks.

You will need:

- 1 x 10½ in. x 13 in. (26 cm x 33 cm) sheet of 10-count clear plastic canvas

- tapestry needle

For the Table Centerpiece

- circle of 7-count clear plastic canvas, 9½-in. (23-cm) diameter, for the base

- 6-strand cotton embroidery floss, 5 skeins in purple, 3 skeins in light green, 2 skeins in red, and 1 skein in dark green

- wet-type florist's foam

- shallow container

- candle and foliage of your choice

For the Serving Dish

- circle of 10-count clear plastic canvas, 4.5 in. (12 cm) diameter, for the base

- 6-strand cotton embroidery floss, 2 skeins in red and 1 skein in each of purple, and light green

For the Table Centerpiece

1 Each colored square on the chart shown on page 269 equals one cross-stitch worked over one square of the plastic canvas. Follow the key for the colors to use.

2 Using all six strands of embroidery floss in the needle, work three 10½ in. x 2¼ in. (25 cm x 5.5 cm) strips of the border as shown on the color chart. When all the cross-stitching is complete, cut out the strips leaving several unworked holes free all around.

3 Using purple thread, cross-stitch the strips together to join them into one length. Fit this strip around the circular base and mark where the seam falls for a snug fit, then, if necessary, work extra squares in purple to fill. Sew the ends together to make a circle.

4 Trim the circle of plastic canvas to fit the base. Using six strands of red, oversew the border onto the base, working through the unworked row of holes. Finish the top edge by oversewing through the unworked row of holes in red.

5 Secure a piece of soaked florist's foam in a shallow container. Push the candle into the center so that it is firmly in position. Place the container in the embroidered base, then add your choice of foliage and flowers.

For the Serving Dish

Work as given for the table centerpiece, repeating the design as necessary on two 8 in. x 1½ in. (20 cm x 4 cm) strips. Note that you will need to create a strip for the dish border measuring approximately 14¼ in. x 1½ in. (38 cm x 4 cm).

tip

Plastic canvas makes a rigid structure. It is available in several counts (squares to the inch/2.5 cm)—here 10-count is used for the stitching but the base is a 7-count radial circle, not stitched. The canvas is very durable and the various sheet sizes makes it ideal for boxes. Work with all six strands of strand cotton, or with tapestry wool to cover the plastic.

Gilded Christmas Pots

An array of pots painted in a festive red and gold harlequin pattern make attractive containers to store cutlery, napkins and Christmas ornaments. These will make an excellent addition to a buffet-style festive meal.

You will need:

- terracotta pots in various sizes
- ³⁄₄ in. (2 cm) flat paintbrush
- white primer (undercoat)
- fine sandpaper
- tracing paper
- craft knife and cutting mat
- medium-sized round paintbrush
- masking tape
- cardboard
- acrylic paints in gold and red
- flat (matte) varnish

1 Using a ³⁄₄ in. (2 cm) flat paintbrush, apply white primer all over the pots to form a base for painting the design. Leave to dry, then smooth with fine sandpaper.

2 Trace the star and fir tree templates below and transfer them onto white paper. Using a craft knife and cutting mat, carefully cut out the shapes to make stencils.

3 Using a pencil, draw a vertical line on opposite sides of each pot, from the top to the base. Paint the inside of the pots gold. Paint one half of each pot red, and the other half gold, using a medium-sized round paintbrush. Brush the paint smoothly in one direction around the curve of the pots, making a neat line where the two colors meet. If there is a rim on the pot, reverse the colors on the rim to give a checkered effect.

4 Referring to the photograph opposite as a placement guide, and aligning the stencils on the vertical lines, secure the stencils to the pots with masking tape. Secure a piece of cardboard down the center of each shape and stencil one half in gold; remove the cardboard, and wait for the paint to dry.

5 Place a new piece of cardboard on the painted side of the motif and stencil the other half in red. Remove the cardboard and stencil and allow to dry. To protect the pots, give them a coat of clear flat varnish.

tip

Remove the stencil and cardboard while the paint is damp, or they may pull the paint off when you remove them. However, wait until the paint is completely dry before applying the next color.

Patchwork Tablecloth

A patchwork design based on four star blocks sets the mood for Christmas. The central panel is enhanced by three borders in different widths, and the tablecloth is lightly padded and quilted.

You will need:

For a tablecloth measuring 39 in. x 39 in. (1 m x 1 m) All fabric is 45 in. (115 cm) wide, 100 percent cotton

- tracing paper
- thin cardboard
- fabric A (gold): ½ yd. (0.45 m)
- fabric B (red): 2 yd. (1.85 m)
- fabric C (green): ⅝ yd. (0.60 m)
- fabric D (green floral): ¼ yd. (0.25 m)
- fabric E (red floral): ⅞ yd. (0.80 m)
- 42 in. x 42 in. (105 cm x 105 cm) low-loft batting
- matching sewing thread
- matching quilting thread

1 Trace the patch shapes A–E from page 269 and transfer onto thin cardboard. Cut out one of each shape as templates for cutting out the patches. A seam allowance of ¼ in. (0.75 cm) is included on the templates.

2 The tablecloth consists of four blocks, each measuring 12½ in. x 12½ in. (32 cm x 32 cm), excluding seam allowances. Cut out the required number of patches for the first block as marked on the patch shapes on page 269. For patch shapes B and C, cut four as given and four as mirror images (marked B1 and C1).

3 Following the stitching plan on page 269, assemble the block in sections, taking a ¼ in. (0.75 cm) seam allowance throughout. Begin by stitching A to B1 and B to D. Then pin and stitch these two units together, matching the seams exactly. Next, stitch A to C1 and C to E. Pin and stitch these two units together. Finally, stitch the two completed units together to form the first section of the star block.

4 Repeat step 3 to make the next section of the star block. Matching seams, pin and stitch the two sections together to make half the star block.

5 Following the stitching plan, repeat steps 3 and 4 to form the second half of the star block. Matching seams, pin and stitch the two halves together. Repeat steps 3 to 5 to make three more star blocks. Pin and stitch the blocks together in pairs, matching seams. Then join the pairs together.

6 Refer to page 269 for the lengths of border strips to cut. Fold each strip in half lengthwise, and match the center of the two shorter strips to the center of the panel. Pin and stitch; trim ends to fit. Pin and stitch the two longer strips of border 1 to top and bottom of the panel in the same way.

tip

Press all seam allowances as you go along. Where possible, press them toward the darker fabric so that they do not show through to the right side of the cloth.

7 Repeat step 6 using the strips for borders 2 and 3. (To make border 3, stitch alternate red and green squares together: you need 18 squares for the short strips, and 20 squares for the long strips.)

8 Sandwich the batting between the patchwork and backing, pin and tack in a grid. Quilt around the patches. Trim the excess batting and backing. Pin and stitch the shorter binding strips to the sides of the cloth. Turn under the long raw edge, turn binding to the back and slip stitch. Repeat at top and bottom, turning under the short ends and slip-stitching closed.

Silk Table Runner

A little freehand drawing, a tube of relief paint and minimal
sewing is all that's required to make this elegant silk runner.
It's a really personal addition to your Christmas table.

festive home

You will need:

- 1²/₃ yd. (1.5 m) of pale gold dupioni silk , 44 in. (112 cm) wide
- soft pencil
- green relief paint
- pale gold sewing thread
- selection of beads and sequins in red, gold and green, including red star-shaped sequins

1 Cut a rectangle 60 in. x 19 in. (150 cm x 48 cm) from the pale gold dupioni silk. Using the picture opposite as a guide, draw a wavy border 2 in. (5 cm) above each of the short edges, using a soft pencil.

2 Following the template on page 270, practice drawing simple Christmas trees, using wavy lines. With a soft pencil, mark the center point of the silk runner 1¼ in. (3 cm) above each of the wavy lines, then another point 4 in. (10 cm) above that. Draw the first tree between these two points, to give a tree roughly 4 in. (10 cm) high. Draw a smaller tree, roughly 3 in. (7.5 cm) high, on either side of the first.

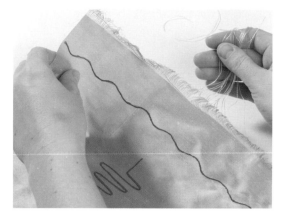

3 Go over the wavy border and each of the drawn trees with the green relief paint. Squeeze the tube steadily to give an even line. Set the runner aside until the paint dries completely.

4 Fray the short edges as far as the wavy border. Turn under a ⅝ in. (1.5 cm) double hem on each of the long edges and machine- or hand-stitch.

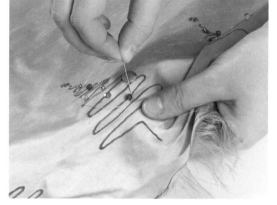

5 Sew a red star-shaped sequin above one tree, then sew beads and sequins randomly to the tree to represent decorations. Repeat on the other trees. Sew sequins in a random pattern to the rest of the runner to give a glittering finish.

tip

Practice using the relief paint on scraps of fabric before starting on the runner. If air bubbles appear, prick them with a pin, and hide any blobs with sequins.

Beaded Napkin Rings

Dress up your Christmas dining table with delicate napkins and matching napkin rings. The pretty red beads are reminiscent of holly berries, enhanced by golden bells and green ribbons.

1 For the basic napkin, fold the square of white cotton with right sides facing. Miter the corners by folding the square across the diagonal and then sew a seam at a right-angle to the fold 1 in. (2.5cm) from the end to ¼ in. (5 mm) to the raw edge. Trim off the corner triangle and repeat with the other three corners.

2 Turn the napkin the right side out and press the corners. Turn each edge under ¼ in. (6 mm) and slip-stitch all the way around.

For the Napkin Ring

1 Iron a piece of interfacing 1³/₄ in. x 6 in. (4.5 cm x 15 cm) onto the linen. Trim linen to ½ in. (12 mm) around the interfacing. Zig-zag stitch the raw edges to prevent them fraying. Fold over the two long edges and slip-stitch in place. Press.

2 Starting on one long edge, insert the needle into the edge of the fabric, ½ in. (12 mm) from one end, then

thread on a red and a gold bead. Take the thread around the gold bead and back through the red one to secure. Repeat along edges of the napkin ring, spacing the beads ½ in. (12 mm) apart.

3 Trace the stencil template on page 270 and transfer onto stencil cardboard. Cut out with a craft knife. Make one stencil for the ribbons and one for the bows. See tip for how to use the registration marks. Measure to find the middle of the napkin ring and position the bell stencil toward the bottom, allowing space for the ribbons above. Apply gold stencil paint.

4 Position the ribbon stencil on the napkin ring and apply green stencil paint. Add a fine gold outline to the ribbons with gold paint. Allow to dry, then slip-stitch the short ends together to form the ring.

5 Repeat the stenciling on a napkin corner and add beads as shown.

Call a truce, then, to our labors—let us feast with friends and neighbors.

Rudyard Kipling

Festive Floral Linen

This beautifully embroidered tablecloth with coordinating napkins will create just the right atmosphere for your Christmas meal when dining with friends and family. It is sure to become a family Christmas keepsake.

festive home

You will need:

- 6-strand cotton embroidery floss, 5 skeins in medium green, 4 skeins in dark green, 3 skeins in white, and deep coral, 2 skeins in medium pink, dark pink, 1 skein in each of the following colors: pale orange, beige/gray, pale beige/gray, burgundy, pale green, buttermilk, and pale pink
- tapestry needle
- embroidery hoop
- white sewing cotton

For the Tablecloth
- 56 in. (142 cm) square white 28-count evenweave linen fabric

For the Napkins
- 14 in. (35 cm) square of the same fabric for each

Finished sizes
Tablecloth measures 54 in. (137 cm) square and napkin measures 12 in. (30 cm) square

For the Tablecloth

1 First neaten the raw edges of the tablecloth. Fold the fabric edge in ½ in. (1 cm) twice to make a double hem all around the outer edge and machine-stitch in position.

2 Fold the cloth in half lengthwise and run a tacking thread along the fold, through a row of holes. Repeat widthwise; the point where the two lines of tacking cross marks the center of the cloth.

3 Each colored square on the charts found on page 270, equals one cross-stitch worked over two threads of evenweave linen in each direction. The colors of cotton embroidery floss to use are given in the key. For easy reference, tape a piece of each color next to its corresponding number in the key.

4 Stretch the fabric in the embroidery hoop to keep it taut during stitching. This will help you to achieve an even tension. Remember to remove the hoop after each stitching session to prevent the fabric from becoming marked.

5 To mark the starting point for stitching the central motifs to correspond with the marked stitch on the chart, measure down 6½ in. (17 cm) from the center point along each tacked line. Work one central motif in each of the four marked positions.

6 To mark the starting point for stitching the corner motifs to correspond with the marked stitch on the chart, measure 8½ in. (22 cm) diagonally in from each corner of the cloth. Work one motif in each corner.

7 Use two strands of embroidery floss for the cross-stitching. When all the embroidery is complete, add the details on the leaves in straight stitches using two strands of buttermilk-colored floss. Gently press the completed tablecloth from the wrong side using a damp cloth over a padded surface.

For the Napkins

For the napkins, make a double hem all around each napkin, working as described. To mark the starting point for stitching the motif to correspond with the marked stitch on the chart, fold the napkin into four diagonally and measure 2 in. (5 cm) in along the fold line from one corner. Work the embroidery in one corner only, then press, following the instructions given for the tablecloth.

Spicy Pomanders

A perfect pastime for winter nights, these oranges are studded with cloves using a variety of decorative patterns. Give these pomanders as gifts to perfume a room or add fragrance to a cupboard.

You will need:

- black felt-tip pen
- 8-10 unwaxed oranges
- small knitting needle or wooden tooth pick
- jar of whole cloves
- 8 tsp. ground cinnamon
- 8 tsp. ground nutmeg
- 4 tsp. ground orrisroot
- 8-10 paper napkins
- large paper bag

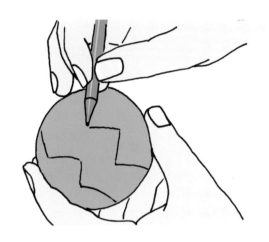

1 Using a felt-tip pen, draw a pattern or design on each orange skin to act as a guide. Let the outlines dry for 5–10 minutes to avoid smudging. If you are sufficiently confident to create a freehand pattern, begin with Step 2.

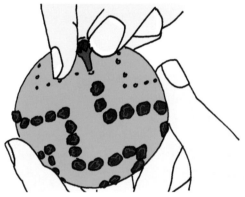

2 Using a knitting needle or tooth pick, pierce holes in the orange skins for each clove. Carefully push the cloves into the holes until you have completed the design.

3 Sprinkle the cinnamon, nutmeg and orrisroot powder on a plate. Mix them together and then roll the oranges in the spices. Wrap each orange in a paper napkin and leave in a warm place for 4 weeks to enhance the fragrance. Dust off any excess powder and display in a bowl or plate.

tip

It is best to use oranges with thick, unwaxed skins as the cloves will remain firmly studded for longer. The natural zest will also release a more vibrant, citrus perfume. Use a thimble to push the cloves into the orange to avoid hurting your fingers.

Quartet of Candles

This up-to-date centerpiece in a bold, shiny metal container is simplicity itself to assemble and looks stunning. The quartet of closely grouped thick candles creates a magical light.

You will need:

4 candles approximately 4 in. (10 cm) high and 2½ in. (6 cm) across

square metal container 11 in. x 11 in. (28 cm x 28 cm)

small pine cones

selection of fruit and dried flowers, such as small pomegranates, kumquats, and Chinese lanterns

1 Place the four thick candles into the metal container so that they touch one another to form a group in the center.

2 Fill the remaining space in the container with small pine cones, and your selection of small fruits, making sure the mixture ends well below the top of the candles.

CHAPTER TWO

JOY OF GIVING

Finding the perfect present for everyone on your
gift list is no problem if you make them yourself.
Here are some great ideas using fun techniques—
including knitting, patchwork, and tin work—plus
ideas for wrapping up everything in style.

★ have a merry christmas ★

Advent Stocking

This stocking isn't just for Christmas morning. Tuck a tiny present or candy into each pocket for the excitement of a surprise every day leading up to Christmas Eve.

You will need:

- tracing paper
- ½ yd. (0.50 m) of white felt, 36-in. (90-cm) wide
- scraps of felt in shades of pink, red, purple, and crimson
- matching sewing thread
- gold relief fabric pen
- 14 in. (35 cm) each of pink organdy ribbon, 3-in. (8-cm) wide, and gold organdy ribbon, 1½-in. (4-cm) wide
- 25 in. (64 cm) white faux fur strip, 5-in. (16-cm) wide
- white sewing thread

1 Trace the stocking template on page 271 and cut out. Fold the felt in half widthwise, pin on the pattern and cut out two stocking pieces.

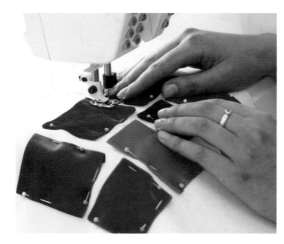

2 Using the templates on page 271 as a guide, cut out 24 pockets from pink, red, purple, and crimson felt. Pin to the stocking front in the order shown on the placement diagram. Using matching thread, stitch around the sides and base of each pocket.

3 Using the gold relief fabric pen, write numbers 1–24 at random on the pockets. With right sides of fabric facing, and taking a ½ in. (1 cm) seam allowance, stitch the stocking front and back pieces together around the sides and base. Turn fabric right side out.

4 Place the narrow ribbon centrally along the wide ribbon and fold in half. With raw edges matching and right sides facing, hand-sew the ribbon to the top corner of the back stocking piece.

5 Fold the strip of fur fabric in half, wrong sides together, and pin around the top of the stocking. Hand-sew in position, tucking in the raw edges at each end.

Full of Surprises

Make these adorable stockings for the children. With their bright designs, they're sure to serve double-duty as Christmas gift bags as well as whimsical mantel decorations.

You will need:

For the Star Stocking

- 1 x 50 g ball (60 yd./ 55 m) of Schachenmayr Boston in each of pink (color A-35) and pumpkin (color B-26)

- 6-strand cotton embroidery floss, 1 skein in pumpkin (Anchor 324)

- set of US size 10½-11 (6.5 mm-8.0 mm) double-pointed needles, or size to obtain gauge

- US size I/9 (5.50 mm) crochet hook

- 1 star button

- 4 in. (10 cm) square of felt in dark pink

For the Star Stocking

Size

Leg to heel, approximately 9 in. (23 cm)
Heel to toe, 8 in. (20 cm)

Gauge

12 sts and 18 rows/rounds to 4 in. (10 cm) over st-st with 10½–11 needles or size to obtain gauge.

To make

With A, cast on 32 sts and divide sts on four needles with 8 sts on each needle. K 3 rounds. Join in B. Using Jacquard (stranded) technique, work in rib patt as foll:

Next row: P1 A, *k2 B, p2 A, rep from * to last 3 sts, k2 B, p 1 A. Work 5 more rounds as set. Cont in st-st (every round k), work 20 rounds with B.

Join in A. Work 2 rounds Jacquard patt and 2 rounds st-st with A. (Leg measures about 7 in. (18 cm) long.)

Work heel

Work 2 rounds with A. Cut off A. Begin to work back and forth in rows across 16 sts on 4th and 1st needles only. Rejoin A to the first of 8 sts on 4th needle and shape heel as foll:

1st row Sl 1, k15, turn.

2nd row Sl 1, p14, sl 1 wyif, yb, turn.

3rd row Sl 1, yb, k13, yf, sl 1, yb, turn.

4th row Sl 1, p12, sl 1 wyif, yb, turn.

5th row Sl 1, yb, k11, yf, sl 1, yb, turn.

6th row Sl 1, p10, sl 1, wyif, yb, turn.

Cont as set until the row 'sl 1, yb, k5, yf, sl 1, yb, turn' is worked.

Next row Sl 1, p6, sl 1wyif, yb, turn.

Next row Sl 1, yb, k7, yf, sl 1, yb, turn.

Next row Sl 1, p8, sl wyif, yb, turn.

Cont as set until the row 'sl 1, k14, yf, sl 1, yb, turn' is worked.

Next row Sl 1, p15, turn.

Next row K16, now work across 16 sts from 2nd and 3rd needles.

Cont in rounds, work 2 rounds in A, 2 rounds in Jacquard patt and 11 rounds in B and 2 rounds in Jacquard patt. Cut off B and cont in A only.

Shape toe

Next round On needle 1, k to last 3 sts, k2tog, k1; on needle 2, sl 1, k1, psso, k to end; work sts on needle 3 same as needle 1; work sts on needle 4 same as needle 2.

Rep last round on 2 foll alt rounds, then on next 2 rounds. Cut off yarn, leaving a long end. Fold over final yarn end and draw a double strand through rem 8 sts. Fasten off securely.

Finishing off

With crochet hook and A, make a hanging loop at center back as foll: attach yarn, work 11ch and ss into edge of sock. Work 1 turning ch, then 1sc into each ch, ending with 1ss into edge of sock.

Using the template below, cut a star from felt. Position on the sock as shown in the picture and sew in place around outer edges using running stitch and three strands of embroidery floss. Sew button to center of the star.

tip

To work in rounds, cast on the number of stitches required evenly across four double-pointed needles. The round change is at the center back, between needles four and one, and the position is marked with the initial end of yarn.

You will need:

For the Christmas Tree Stocking

- 2 x 50 g balls (98 yd./ 90 m) of Schachenmayr Brazilia in golf green (78)

- scraps of Brazilia Lamé in silver (81) and Boston in pumpkin (25) and pink (35)

- set of US size 7–9 (4.5–5.5 mm) double-pointed needles or size to obtain gauge

- J/10 (6.0 mm) crochet hook

For the Christmas Tree Stocking

Size
Leg to heel, approximately 9 in. (23 cm)
Heel to toe, 8 in. (20 cm)

Gauge
18 sts and 28 rows/rounds to 4 in. (10 cm) over st-st with 7-9 (4.5–5.5 mm) needles or correct size to obtain gauge.

Abbreviations
See page 66.

To make
With green, cast on 48 sts and divide sts on four needles with 12 sts on each needle. Work 5 rounds in k2, p2 rib patt, then cont in st-st until leg measures 8 in. (20 cm).

Work heel
Begin to work back and forth in rows across 24 sts on 4th and 1st needles only. Rejoin yarn to the first of 8 sts on 4th needle and shape heel as foll:
1st row Sl 1, k23, turn.
2nd row Sl 1, p22, turn.
3rd row Wyif sl 1, yb, k21, yf, sl 1, yb, turn.
4th row Sl 1, p20, sl 1 wyif, yb, turn.
5th row Sl 1, yb, k19, yf, sl 1, yb, turn.
6th row Sl 1, p18, sl 1 wyif, yb, turn.
Cont as set until the row 'sl 1, yb, k9, yf, sl 1, yb, turn' is worked.
Next row Sl 1, p10, sl 1 wyif, yb, turn.

Next row Sl 1, yb, k11, yf, sl 1, yb, turn.
Next row Sl 1, p12, sl 1 wyif, yb, turn.
Cont as set until the row 'sl 1, k22, yf, sl 1, yb, turn' is worked.
Next row Sl 1, p23, turn.
Next row K24, now work across 24 sts from 2nd and 3rd needles.
Cont in rounds, work a further 4 in. (10 cm) in st-st.

Shape toe
Next round On needle 1, k to last 3 sts, k2tog, k1; on needle 2, sl 1, k1, psso, k to end; work sts on needle 3 same as needle 1; work sts on needle 4 same as needle 2.
Rep last round on foll 4th rounds twice, then on alt rounds 3 times and every round 4 times. Cut off yarn, leaving a long end. Fold over final yarn end and draw a double strand through rem 8 sts. Fasten off securely.

Finishing off
With crochet hook and green, make a hanging loop at center back as foll: attach yarn, work 15ch and ss into edge of sock. Work 1 turning ch, then 1sc into each ch, ending with 1ss into edge of the sock.
Make 14 decorations in pink and 12 in each of pumpkin and silver. For each decoration, with crochet hook, make 3ch, (yrh, insert hook in 1st ch, yrh and draw a loop through, yrh and draw through first 2 loops on hook) 4 times, yrh and draw through all 5 loops, work 1ch, fasten off. Sew on decorations.

Picture Advent Calendar

Children will love finding new surprises hidden in the little finger-sized pockets of this appealing cross-stitch Advent calendar. It is sure to be in demand for many Christmases to come.

You will need:

- 20½ in. x 11 in. (52 cm x 28 cm) white Aida fabric

- 6-strand cotton embroidery floss, one skein in each of dark green, light green, red, golden brown, and black

- 6-strand metallic embroidery floss in gold

- tapestry needle

- 16 in. x 14½ in. (40 cm x 37 cm) 14-count red Aida fabric

- white sewing thread

- red sewing thread

- 17½ in. (45 cm) of 1-in. (2.5-cm)-wide dark green tape

- 15¾-in. (40-cm) length of wooden dowel rod or bamboo cane

Finished size

14½ in. x 12¾ in. (37 cm x 32 cm)

1 To stitch the pockets, cut the white Aida fabric into four pieces each 5 in. x 11 in. (13 cm x 28 cm). Fold each piece in half widthwise and mark the crease line with stitches in a brightly colored sewing thread.

2 There are three charts for the embroidery on the white Aida fabric on page 271. Chart A shows the six motifs in the top row of pockets. The same motifs are used for all the other rows, but in different orders as shown on diagram 1, also on page 271. Chart B shows the borders around the numbers and the positions for single and double numbers are indicated by dotted lines. Chart C shows the numbers.

3 Each colored square on the charts equals one cross-stitch worked over one square of the Aida fabric. The solid lines show where to work back stitches or straight stitches and the small dots represent French knots. On chart A, the vertical center line is marked with arrows. The colors of cotton and metallic embroidery floss to use are given in the key. For easy reference, tape a small piece of each color next to its corresponding number on the key.

4 Work each panel of pockets as follows. Start centrally ½ in. (1 cm) from the top edge of the fabric, and begin by stitching the light green border. Then stitch the motifs, using diagram 1 as a guide to placing them correctly for each panel. The metallic gold stars are worked as two triangles of straight stitches, one over the other.

5 To stitch the pocket borders and numbers, you will need to work on the back of the fabric as well as turning it upside down, so that the numbers are the right way up when you fold the pockets. Following chart B and repeating it three times, stitch the light green borders, starting ½ in. (1 cm) up from the bottom edge of the fabric. Make sure that the vertical lines even up with the ones on the other side of the fabric when the pockets are turned up. Following chart C, add the numbers to the pockets.

6 To stitch the border, follow chart D on page 271. Find and mark the center of the red Aida fabric. Beginning at the center of the top edge, stitch a small gold star 12 Aida squares down. The stars are worked in the same way as those on the white panels. The holly leaves are dark green straight stitches.

9 Matching the center lines on the red Aida fabric background and on each pocket section, sew the first pocket in place. Use white sewing thread and small slip stitches for this, making sure you work a few extra stitches at each corner to strengthen it.

10 To form the divisions between each numbered pocket, work a line of backstitch through the center of each dividing line of green cross-stitches. Start and finish off securely at each end by working a few stitches on top of each other at these points.

11 Neaten the edges of the red Aida background fabric by turning the excess to the wrong side, two squares from the edge of the gold stars. Slip stitch in place using red cotton sewing thread. Miter the fabric at the corners to create a neat edge.

12 Cut the piece of green tape into three equal lengths. Fold each one in half and iron. Position one loop at each end and one in the middle of the top edge. Slip stitch securely in place on the wrong side. Thread the dowel rod or cane through the tape loops and hang suspended from a picture hook or supported on cup hooks screwed into the wall.

7 To make up the calendar, trim the excess white Aida fabric from around the pocket pieces to leave ½ in. (1 cm) all round. Turn this to the wrong side along the top edge of the numbers and tack, then slip stitch in place along the edge of the light green cross-stitches.

8 Fold the number section up to the right side along the bottom row of green cross-stitches and iron. Turn the excess fabric to the wrong side around the remaining three sides and tack in place. Iron from the wrong side.

Christmas Robin

Nothing says "Merry Christmas" like a handmade card. Let your imagination go wild and personalize each Christmas card with metallic glitter or other embellishment.

You will need:

- 11 in. x 5½ in. (28 cm x 14 cm) of green cardstock
- 4½ in. x 5½ in. (12 cm x 14 cm) of matte gold paper
- 3¼ in. (8 cm) square of red corrugated cardstock
- small piece of black paper for the beak
- 2 plastic eyes
- compass
- spray adhesive
- craft knife
- superglue

1 Score the green card in the center and fold to make a 5½ in. (14 cm) square.

2 Trace the bird's body from the templates on page 272 and transfer onto gold paper. Cut out using a craft knife.

tip

If making a number of cards at a time, speed up the process by using a circle cutter to cut a perfect circle every time.

3 Using a compass, draw a 3¼ in. (8 cm) circle on the reverse of the red corrugated cardstock. Trace the beak shape and transfer onto the black paper. Cut out both the circle and the beak with a craft knife.

4 Starting with the gold paper, glue the body shape onto the front of the green cardstock. Add the red breast and beak. Finally add the two plastic eyes using superglue.

Heavenly Angel

Bring a touch of heaven to your Christmas greetings. The silk of the angel's dress has zig-zag stitching to stop the edges fraying, but all the other details are just glued on, quick as a flash.

You will need:

- 9 in. x 8 in. (23 cm x 20 cm) of blue tissue paper
- 9 in. x 8 in. (23 cm x 20 cm) of white cardstock
- spray adhesive
- 3½ in. (9 cm) square of pale pink silk
- 9 pale blue 1/16 in. (2 mm) glass beads
- 2 pink wooden beads
- 2 pieces of 1/8 in. (3 mm) pink ribbon, 2-in. (5-cm) long
- double-sided tape
- 2½ in. (6 cm) square of decorative net
- 2 pieces of gold cord, 5 in. (13 cm) long
- 10 clear 1/8 in. (3 mm) glass beads
- 5/8 in. (15 mm) clear flat-backed bead
- superglue

1 Stick the blue tissue paper onto the white cardstock with spray adhesive. Fold in the center to make a card 8 in. x 4½ in. (20 cm x 11.5 cm).

2 Trace the angel body shape from the templates on page 272 and transfer onto the pale pink silk. Using a sewing machine and white thread, follow the outline with a close, narrow zig-zag stitch. Trim out with scissors taking care not to cut the stitching.

3 Sew the pale blue seed beads in a zig-zag pattern on the bottom of the body; pull the thread across the back of the fabric and tie off securely.

4 Make the legs by attaching the pink beads to one end of each ribbon with superglue. Attach the legs to the back of the body using double sided tape, then stick the body to the card with spray adhesive.

5 Using the template as a guide cut out the wing from the net fabric and glue it in place with a small amount of superglue in three places. Glue the flat-backed bead for the head in place with superglue.

6 Take one of the pieces of gold cord and glue the end on the inside of the card ½ in. (12 mm) from the top. Once stuck, stretch the cord across the top of the card and over onto the back. Glue in place. Next glue the five clear beads underneath the cord, spacing them evenly across the card.

7 Repeat step 6 at the bottom of the card but postioning the beads above the cord.

Dangling Ornament

Cut a window from your card and hang a shiny ornament in it. This clever design is sure to surprise and delight the recipient. You can further enhance your card by punching a line of Christmas trees along the bottom.

You will need:

- 6 in. x 8 in. (15 cm x 20 cm) of thick white watercolor paper folded to 3 in. x 8 in. (7.5 cm x 20 cm)
- Christmas tree motif paper punch (optional, available from craft store)
- 3 in. x 2 in. (7.5 cm x 5 cm) of green heavy-duty foil
- 6 in. (15 cm) of silver thread
- 5/8 in. x 2 in. (15 mm x 50 mm) of gold card
- 3 red flat-backed gems
- craft knife
- double-sided tape
- superglue

tip

To cut a neat window, use a small piece of cardboard cut to the correct size, position this centrally on the front of the card and cut around it, like a stencil.

1 Cut out a square 3 in. x 2 in. (7.5 cm x 5 cm) 2¼ in. (5.5 cm) from the top of the card and ⅝ in. (15 mm) in from the each edge.

2 On the front of the card, position the punch (if using) at the bottom left-hand side and press to cut out motif. Repeat process on the bottom right-hand side of the card. Finally position the punch exactly in the center of the two motifs and press to cut out final tree shape.

3 Transfer the ornament template from page 272 onto the reverse of the green foil. Cut out using a craft knife. Fold along the dotted line and stick the flap down with double-sided tape trapping the silver thread between the two pieces of card. Tie a knot in the silver thread.

4 Stick the gold band centrally on the ornament and trim off the excess on either side following the curve of the ornament. Superglue three gems evenly spaced on the center of the gold band.

5 Hang the ornament in the window of the card and stick in place on the reverse with sticky tape.

Sprightly Santa

Here's a Santa with a stylish attitude, but he'll still bring lots of presents. Make him from felt squares, readily available from craft stores, or you may have scraps of felt in your ragbag.

You will need:

- 3 in. x 5 in. (7.5 cm x 13 cm) red felt
- 2½ in. (6 cm) square of white felt
- 1¼ in. (3 cm) square of pink felt
- 2 in. x 3½ in. (5 cm x 9 cm) of beige felt
- 1¼ in. (3 cm) square black felt
- 9 in. x 8 in. (24 cm x 20 cm) of silver card folded to 4½ in. x 8 in. (12 cm x 20 cm)
- fabric glue

1 Using the photograph as a color guide, transfer the shapes from the template on page 272 to the different colored felts. Cut out with scissors.

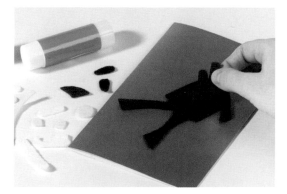

2 Starting with the body, position and glue in place on the card. Position the legs and right arm and glue in place.

3 Next position the face, hands and hat and glue in place. Add the present bag.

4 Glue all the white felt in place and finally add the shoes.

Citrus Ribbon Wrap

Everyone enjoys giving as well as receiving presents. And a gift wrapped with thought and a little imagination makes the occasion even more memorable.

You will need:

- 1 orange
- 4 paper towels
- handmade paper
- double-sided tape
- ribbon, sufficient in length to wrap around your gift and form a bow
- scissors
- glue gun

Did you know?

Gifts have been wrapped since the invention of paper circa 105 A.D. in China. Decorative gift wrap didn't take off until Christmas 1917, when the Hall Brothers' store in Nebraska, USA, sold out of tissue for customers to wrap holiday packages. As a substitute, they sold decorative French envelope lining.

1 Cut the orange into slices, about ³⁄₈ in. (8 mm) thick. Cover a microwaveable plate with paper towels. Place the orange slices on top and cook in microwave at 50 percent power (medium) for 3 minutes. Turn over and repeat for a further 2 minutes. Leave to air-dry for 2–3 days.

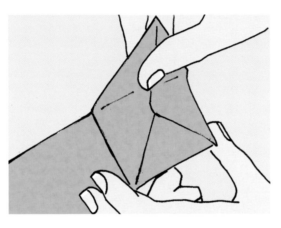

2 Cut a piece of handmade paper large enough to fit around your gift, allowing extra for an overlap. Place double-sided tape on the right-hand top and bottom edges. Remove the backing paper from the tape and wrap the paper tightly around the gift. Press down the edges to secure.

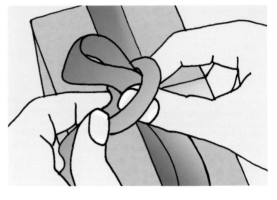

3 Fold the ribbon in half. Center it lengthwise over the top of the box, wrap around the edges, twist at the back and then bring it back up to the top of the gift to knot. Tie the ribbon in a bow, trimming the ends to match each loop. Arrange the bow so that the ribbon is not twisted.

4 Using a glue gun, place two small dabs of glue, about 4 in. (10 cm) apart, on the long length of ribbon next to the bow. Place two dried orange slices on top of the glue and leave until completely dry.

tip

Handmade paper tends to be quite thick. To achieve crisp folds when using it as gift wrap, fold the paper around the edges of the gift, then remove it. Using a paper folder, crease the folds to give more defined edges, before securing the paper back around the gift.

Snowflake Gift Wrap

A pile of beautifully wrapped presents placed under a
Christmas tree really sets the scene. This impressive handmade
gift wrap adds that extra-special touch to your carefully chosen
gifts. Make your own snowflake stencil or use a stamp for the
decoration, then tie with matching string.

joy of giving

You will need:

- 17 in. x 11 in. (43 cm x 28 cm) sheet of thin cardboard
- 1 large sheet of plain white paper
- red acrylic paint
- stencil brush
- 1 large sheet of red paper
- various snowflake stamps (available from craft store)
- pencil
- craft knife
- white acrylic paint
- 2 yd. (2 m) red and white festive string

1 Take a piece of thin cardboard and trace one of the snowflake templates (see page 273) onto it. Using a craft knife, carefully cut out the areas of the template to make the stencil. There are different shapes and sizes to choose.

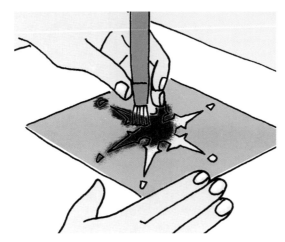

2 Take the white paper and pour some red acrylic paint onto an old plate. Decide if your gift wrap will have a random pattern, or if the snowflakes will be in a line or block pattern. Working from the top left corner of the sheet, position the stencil where the first flake should be, then dip a stencil brush into the paint and dab over the stencil. Ensure that all of the white paper inside the stencil is covered with paint. Carefully remove the stencil before the paint dries.

3 Alternatively, if you have some snowflake stamps you can use these to decorate your gift wrap. Using the red paper, dip the stamp into the white acrylic paint, blot any excess paint on a paper towel to avoid smudging the stamp, then press firmly onto the paper. Always practice on scrap paper before stamping onto your special gift wrap paper.

4 Once you have finished stenciling or stamping, put the sheet of gift wrap to one side and allow to dry completely.

Finishing touches

When your gift wrap is completely dry, wrap your gift. Use jolly red-and-white festive string for a matching bow to finish off your gift.

tip

Avoid using too much paint on your stencil brush as this may cause your gift wrap to crinkle. Always test your stencil on scrap paper before stenciling onto special paper. You can use some low-tack tape to hold your stencil in position before adding paint.

Did you know?

Wrapping Christmas presents is quite a recent tradition. In the 19th century, unwrapped gifts were put under a Christmas tree, or hung on the branches. Sometimes, people would even hide a gift to prolong the excitement of finding out what it was.

❄ *Did you know?*

Baboushka is a Russian gift-bringer, an old woman who, according to custom, would not go with the Wise Men to visit the baby Jesus. She later realized she should have traveled with them, and so she still searches for the baby. On the eve of Epiphany (January 5th) she visits sleeping children to leave them gifts.

Organdy Wrap

Make even the simplest present look luxurious by enveloping it in gleaming gold organdy. This quick and easy gift wrap can also be hung as a tree decoration.

You will need:

For two gifts

- ½ yd. (50 cm) of gold organdy, 36-in. (90-cm) wide
- 2½ yd. (2.30 m) gold ribbon, 1-in. (2.5-cm) wide
- pinking shears (optional)

1 From the gold organdy, cut two 16-in. (40-cm) squares. If you wish, use pinking shears to create a non-fraying zigzag edge.

2 Cut the gold ribbon in half to give two 45-in. (114-cm) lengths. Trim the ends at a diagonal.

3 Place each present in the center of a square of organdy and gather the fabric up evenly around it. Tie with the ribbon and make a lavish bow with long trailing ends. Adjust the corners of the fabric so that they stand up stiffly and attractively.

joy of giving

Velvet Rose Trim

This stunning velvet rose would make any present look even more irresistible. Made of soft, smooth velvet, the petals and leaves are stiffened with wire to give them body.

1 Trace the petal and leaf shapes shown on page 273 and cut out to use as templates. From the dark pink velvet, cut six large and six small petals. From the lime green velvet, cut six leaves, adding a ¹⁄₄-in. (6-mm) seam allowance all around.

2 Fold each petal with right sides together. Stitch ¹⁄₈ in. (3 mm) away from the fold to create the central vein channel. Cut a 4³⁄₄-in. (12-cm) length of red wire and insert it into the channel, leaving the end emerging at the base.

3 Place two leaves right sides together and, taking a ¹⁄₄-in. (6-mm) seam allowance, stitch around the edge, leaving an opening at the base. Turn through to the right side. Cut a length of wire long enough to go all around the leaf plus about 4 in. (10 cm). Bend the wire in half, insert it into the leaf and spread it out to take the shape of the leaf and stiffen it.

4 Close the opening in the leaf with slip stitch, leaving about 2 in. (5 cm) of wire emerging at the base. Using two strands of cotton embroidery floss, stitch veins in stem stitch. Repeat steps 3 and 4 to make two more leaves.

5 Cut 14 lengths of wire 4³⁄₄-in. (12-cm) long and, using superglue, stick a bead to the end of each wire to make stamens (central part of flower). Hold the stamens together in a bunch and arrange the small petals, then the large petals, and finally the leaves around them. Wind a length of wire several times around the base of the flower to secure it.

6 From the lime green velvet, cut a quarter-circle with a radius of 2 in. (5 cm). With right sides together and taking a ¹⁄₄-in. (6-mm) seam allowance, stitch along the straight edge and turn through to make a cone. Slip the cone over the base of the flower to hide the wires. Tie the green satin ribbon around the cone, and tie to the top of your present.

For a Beautiful Corsage

Make up the rose in the same way and secure the ribbon to the cone and wires with a little neat oversewing at the back of the flower to keep everything secure. Then sew a brooch pin to the back to make a beautiful corsage. The colors of the fabrics can be varied to match a favorite dress or suit, and contrast beads used to emphasize the stamens.

Ways with Tags

A hand-crafted tag is the finishing touch to a beautifully wrapped gift. Why not try some of these simple tags to make your gift-giving extra special? They are quick-to-make and inexpensive too.

You will need:

- 4½ in. (11 cm) square of green corrugated cardstock
- craft knife
- 12 in. (30 cm) of medium-gauge silver wire
- wire cutters
- 20 in. (50 cm) of fine-gauge silver wire
- small silver star
- 7 in. (18 cm) of ¼ in. (5 mm) red ribbon
- double-sided tape

For the Star Tag

1 Trace the star template from page 273 and transfer onto the green cardstock. Cut out with a craft knife. Using the template as a guide, bend the medium-gauge wire into a star shape. The two ends should overlap slightly, but trim off any excess wire.

2 Wrap the fine-gauge wire evenly around the star shape. Ensure the two ends are tucked inside the binding. Trim off any excess wire.

3 Wrap a short length of fine-gauge wire around one of the points, leaving two short pieces of wire at the back. Make a small hole in the green star and poke the ends of the wire through. Bend ends over to secure. Trim off any excess. Repeat at the base of the star.

4 Glue the small silver star in the center of the tag. Fold and stick the red ribbon in place on the back of the tag using double-sided tape.

tip

It's great to be able to reuse old Christmas cards to make stylish gift tags. To try these quick ideas, you'll need some old cards, cord, and corrugated cardstock.

1 Cut out motifs you want to use from old cards using scissors or a craft knife.

2 Take a motif and place onto a piece of corrugated cardstock, with the stripes running vertically. Mark out a rectangle around the motif, leaving a minimum 1/8 in. (3mm) border. Double the size of the rectangle to make a folded tag and cut out.

3 Fold the card in half and make a hole in the top left-hand corner with a hole punch.

4 Affix some double-sided adhesive spacers to the back of the motif to give a 3D effect when applied to the tag. Using double-sided tape will give a flatter finish.

5 Cut a length of cord, thread through the hole and tie off.

You will need:

- 6¼ in. x 2½ in. (16 cm x 6 cm) of thin blue cardstock
- 6¼ in. x 2½ in. (16 cm x 6 cm) of tracing paper
- 8 in. (20 cm) of 1/8 in. (3mm) blue ribbon
- white acrylic paint
- mapping pen

For the Snowflake Tag

1 Trace the tag shape and snowflake design from the templates on page 273. Transfer tag shape onto the thin blue cardstock and cut out.

2 Using a mapping pen, draw over the snowflakes with thinned white acrylic paint, see tip left. When the paint is dry, erase any visible pencil lines.

3 Trace the overlay shape from the templates and transfer to tracing paper. Cut out. Position the tracing paper on top of the card and make a hole through both using a hole punch.

4 Secure both parts of the tag together by threading a ribbon through the holes. Secure, then use this ribbon to attach the tag to your gift.

tip

Mix your acrylic paint so it has the consistency of light cream. This will mean it will be free-flowing in your mapping pen. Keep a piece of paper towel close by to dab off any excess before starting to draw.

Baby's Santa Bib

Baby's first Christmas will be made extra special with this fun and cheerful cross-stitch Santa bib. Have a camera ready for plenty of adorable snapshots!

You will need:

- 6-strand cotton embroidery floss, two skeins in grass green and one skein in each of the following colors: black, apricot, white, purple, yellow, and red

- white bib with 14-count Aida fabric band border

- tapestry needle

1 Fold the bib in half widthwise, and run a tacking thread along the fold through a row of holes. Repeat lengthwise and tack; the point where the two lines of tacking cross marks the center of the design. Mark the center lines of the chart in pencil to correspond.

2 Each colored square on the chart equals one cross-stitch worked over one square of the Aida fabric band. The colors of embroidery floss to use are given in the key.

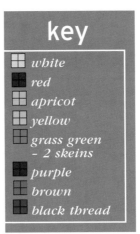

key

- white
- red
- apricot
- yellow
- grass green – 2 skeins
- purple
- brown
- black thread

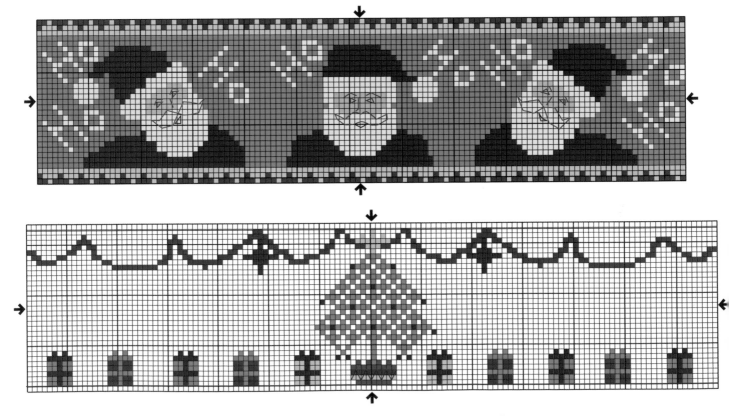

joy of giving

3 Start at the center and use three strands of embroidery floss throughout for the cross-stitching. When all the cross-stitching is complete, add the backstitch details to Santa's face using two strands of black thread.

4 Press the finished work from the wrong side over a lightly padded surface such as a terrycloth towel.

"We shall find peace.
We shall hear angels,
we shall see the sky
sparkling with diamonds."
Anton Chekhov

joy of giving

Sequined Scarf

Sparkling beads and light-as-a-feather silk chiffon make this scarf perfect to dress up a casual outfit or add the finishing note to an elegant one. What girlfriend wouldn't be thrilled with this gift?

You will need:

- 12 in. x 62 in. (30 cm x 160 cm) silk chiffon
- matching sewing thread
- beading needle
- approx. 200 translucent blue cup sequins, ranging from 1/4 in. to 3/8 in. (5 mm to 8mm) diameter
- 1/4 oz. (6 g) blue metallic bugle beads
- 4 mm and 8 mm matte blue faceted glass beads
- 1/4 oz. (6 g) 2 mm clear seed beads
- 1/4 oz. (6 g) 2 mm clear blue seed beads

1 Trim the edges of the chiffon so that they are square, then neaten the entire scarf with a hand-rolled hem sewn in matching thread.

2 Thread the beading needle with matching thread and fasten on at the bottom corner, about 1/3 in. (15 mm) from the long edge. To add a bead, bring the needle to the right side, thread it through a bugle bead, and take the needle back to the wrong side. Bring the needle out again 1/4 in (5 mm) away and parallel to the long edge. Sew on another bead. Continue to sew bugle beads in a line about 8 in. (20 cm) long and then fasten off securely with a double stitch.

3 Next sew a line of beads parallel to the bugle beads and about 3/4 in. (2 cm) away. For this line, sew about 12 clear seed beads, then a few 4-mm faceted glass beads, and some 8-mm faceted glass beads with blue seed beads either side. Repeat the sequence, then finish off.

4 For the third row, spaced as before, sew approximately 8 seed beads, then add a variety of sequins, with seed beads in each center. Bring the needle up in the center hole of the sequin, thread on a seed bead and take the needle back through the center hole of the sequin again to the wrong side.

5 Continue sewing lines of beads across the short end of the scarf, making the lines different lengths and starting at varying distances from the end, to give your scarf a freestyle effect.

6 Repeat steps 2–4 to decorate the other end of the scarf in the same way, fastening off each row securely. Make sure the two ends are decorated to a similar degree.

tip

The informal way of working used for this scarf is applicable to many other items— simply stitch straight lines of different beads in various lengths across the fabric you are working on to create a haphazard, unstudied feel.

Fun Animal Jigsaw

Nostalgic and handmade, these wooden puzzles painted with colorful animals will thrill young children at Christmas.

You will need:

- 9 blocks of wood, 1¼ in. (33 mm) square
- small and medium paintbrushes
- acrylic paints: dark pink, light pink, yellow, dark green, light green, dark blue, light blue, orange, red, purple, black, white
- tracing paper
- thin cardboard band to hold block together when transfering template designs

1 Paint each side of your block in a different color: dark pink, yellow, dark green, light blue, orange, and red. Allow to dry between colors.

2 Trace the animal templates from page 274 onto tracing paper.

3 Put all the blocks together to make a dark pink square. Secure by placing a band of cardboard around the edge of the block and taping in place. Transfer the elephant design to the surface of the blocks by tracing over the template. Make sure the outlines line up across the blocks. Paint the elephant using light pink paint and allow to dry. Add the eye and toe detail in purple.

4 Repeat step 3 to transfer the snake design onto the yellow side. Paint the main body in light green, add red spots with black outlines. Don't forget to add eyes and nostrils in black, and a forked tongue in red.

5 Repeat step 3 to transfer the giraffe onto the dark green side. Paint the main body in orange and add the yellow patches when the orange paint has dried. Add eyes in black.

6 Repeat step 3 to transfer the penguin stencil to the light blue side. Paint around the outside edge of body and head in dark blue. Allow to dry. Paint the feet in yellow and the middle of body in white. Add eyes in white and beak in yellow with a small brush.

7 Repeat step 3 to transfer the hippo design onto the orange side. Paint the body in light blue. Allow to dry. To paint the head in a slightly lighter shade, add a small amount of white to the blue and mix in well. Add ears and jaw line in the first colour with a small brush, then add eyes and nostrils in dark blue.

8 Repeat step 3 to transfer the lion design onto the red side. First paint the body and head yellow, then when dry add the mane, inner ears and tip of the tail in orange. Finally, add eyes, nose, and mouth in black.

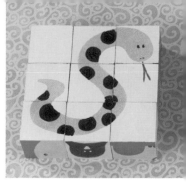

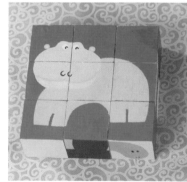

Pretty Padded Hangers

A thoughtful gift for a grandmother or a favorite aunt, these
hand-stitched treasures trimmed with lace will help make laundry
day a pleasure.

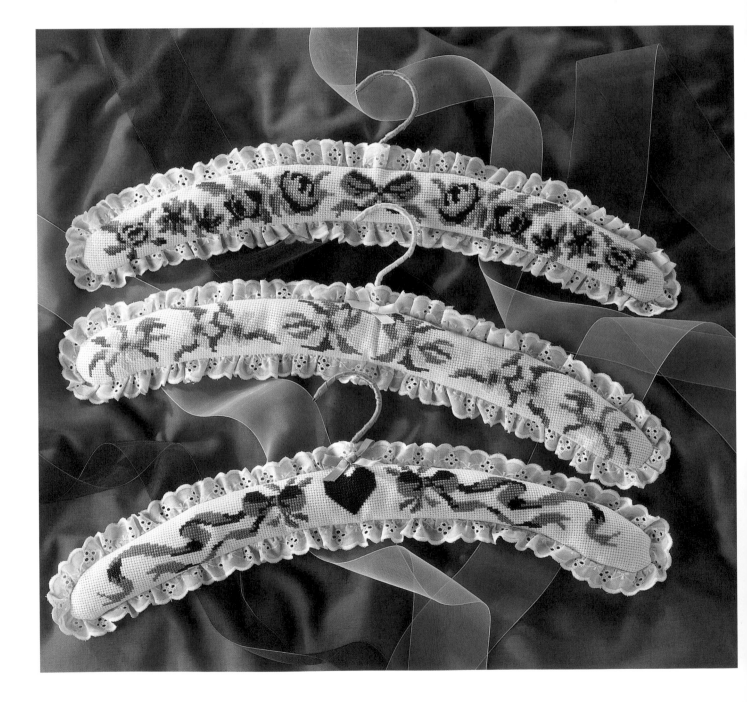

You will need:

- 18½ in. x 5¼ in. (47 cm x 13 cm) white 14-count Aida fabric for each hanger
- 6-strand cotton embroidery floss, one skein each of cerise, rose pink, pale pink, scarlet, royal blue, mid blue, lime green, mid green, bright yellow, pale yellow, light terracotta, pale orange
- tapestry needle
- tracing paper
- wooden coat hanger, about 16 in. (40 cm) long
- 18½ in. x 5¼ in. (47 cm x 13 cm) cotton backing fabric
- polyester batting
- 1¼ yd. (1.1 m) of white cotton eyelet trim, 1¼ in. (3 cm) wide
- narrow ribbon for hook and bow

1 Find the center of the Aida fabric by folding it lightly in half widthwise. Mark the crease line with running stitches in a contrasting color. Now mark the center point of the design on this fold line about 2 in. (5 cm) from the top edge. Work the design outward from this point.

2 Oversew the edges of the Aida fabric to prevent them from fraying when stitching. Each symbol on the chart equals one cross-stitch worked over one square. The key shows which colors of stranded floss to use.

3 Using two strands of embroidery floss for the cross-stitching, start at the center of the chart and work each half from the middle outward.

4 Using the template on page 275 make a hanger pattern by drawing it onto tracing paper (this allows you to see that the embroidery is centered on the hanger). Check that this template fits the hanger you are using, as they vary in shape. If necessary, adjust the template. Use the pattern to cut out hanger shapes from the embroidered fabric, the backing fabric, and two pieces of batting.

tip

The template for the hanger found on page 275 is just one half of the hanger. When you cut it out, fold the fabric in half and make sure you position the straight grain on the fold to make one complete shape.

5 Hand- or machine-stitch two rows of gathering thread along the white cotton eyelet trim, the first ½ in. (1 cm) away from the raw edge and the second ¼ in. (5 mm) away from the first. Mark the quarter points along the outer edge of the embroidered Aida fabric and along the length of the trim with pins, then draw up the gathering threads so the trim fits evenly all around the outer edge of the Aida fabric. With right sides facing and raw edges and pins matching, sew the trim in place, working the stitching between the lines of gathering. Remove the gathering threads once the stitching is complete.

6 With right sides facing, place the backing piece on top of the frilled front section, then lay a piece of batting on each side and tack in position. Machine-stitch around the lower edge and curves, working as close as possible to the original stitching line and leaving the top edge open. Trim the batting close to the stitching all around, clip the corners and notch the curves. Turn right sides out. Stitch a small bow in place at the base of the hook.

7 Bind the metal hook of the hanger with ribbon to match the bow. Apply a small piece of clear adhesive tape to the top of the hook and start off by working the ribbon over it. Tape the opposite end of the ribbon to the hanger. Insert the hanger, turn under the raw edges and close the top edges by slip-stitching together.

Mosaic Coaster

Coasters make a practical hostess gift, and will appeal to just about anyone because you made it yourself. Alter the tile colors to suit the person's decor.

You will need:

For one Coaster

- 4½ in. (11 cm) square MDF base
- 13 x ¾ in. (2 cm) blue tiles
- 12 x ⅜ in. (1 cm) white tiles
- 4 x ⅜ in. (1 cm) blue tiles
- 16 x ⅜ in. (1 cm) light green tiles
- 16 x ⅜ in. (1 cm) dark green tiles
- white (PVA) glue
- pale gray grout

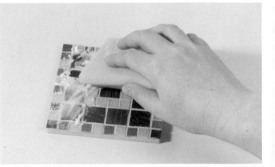

1 Find the center of each side of the coaster base and mark two intersecting lines in pencil. Position a ¾ in. (2 cm) blue tile centrally over the cross, and draw around the edges, extending the lines so they can be used as a guide for the smaller tiles later. It can be helpful to lay out all of the tiles onto the base before gluing any down to get a feel for the spacing.

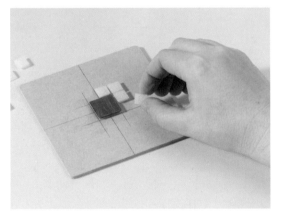

2 Glue a single ¾ in. (2 cm) blue tile in the center of the coaster base. Then glue a border of ⅜ in. (1 cm) white tiles all around it, leaving a small even gap between each tile for the grout to be added later.

3 Surround the white tiles with a border of ¾ in. (2 cm) blue tiles. Add a small ⅜ in. (1 cm) blue tile at each corner.

4 Finish each side by alternating dark and light green ⅜ in. (1 cm) tiles between the corners. Allow to dry.

5 Cover all the tiles with grout, smoothing it into the cracks. Once the grout has set, clean off the excess with a damp cloth, then buff with a soft cloth to polish up the tiles.

tip

If you can't find any small tiles, the large tiles can, with practice, be cut down to size using tile cutters. Wear protective eyewear when cuttng glass tiles.

" *Who shall for the present delight here...* **"**
Robert Herrick

Filigree Jewelry

These pretty filigree jewelry pieces are an ideal Christmas gift for a female family member or friend. Add a personal touch by stitching these dainty brooch and pendant designs yourself.

You will need:

For each Design

- 5 in. (13 cm) square cream 22-count Aida fabric
- 6-strand cotton embroidery floss in the following colors: deep pink, rose pink, pale pink, blue, pale green, green, gold, and slate gray
- tapestry needle

For the Brooch

- purchased round frame 1¼ in. (3 cm) with a bow

For the Pendant

- purchased oval frame 2¾ in. x 1½ in. (7 cm x 4 cm)

Finished sizes

Brooch
- 1¼ in. (3 cm)

Pendant
- 1³/8 in. across x 1½ in. (3.7 cm x 5 cm)

For the Brooch

1 To stitch the brooch, fold the Aida fabric in half lengthwise and mark the crease line with tacking stitches through a row of holes, using a contrasting floss. Repeat widthwise: the point where the two lines of tacking cross marks the center of the design. Mark the center of the chart (see page 276) in pencil to correspond.

2 Each colored square on the chart on page 276 equals one cross-stitch worked over one square of the Aida fabric. Follow the chart for the colors to use.

3 Start at the center and use one strand of embroidery floss throughout for the cross-stitching. When all the cross-stitching is complete, backstitch the filigree pattern surround indicated by the solid lines on the chart using one strand of the slate gray embroidery floss.

4 Iron the finished embroidery from the wrong side over a lightly padded surface, taking care not to flatten the stitches. Trim the Aida fabric to fit the mount and insert the design.

For the Pendant

1 To stitch the pendant, work as given for the brooch, noting that you should work the filigree heart in backstitch at the center of the design first, before completing the design in cross-stitch.

2 When all the cross-stitching is complete, backstitch flower stems around the central heart using one strand of dark green embroidery floss. Trim the Aida fabric and insert into the mount.

tip

Don't worry if you have trouble finding an exact match for the brooch or pendant, as long as it is a similar size and shape, you'll still be able to complete this project.

Flavored Gift Oils

You will need:

- sterilized glass bottles with corks or lids

For Fresh Herbal Oil

- 2 sprigs fresh oregano
- 4 large basil leaves
- 2 bay leaves
- 2 sprigs fresh sage
- 1 large garlic clove, peeled and sliced
- 6 black peppercorns
- 5 cups (2 pints/1.2 liters) extra virgin olive oil

For Fiery Chili Pepper Oil

- 12 dried red chilies
- 2½ cups (1 pint/600 ml) light olive oil or corn oil
- 2 tsp cayenne pepper

For Fragrant Lemon Oil

- 1 lemon
- 3-4 sprigs of fresh thyme
- 2½ cups (1 pint/600 ml) extra virgin olive oil

The oils will keep for up to 4 weeks when stored in a cool place.

Oils infused with herbs, spices or citrus fruits can be added to marinades, dressings, sautés, and stir-fries or drizzled over pizzas. They make original presents for your food-loving friends.

For Fresh Herbal Oil

1 Gently rub the oregano, basil, bay leaves, sage, and garlic between your fingers to release their aroma. Divide between sterilized bottles with the peppercorns.

2 Pour in the oil to within ⅛ in. (3 mm) of the top of the bottles, making sure the herbs and garlic are completely covered.

3 Seal the bottles tightly with corks or screw caps and shake well. Store in a cool cupboard for 2 weeks before using so that the flavors have time to develop.

For Fragrant Lemon Oil

1 Peel the zest from 1 lemon in thick strips and dry for 1¼ hours in the oven on its lowest setting.

2 Place in sterilized bottles with the sprigs of fresh thyme and pour in the extra virgin olive oil. Store for 1-2 weeks before using.

For Fiery Chili Pepper Oil

1 Chop the red chilies and place in a saucepan with the light olive oil or corn oil and the cayenne pepper. Simmer for 10 minutes. Do not allow the oil to get too hot or it will not keep for as long.

2 Leave to stand and cool for 12 hours before straining into sterilized bottles. Add an extra dried chili if desired. The oil is ready for use.

Snowflake Frosted Vase

The most inexpensive items can be transformed into works of art with creativity and a bit of time. Anyone you give this vase to will be thrilled with your gift and so amazed.

You will need:

- tracing paper
- masking film
- craft knife
- straight vase
- etching spray

1 Trace the snowflake designs from page 276 and transfer them directly onto the reverse of the masking film. Depending on the size of your vase, trace a suitable number of snowflakes to make a pleasing pattern.

2 Cut out the snowflakes from the masking film with a craft knife. Peel the backing from the film and position the snowflakes randomly over the vase. The film is very low-tack and easy to lift off and reposition. Move the snowflakes around until you have a well-spaced design.

3 Working in a well-ventilated area and following the manufacturers' instructions, apply etching spray over entire surface of the vase.

4 Remove the masking film to reveal the snowflake design. Allow the etching spray to dry completely, then polish lightly with a soft cloth.

tip

The patterns on etched glass are shown off to best effect against a colored backdrop. For gift giving, this is easily achieved by partially filling the glass container with a contrasting material, for example, wrapped candies, colored bath oil, or simply an attractive plain tissue paper.

" I should hardly admire more if real stars fell and lodged on my coat. "

Henry David Thoreau

Heart-Embossed Diary

This pretty hand-embossed and bejeweled diary has a precious quality that's in keeping with the thoughts and secrets that may be written within. Made by pricking out a heart design in foil, it's a wonderful gift for a teenage girl.

You will need:

- tracing paper
- 1 sheet of heavy-duty aluminum foil, 11½ in. x 7¼ in. (18.5 cm x 29 cm)
- used-up ball-point pen, or embossing tool, available at craft stores
- double-sided tape
- 8 in. x 10.5 in. (20 cm x 27 cm) sheet of cardboard
- plain 8 in. x 10.5 in. (20 cm x 27 cm) diary
- 1-in. (2.5-cm) clear heart gem
- 2 x ⅝-in. (17-mm) pink gems
- ½-in. (12-mm) clear gem
- white (PVA) glue

1 Trace the design from the template on page 277. Attach the tracing to the dull or wrong side of the foil (if there is a difference) and place on a soft surface. Trim foil with sharp scissors to leave a ¾ in. (2 cm) border around the template. With a used-up ball-point pen, go over the design with a series of dots. You could also use an embossing tool with a blunt tip, available from most craft stores.

3 Fold the two short foil edges up and trim the corners with scissors so the foil folds over neatly. Stick the edges down with double-sided tape.

4 Fold the two long foil edges up and trim the corners with scissors. Stick in place as in step 3.

2 Apply double-sided tape to one side of the cardboard, sticking it along each edge and through the center. Remove the tracing from the foil and turn the foil over. Position the foil so the wrong side of the design is centrally over the cardboard and the raised dots are visible. Stick the foil to the surface of the cardboard.

5 Using double-sided tape, position and stick the foil-covered cardboard to the front cover of the diary. Finish by attaching the gems to the cover with white (PVA) glue.

tip

When transferring the design, use only light pressure to avoid making a hole right through the foil.

Framed Flowers

Any garden enthusiast would be thrilled to receive this pretty framed cross-stitch picture for Christmas. The matching potpourri sachets will make a great addition to the gift.

Refer to the chart on page 278.

You will need:

For the Sampler

- 16 1/2 in. (42 cm) square white 14-count Aida fabric

- 6-strand embroidery cotton, two skeins in each of Christmas green and pale green; one skein each of black, olive green, dark red, red, bright pink, gray/green, light Christmas green, light green, pale peach, pale yellow, yellow, green, bright Christmas green, gray, light gray, white, orange, pale pink, pink, dark pink

- tapestry needle

For the Potpourri Sachets

- 5 1/8 in. x 7 1/4 in. (13 cm x 18.5 cm) 14-count Aida fabric

- 5 1/8 in. x 7 1/4 in. (13 cm x 18.5 cm) cotton fabric for backing

- sewing thread

- narrow lace for trimming top edge

- lengths of 1/2-in. (1-cm) and 1/4-in. (0.5-cm) wide ribbon

For the Sampler

1 Before you begin the cross-stitch, find the center of your fabric by folding it lightly in half each way. Mark the resulting crease lines with running stitches worked in a brightly colored sewing thread.

2 Mark the vertical center line of the chart as indicated by arrows at the side of it, in pencil to correspond. Oversew the edges of the Aida fabric to stop them from fraying as you stitch.

3 Refer to the chart on page 278. Each colored square on the chart equals one cross-stitch worked over one Aida fabric square. The solid lines indicate backstitching. The key shows which colors of embroidery cotton to use.

4 Using two strands of the embroidery thread for the cross-stitching, start with the central horizontal line dividing the two lines of motifs and work it in pale and Christmas green. Continue using these two colors for the outer border and lines separating the flower pictures. Then, work each flower motif within its individual frame.

5 As the cross-stitching for each flower motif is finished, backstitch the details as indicated on the chart. Use one strand of embroidery thread and colors as follows: Christmas green for the snowdrop stems and outlining the flowers; black for outlining the tulip blooms, leaves, and stalks; orange for highlighting the rosebuds and Christmas green for details on their leaves; black for all the details on the pansies, pinks, and primulas.

6 To finish, iron the finished embroidery on the wrong side over a lightly padded surface, and frame as desired.

For the Potpourri Sachets

1 Fold the Aida fabric in half lengthwise and mark the crease line with running stitches in a contrasting color. Measure 1 1/2 in. (3.5 cm) down from the top edge and 5/8 in. (1.5 cm) up from the bottom edge. Mark with pins.

2 Fold the remaining section of the fabric in half widthwise and mark the crease with another line of contrasting running stitches. Mark the center lines of the required motif on the chart in pencil to correspond.

3 Start at the center and use two strands of embroidery thread throughout. When all the cross-stitching is finished, work backstitch details in colors as given for the sampler with one strand of embroidery thread.

4 Place the Aida fabric and cotton backing with right sides together, and taking ⅝ in. (1.5 cm) turnings, sew around three sides of the sachet, leaving the top edge open. Trim the seams and corners. Turn the sachet right side out and iron, taking care not to flatten the embroidery.

5 Turn under a ½ in. (1 cm) hem all around the top edge and stitch in place. Slip-stitch a narrow lace trim around the top, starting and ending at one side of the seam edge.

6 Position the wider ribbon about ¾ in. (2 cm) from the top edge. Turning under the row ends to neaten, and starting and ending at the center front of the sachet to leave a gap, neatly slip-stitch the ribbon in place in position around the sachet to form a casing. Thread the narrow ribbon through the casing to tie at the front. Alternatively, choose a contrasting colored ribbon instead of a matching one.

Winter Wear for Walks

Don't forget to give your precious pooch a gift at Christmastime. This handsome red-and-black felt coat is perfect for keeping small dogs warm in cold weather. Your dog will look stylish when out walking.

"Over the river and through the woods, Trot fast my dapple gray: Spring o'er the ground just like a hound, For this is Christmas Day."

Lydia Maria Child

You will need:

- tracing paper
- 22 in. x 16 in. (55 cm x 43 cm) piece of red felt
- tailor's chalk
- tacking thread
- 24 in. x 4 in. (60 cm x 10 cm) piece of 14-count waste canvas
- 6-strand cotton embroidery floss, one skein in black
- tapestry needle
- 2½ yd. (2.5 m) single fold bias tape in black
- 4 in. (10 cm) Velcro tape
- black sewing thread

tip

Once you have stitched your motif, you can remove the waste canvas. Start by removing any stitches holding the canvas in place, then dab the motif lightly with water. The canvas is held together with a starch-based glue. The water dissolves the glue, allowing you to pull out the canvas threads.

1 You will find a half-size pattern for the dog's coat on page 279. Enlarge it to 200 percent on a photocopier, then copy the outline onto tracing paper, with crosses marking the position of each paw motif. The small arrows on the pattern show the direction in which each motif is placed and need not be marked on the tracing paper. Cut out the paper pattern.

2 Cut a strip of red felt 10 in. x 2 in. (25 cm x 5 cm) and set aside for making the fastening straps. Pin the pattern on the remaining felt. Draw around the outline with tailor's chalk (do not cut felt at this stage). Mark the crosses in position with short lines of tacking stitches in a contrasting color, stitching through both paper and felt. Tear the paper away carefully.

3 For each paw motif, cut a 2 in. (5 cm) square of waste canvas and mark the center. Pin the waste canvas over one of the tacked crosses on the felt, matching the center lines to the tacking. Tack the waste canvas in position around the edges.

4 The center lines on the waste canvas correspond to the center lines marked by arrows on the chart. Each motif should be worked in the direction indicated by the arrows on the chart on page 279, matching these arrows to the top arrow on the chart.

5 Using two strands of the black embroidery floss throughout, work all the cross-stitching, then outline each area of cross-stitch in backstitch as indicated. When the embroidery is finished, remove the waste canvas (see tip box for further instructions).

6 Iron the embroidery on the wrong side over a lightly padded surface. Cut out the main shape following around the chalk outline and bind the outer edge with bias tape. From the long strip of felt, cut two pieces each 5 in. x 2 in. (12.5 cm x 5 cm)—or shorter if required—allow for a 2 in. (5 cm) overlap under the dog's tummy. Trim one end of each piece to a smooth curve. Bind the edges with bias tape, leaving the straight end free. Sew one strap to each side of the coat under the bound edge as indicated on the outline diagram.

7 Cut the Velcro tape in half to make two pieces each 2 in. (5 cm) long. Pull one piece apart and sew one side to the end of one strap, on the right side, and the other to the underside of the other strap. Sew the two sides of the other piece of Velcro tape to the ends of the collar section of the dog's coat.

Floating Necklace

Tigertail—the delicate nature of the wire makes the beads appear to float around the neck. It's a perfect present for any glamour girl.

joy of giving

You will need:

- 5 ft. (1.5 m) tigertail nylon-covered jewelry wire (.012-.015 gauge)
- 2 calottes (necklace ends)
- 2 crimp beads
- 10 irregular-shaped glass beads in lilac
- 10 metallic ball beads in pale green
- 10 metallic circular beads in copper
- clasp
- jump ring
- flat-nose pliers

1 Cut your length of tigertail into three. Treating the three lengths as one, push the ends through the hole at the base of the calotte, through one crimp bead and then squeeze the crimp bead with your flat-nose pliers to secure the tigertail.

2 If there is any excess tigertail, trim, then squeeze the calotte closed around the crimp bead. Slide the clasp onto the end of the calotte and use the pliers to close.

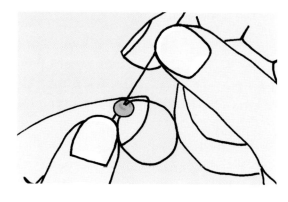

3 Thread one round bead to 4 in. (10 cm) from the clasp end of one length. Once in postion take the tigertail back through the hole and pull the coated wire taut.

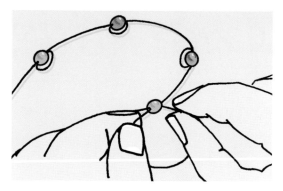

4 Continue to work along one length of tigertail, leaving about 2 in. (5 cm) space between the beads. Work with the colors and add in the irregular-shaped beads randomly—do not work in sequence. String ten beads on each length.

5 Work your second and third lengths of tigertail in a similar way, ensuring that the beads are offset with each other, so they don't line up.

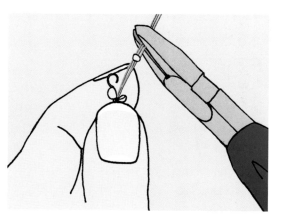

6 Pull all three ends taut and thread on a calotte, then a crimp bead. Squeeze the crimp bead to secure. Trim off any excess wire, move the calotte up to enclose the crimp bead and squeeze to close. Finally, add a jump ring to the end.

tip

Be careful not to kink your tigertail as you work. If you want to tighten the loops around the beads, gently squeeze the wire round them —but only once your necklace is completed.

Charming Cat Pillow

Amuse your cat-loving friends with a present of this whimsical cat in Christmas colors. He's such fun, he'll have pride of place all year round. Simple sewing skills are all you'll need to complete the project.

You will need:

- 12 in. (30 cm) square red printed cotton
- 2 pieces red printed cotton 16 in. x 11 in. (40 cm x 28 cm)
- 4 strips green/red check cotton 12 in. x 3 in. (30 cm x 7.5 cm)
- 4 squares pale green printed cotton 3 in. x 3 in. (7.5 cm x 7.5 cm)
- 12 in. (30 cm) square cream printed cotton
- 6 in. (15 cm) square gold cotton
- 2 black oval beads or buttons
- dark-gray 6-strand cotton embroidery floss
- 16 in. (40 cm) square pillow form

1 Using the template on page 279, cut out a cat, back leg, and two ears from the cream print cotton, and a bow from the gold cotton.

2 Using a ½ in. (1 cm) seam allowance, sew a strip of the checked fabric to two opposite sides of the red printed square. Sew a pale green printed square to each end of the remaining two strips. Sew these strips to the top and bottom of the other pieces, matching seams carefully. Press with an iron.

3 Using the pillow diagram as a guide, pin and tack the ears and back leg in place. Sew in place onto the pillow front using a slip stitch and turning under approx. ¼ in. (5 mm) as you work.

4 Pin the rest of the cat in place and stitch down in the same way. Repeat this step for the bow and then add the knot on top of the bow.

5 Using the template on page 279 as a guide, mark the details onto the cat's face, ears, and paws.

6 Embroider all the details by laying two strands of dark gray embroidery floss over the lines, then securing the thread with small stitches worked over it (this technique is called couching). For the bow details, use only one strand. Work a closely spaced satin stitch for the nose and sew the beads or buttons in place for the eyes.

7 To make the back of the pillow, take the other pieces of red print fabric and turn a ½ in. (1 cm) double hem on one long edge of each and machine-stitch. Overlap these two machined edges, both right side up until they match the size of the pillow front and pin at each end—these edges will form the envelope opening on the pillow back.

8 Place pillow back and front, right sides together. Pin, tack, and machine-stitch around all four edges. Remove the tacking, turn right side out and push the corners out with a knitting needle. Iron lightly, insert the pillow form.

Gift for a Party-Goer

Enter into the party spirit with this stunning beaded silk clutch bag. Simple to make, it is the ideal present for anyone who enjoys dressing up for the party season.

You will need:

- 15 in. x 10 in. (38 cm x 25 cm) rectangle of drapery interfacing
- 1/3 yd. (30 cm) of pale gold dupioni silk, 44 in. (112 cm) wide
- tracing paper
- 1/3 yd. (30 cm) of cream lining, 44 in. (112 cm) wide
- tacking thread
- gold sewing thread
- 3 clear sew-on jewelry stones, 1/4 in. (5 mm) in diameter
- 24 cranberry bugle beads
- 1/4 oz. (10 g) cranberry rocaille beads
- 6 clear sequins
- snap fastener

1 First of all, begin by preparing the interfacing. Fold up 4 in. (10 cm) at one end of the interfacing for the flap on the clutch bag, and iron along the fold. Repeat at the other end, folding up 5 in. (13 cm) for the front of the bag. Iron. Open the interfacing out flat again.

2 Cut a rectangle 17 in. x 12 in. (41 cm x 28 cm) from pale gold dupioni silk. Pin the interfacing centrally on the fabric with the right side of the fabric outermost. Fold the raw edges of the fabric over the interfacing and tack in place.

3 Trace the beading design from the pattern on page 280, and go over the pencil lines again on the reverse of the tracing paper. Pin the tracing on the silk so that the front edge of the pattern lines up with the front edge of the flap. Transfer the design by redrawing the pencil lines. Remove the tracing paper.

4 Sew the three jewelry stones to the silk using gold thread, where indicated by the crosses. Complete the beading by sewing 12 bugle beads radiating outward from each jewelry stone. Sew rocaille beads along the curved lines. Sew a sequin at each dot with a rocaille bead on top. Randomly dot rocaille beads around the design.

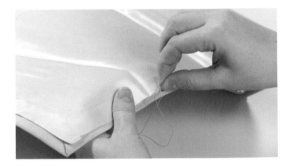

5 Cut a rectangle 16 in. x 11 in. (40 cm x 27 cm) from cream lining. Iron under 1/2 in. (1 cm) on the raw edges. Pin the lining centrally to the underside of the bag. Slip-stitch the lining in place.

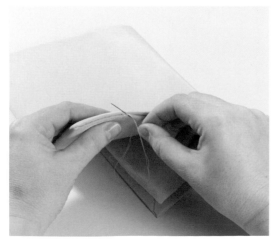

6 Fold up the front of the bag. Slip-stitch the side edges in together, using matching gold thread and finishing off with a few oversewing stitches on the inside of the bag for strength. Position one part of the snap fastener centrally on the underside of the flap and sew in place. Stitch the other part to the front flap so the bag can be closed securely.

Clever Boxes

Some presents may seem difficult to wrap, so the best way to solve this is to make a custom package. Equally, you can jazz up a homemade Christmas gift with a handmade fancy box or bag.

You will need:

- 2 x 7½ in. (19 cm) square sheets of medium-weight white cardboard

- 23½ in. x 2 in. (59 cm x 5 cm) strip of medium-weight white cardboard for box sides

- 24½ in. x 1 in. (62 cm x 2.5 cm) strip of medium-weight white cardboard for lid

- double-sided tape

- white (PVA) glue

- sheets of white and/or colored tissue paper for covering and lining the box

For the Star-Shaped Box

This snow-white star-shaped box is sure to delight the recipient.

1 Trace the templates from page 280 onto cardboard and cut out.

2 To make the box, score along the tabs on the star base and bend them upward. Score the strip as indicated on the template and fold along the score lines to fit the base. Use pieces of double-sided tape to secure the base to the inside of the strip that will make up the box sides. Secure the ends of the strip together. Repeat to make the lid.

3 Cut the tissue paper into pieces approximately 2 in. (5 cm) square. Apply white (PVA) glue to the sides of box and smooth the tissue paper into place. Leave the large flat areas until last, but take care not to cover the lid in too many layers, otherwise it may not fit the box. Make sure all edges are neatly covered.

Finishing Touches

For a truly individual look, use strips of tissue paper in contrasting colors, or glue craft-store embellishments, such as letters and charms, onto the lid. This petite box is perfect for delicate gifts —but be sure to line it with some colorful tissue paper, not just to display the contents, but also to protect the inside of the box from sharp edges or contents that may mark the interior.

tip

If you plan to give edible gifts, make sure they will last until Christmas Day. Also remember to tell the recipient if the gift needs to be kept away from heat sources like warm Christmas lights. Tissue paper absorbs moisture causing it to discolor or bleed, so store the gift box somewhere cool and dry, rather than in the fridge.

You will need:

For a 9 in. (23 cm) Cake

- 2 x 16 in. (40 cm) square sheets of gold cardboard
- 10 in. (25 cm) square cake board
- double-sided tape
- 55 in. (125 cm) wide red satin ribbon

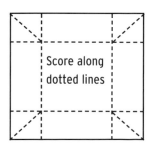

Score along dotted lines

For the Cake Box

1 Measure the height of your cake on the cake board and add ½ in. (1cm). The cardboard for the bottom part of the box will need to measure the diameter of the cake board, plus twice the height. For a cake that is 3 in. (7.5 cm) high and 10 in. (25 cm) wide, your cardboard will measure 16 in. (40 cm) square. Work out the size of cardboard you need and cut out.

2 Place the cake board in the center of the wrong side of the cardboard. Draw a line, from edge to edge on the cardboard, along each side of the cake board. Draw diagonal lines corner to corner, but avoiding the central square. Score the cardboard along all the marked lines.

3 Turn the cardboard over and fold the corners outward along the diagonal. Using double-sided tape, stick the fold against the outer side of the box. Repeat for all four corners.

4 Make the lid in the same way but increase the size of the central area by ⅛ in. (3 mm) on each side and reduce the box depth by 1 in. (2.5 cm) on each side. Add the lid and wrap with the ribbon, finishing in a bow.

Gifts Galore

Create a big impression with a tower of presents. This idea is great for a series of small, light gifts, such as a set of jewelry, ornaments, or even cookies.

Choose three sizes of box that will stack up neatly and buy two of each. Swap the lids of the same sized boxes for a pleasing contrast. Place a strip of double-sided tape at the center of the lid of the largest box and place the base of the medium box on top. Repeat with the medium lid and small base.

Add colorful tissue paper to each box to cradle the gifts. Put the lids onto the boxes to create the tower. Secure with two lengths of ribbon, pulled up from the bottom, and tie together in a bow at the top.

Did you know?

In Scandinavia, the main celebration for Christmas is on the evening of December 24th rather than December 25th. Carols are sung as adults and children walk around the illuminated Christmas tree holding hands, and gifts are exchanged after dinner.

joy of giving

Cookie Cracker

Who wouldn't look forward to opening these intriguing little parcels?
They're so much fun! Place a bunch of cookie crackers in a decorative
bowl near your door as unexpected take-home gifts for your guests.

You will need:

- thin gold cardboard
- waxed paper or tracing paper
- matching plain or patterned cellophane
- double-sided tape
- gold metallic shredded paper
- small rubber bands
- gold metallic thread

1 Measure your stack of cookies, and the circumference of one cookie. Cut the cardboard and waxed paper 2 in. (5 cm) longer than the stack and 2 in. (5 cm) wider then the circumference. Cut out a rectangle of cellophane that is 2 in. (5 cm) wider and twice the length of the cardboard.

2 Roll the waxed paper inside the cardboard, allowing a 2 in. (5 cm) overlap, and tape the sides together using double-sided tape to form a lined tube. Rest on a flat surface and place the cookies inside. Fill each end with gold shredded paper to keep the cookies cushioned and in place.

3 Take care to prevent cookies from falling out as you roll the cellophane around the tube. Tape along the long edge for a close fit.

4 Pinch together one end of the cellophane, close to the end of the tube. Secure the end with a small rubber band. Repeat for the other end. Tie gold metallic thread in a bow around the ends to hide the rubber bands and add extra sparkle to the finished present.

Beautiful Bags

A luxurious velvet bag promises an indulgent gift, while organza and silk add a feminine touch. Experiment with fabrics and ties to create the perfect wrapping for your gifts.

You will need:

For a Wine Bottle Bag

- 20 in. x 13 in. (50 cm x 34 cm) fabric
- tailor's chalk
- 30 in. (75 cm) cord or ribbon
- 8 small metal rings

tip

For wide containers such as preserve or cosmetic jars, allow extra length to the body of the bag as more fabric is required to gather across the lid.

For a Wine Bottle Bag

1 Measure the circumference and height of the bottle. Cut a rectangle of fabric 2 in. (5 cm) wider than the circumference and 6 in. (15 cm taller). Cut out a circle around the base of the bottle allowing for a ¼ in. (6 mm) hem.

2 Fold the rectangle along the longest side, right sides together, to form a tube. Pin, tack, and sew to form a tube. Pin the circle to one end of the tube, right sides together. Sew the two pieces together.

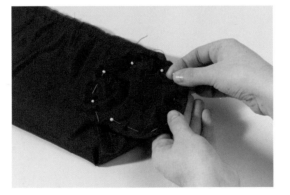

3 Turn the bag right-side out and place the bottle inside the bag. Fold the top of the fabric down inside the tube, until it is 1½ in. (4 cm) higher than the bottle. Pin. Remove the bottle. Turn bag wrong side out again, and slip-stitch edge under to prevent the edges from fraying.

4 Pin a line in the the fabric around the top of the bag where it is to be tied. Sew the metal rings at regular intervals along the pinned circle. Put the bottle in the bag. Thread the cord through the rings and tie in a bow.

Fabrics and Ties

You can make present bags of all different shapes and sizes to wrap bottles, jars, even pillar candles that are difficult to wrap with paper. Choose a fabric strong enough to hold the contents. Selecting fabrics that match or enhance the present inside, such as pretty gauze and silk for cosmetics and perfume or calico and natural cottons for homemade jams and preserves, can give a tantalizing hint as to the contents.

Cord or ribbon can match or contrast with the chosen fabric. Raffia and colored string are especially delightful when linked to a garden-themed gift.

66 *Gold I bring to
crown him again..* 99
John Henry Hopkins

Tastefully Done

Homemade kitchen or garden gifts can be prettily packaged with a natural theme. Fresh herbs or plants make a welcome gift, and are kept upright and protected in a raffia-tied paper bag.

tip

This type of wrapping is best for larger items, as smaller ones may fall out if the bag is knocked over. Different colored paper bags, ribbons, and decorations can change the look. Plain paper bags can even be stamped with jolly motifs to appeal to young or old.

You will need:

- plain brown paper bag with handles
- hole punch or craft knife
- natural raffia and green garden twine
- pine cones and sprigs of fir or artificial leaves
- glue gun

1 Measure 2½ in. (5 cm) down from the top edge of the bag. Use a ruler to help draw a faint pencil line across the bag. Using a hole punch or craft knife, make four evenly spaced holes along the pencil line, cutting through both sides of the bag.

2 Twist together two pieces of raffia and one of green twine, and tie a small knot at both ends. Place the contents in the bag.

3 Starting in the middle and working to one edge, thread the raffia in and out of the holes. Make sure that the raffia goes round each outside edge of the bag. Finish with both ends back at the middle, and tie them in a bow. Tie more raffia strands around the front bow, then glue pine cones and sprigs to them.

Bountiful Baskets

If the presents are too good to hide, nestle them together in a basket wrapped in cellophane for real impact. The basket is part of the gift, so choose one that may be used along with the contents.

You will need:

- basket of suitable size
- several sheets of colored tissue paper
- assorted gift items, such as herb oils, wooden spoons, whisk, tea towel, pepper grinder, bay leaves, bouquet garnis
- cellophane to wrap basket
- red ribbon and gift tag
- glue gun

tip

When placing oil bottles or jars in a basket, prop them up at a slight angle with the lids uppermost. This helps to prevent any leakage while they are in transit.

1 Crunch up the tissue paper and place in the bottom of the basket. Be sure to use plenty of tissue paper to line the base, and support and cushion slender glass items.

2 Fill the basket with gift items, putting in the larger items first and packing smaller ones around.

3 Wrap the basket in cellophane, securing the cut edges on the back of the basket with sticky tape. Cut short pieces of ribbon and stretch across two corners, securing on the back as before. Tie a ribbon bow; attach a gift tag at a top corner with sticky tape, then glue the bow over the top of the tag.

Christmas Cheer

★ have a merry christmas ★

CHAPTER THREE

JUST FOR KIDS

Christmas is all about family fun. Here are
entertaining activities—from puppet making to
holiday baking—you can do with and for your
children, plus some projects they can make
by themselves, with just a little extra help.

Christmas Puppet Show

A Christmas puppet show is a tradition in many households, and it is a great way to get everyone in a festive mood. Why not encourage the children in your family to take a starring role in the holiday entertainment?

Rudolph the Red-Nosed Reindeer

Kids will love putting on a special show at Christmas. The fun begins when you start making the puppets and getting the props and scenery ready. From there you can build up excitement by telling them this well-loved story and explaining the action in the show—just read the script and stage directions on page 125.

This puppet show would be ideal for two or three children to present—enough hands to manage the puppets, backdrops, and props with a little practice.
The adventures of Rudolph are familiar to everyone, but children will also enjoy making up their own stories starring Rudolph, Santa, Elf, and the Tiny Reindeer.

You don't even need to have your own puppet theater to put on this show. Simply find a sturdy table for a stage, and if you're handy, you can use a large cardboard box to make a convincing stage front. Use two tall chair backs to support a rod for the backdrops.

Did you know?

The story of Rudolph is a modern invention that has become a classic. It is based partly on the tale of the Ugly Duckling. There is also a popular song called "Rudolph, the Red-Nosed Reindeer." If you know the words, you can sing it during the show, or play a recording.

just for kids

Making the Puppets

All the puppets are really easy to make from felt and a few common materials. Follow the instructions for Elf to make Santa and Rudolph too.

For Elf, Santa's helper

1 Trace the shapes from the templates on page 281 and cut them out from felt in the colors shown on the templates.

2 Use 6-strand red cotton embroidery floss in chain stitch to make a wide smiling mouth. Then use fabric glue—carefully following the manufacturers' directions—to stick the eyes in place.

3 Now position all the pieces on the front and back body as shown pictured at right. When they are in place, glue them down, making sure that the face overlaps the collar.

4 Let the glue dry completely. Then pin the front to the back, right sides facing out. You are now ready to sew the puppet together.

You will need:

- 2 pieces of 12 in. x 9 in. (30 cm x 23 cm) green felt
- pieces of felt in pink, olive green, red, and yellow
- 6-strand cotton embroidery floss in red and green
- fabric glue
- 2 small plastic eyes

PLEASE NOTE: These puppets are not safe for the use of children under three years old.

tip

Make sure that you spread the fabric glue right to the edge of the felt pieces so they do not lift and gap.

5 Use 6-strand green cotton embroidery floss in running stitch to sew all around the puppet, not going right to the edges on the head and hands as shown, above. Secure the thread well at each end.

just for kids

You will need:

- 2 pieces of 12 in. x 9 in. (30 cm x 23 cm) red felt
- pieces of felt in pink, white, and black
- 6-strand cotton embroidery floss in black and red
- fabric glue
- 2 plastic eyes

For Santa Claus

1 Make Santa as you did the Elf. Glue the beard over the face before stitching a smiling mouth in black floss and gluing on the eyes.

2 Assemble pieces as shown; pay careful attention to which pieces overlap the others—especially the trim on sleeves and hat. Stitch around edges in red floss.

You will need:

- 2 pieces of 12 in. x 9 in. (30 cm x 23 cm) rusty brown felt
- pieces of felt in medium brown, tan, and red
- 6-strand cotton embroidery floss in black and brown
- red thread
- fabric glue
- 2 large plastic eyes
- polyester batting for stuffing the nose

For Rudolph

1 Make Rudolph as you did Elf. Stitch a humorous mouth in black floss and glue on his eyes.

2 To make the nose, run a gathering stitch around the edge of the nose shape and gather up. Fill the center with batting before pulling the thread tight. Use the end of the thread to sew the nose onto the face.

3 Assemble all pieces as shown and glue in place. Stitch around edges in brown floss.

You will need:

- 2 knitted gloves in brown
- pieces of felt in orange and light brown
- 6-strand cotton embroidery floss in brown
- fabric glue
- 16 small plastic eyes
- 8 black beads for noses

For Tiny Reindeer

1 Assemble eight faces as for Rudolph, with a bead for the nose.

2 Glue one face on the "pad" side of each of the glove fingers. Leave thumbs free.

Props and Backdrops

Making these accessories will help put on a good show.
Have them ready to bring on when the action demands.

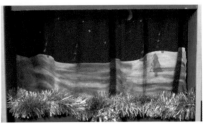

You will need:

For the Props

- 18 in. x 10 in. (46 cm x 25 cm) piece of heavy cardboard
- pieces of felt in the colors shown
- fabric glue
- black felt-tip marker
- glue gun
- 3 x 16 in. (40 cm) wooden dowel for handles

For the Backdrops

- 37 in. x 30 in. (93 cm x 75 cm) each of dark and light blue cotton
- fabric paint in green and white
- length of dowel for hanging backdrop

For the Props

1 To make the rooftops, sleigh, and gifts, trace background shapes from the templates on page 282. Trace them all onto the cardboard and cut out.

2 Trace detail shapes onto felt using the colors shown below and cut out carefully.

3 Glue felt pieces to the front of the cardboard backgrounds as shown below. Let dry and draw outlines around the main shapes with black felt-tip marker as shown. Glue the handles securely to the back.

For the Backdrops

1 Make the "daytime" backdrop from the light blue fabric, with a casing for the dowel at the top and a hem at sides and bottom. Use white fabric paint to make a wavy snowdrift in the bottom half, and when dry use the green paint for some simple, freehand evergreen trees, as shown.

2 Make the "night-time" backdrop from dark blue fabric in the same way. Hang in your puppet theater, or rig up on a suitable length of dowel rod supported between two chair backs.

tip

To make outlines on the props, work slowly and stroke over lines a few times as you work. Practice on scraps first.

just for kids

The Story of Rudolph

This script can be interpreted by the children, or read aloud by parents during the show.

Once upon a time, there lived at the North Pole a young reindeer named Rudolph. He was a lively, happy reindeer and loved playing in the snow. But one day, the other reindeer noticed that he had a very large, bright red nose, and they teased him about it without mercy.

Rudolph was sad because it was Christmas Eve and he was afraid that, because of his shiny nose, he would never be chosen to pull Santa's sleigh. He went to visit Santa and Elf, who were getting all their presents ready. They were always kind to Rudolph and never mentioned his funny nose.

At last, Santa boomed, "Elf, I must go now. Let's load up the presents."

When all was ready, Santa asked, "Where are my eight reindeer? I need their strength to pull my sleigh."

Then Santa looked around him and noticed how foggy the night had become. He was worried that he would not be able to see his way. Suddenly he spied Rudolph with his bright red nose, and he had a very bright idea!

"Rudolph," he cried, "I want YOU—with your shiny nose— to light the way for my sleigh tonight!"

The Tiny Reindeer made way for Rudolph. Now everybody loved him and said what a very special reindeer he was. From then on, Rudolph was Santa's first choice every Christmas Eve.

These stage directions show where to use different puppets and props.

Rudolph frolics in the snow. The Tiny Reindeer come in and laugh at him.

Rudolph is sad and begins to cry. The Tiny Reindeer prance off, still laughing.

Rudolph cheers up and trots off to see Santa and Elf, who are busy with all their presents. He helps them work.

While they work, day turns to night.

Santa and Elf pack up the sleigh, while Rudolph helps them.

The Tiny Reindeer prance onstage and proudly take their places in front of the sleigh.

They get ready to leave but Santa stops them in their tracks. Then everyone's eyes turn to Rudolph, standing alone at the side.

Santa points to Rudolph, and the Tiny Reindeer cheer him.

Santa and Rudolph wave goodbye and fly away over the rooftops of houses, with their sleigh full of Christmas presents.

Stamped Paper and Cards

Children of all ages love to get creative with stamps, and here are a couple of easy projects to brighten plain paper with colors and patterns.

You will need:

- notepaper and envelopes
- Christmas stamps
- colored inkpads

Letter to Santa

1 Lay paper and envelopes on a flat surface. Place face of stamp onto the inkpad and then onto the paper.

2 Press hard and lift up without moving the stamp from side to side. Repeat with different colors and stamps. Practice to discover the most pleasing combinations.

3 When you have decorated the paper, you can write a letter to Santa with brightly colored pencils.

You will need:

- colored paper and envelope
- small and medium potato
- pen and sharp knife to shape potato stamp
- pink and white paint
- scraps of red and white felt
- plastic eyes
- white bobble for hat and pink bobble for nose
- white (PVA) glue
- black felt-tip pen

Potato Print

1 Cut and fold the paper to fit your envelope.

2 Cut the small potato in half—it should be the size of Santa's face. Dip in pink paint and print just below the card center.

3 Cut the medium potato in half. Cut a beard-shaped stamp, dip in white paint, and print over the face.

4 Cut a hat from red and white felt and glue in place. Glue on eyes and bobbles and draw a smile.

just for kids

You will need:

- colored paper and envelopes
- photographs
- scraps of felt and paper
- red bobble for nose
- multicolored sequins
- white (PVA) glue

Photo Christmas Cards

1 Cut a triangle from felt for the tree, and cut out a circle as shown above. Cut antlers from felt, using the templates on page 127 as a guide. Cut a crown from paper.

2 Using the photos as a guide, glue the felt, paper, sequins, and bobble nose in place. Allow the glue to dry before adding your special Christmas message inside.

just for kids

Paper Chains

These chains will look great on the tree. Make them long or short and in the colors of your choosing.

You will need:

- construction and wrapping paper in different colors and patterns

- white (PVA) glue

tip

Make sure the glue on every loop is dry before making the next loop. Otherwise your chain may fall apart.

1 Cut strips of paper 1 in. (2.5 cm) wide and 7 in. (18 cm) long. Try to get a balance of different colors.

2 Put some glue on the end of one strip and form a loop by pressing the opposite end over the glued end. Press together until the glue is dry.

3 Thread the next strip through the loop you have just made, and glue together as before. Continue like this until your chain is long enough.

just for kids

Tree Trimmings

These cheerful ornaments are fun to make with odds and ends you can find around the house.

You will need:

- small piece of cardboard
- various wide ribbons
- narrow ribbon for hanging
- fabric glue
- small piece of colored paper
- hole punch

For the Ribbon Tree

1 Cut a triangle cardboard about 5 in. (12.5 cm) tall and $4^1/_2$ in. (11.25 cm) across the base. Stick a loop of wide green ribbon at the base to form a trunk.

2 Glue ribbon across the bottom tier and trim away excess. Repeat with different ribbons, overlapping each tier, and finishing with paper at the top.

3 Do the same on the reverse. Punch a hole in the top and thread the narrow ribbon through to make a loop.

You will need:

- 2 Styrofoam balls, 1 smaller for the head, 1 larger for the body
- white (PVA) glue
- 1 sheet of white tissue paper
- orange paint and a brush
- 2 small plastic eyes
- 6 black beads for mouth
- 2 purple sequins for buttons
- US no. 5 (1.75 mm) steel crochet hook
- silver thread

For Mr. Snowman

1 Tear tissue in strips and soak in glue mixed with water. Mold tissue around each ball. Roll a carrot nose from tissue and mold it onto the head. Let dry.

2 Push crochet hook through body. Pull through a loop of thread 8 in. (20 cm) long. Push the crochet hook through head from top and pull through the loop of thread from the body. Adjust to form a 5-in. (7.5-cm) loop at top, and secure at body base with a large knot.

3 Paint the nose orange. Glue eyes, beads, and sequins to head and body as shown in the picture at left.

Fun Flower Hair Bands

Any little girl would be delighted by these pretty party hair bands
with their sweet flower and butterfly motifs.

You will need:

- plain elastic hair bands
- scraps of felt
- white (PVA) glue

1 Use the templates on page 283 to cut out all the felt shapes and decorations for the flowers.

2 Glue decorations onto one of the felt flower shapes.

3 Lay another flower shape on a flat surface and spread with glue. Lay a hair band in the center and place the decorated body on top, press securely, and leave to dry.

4 Repeat steps 1 to 3 to make the second flower hair band.

You can also make butterfly hair bands using the templates shown on page 283 and referring to the picture below. Follow the same method. You will also need two short lengths of pipe cleaner; roll one end to form antennae. Place one antenna on either side of the hair band when you insert it between the two layers of felt in step 3.

tip

Adhesive should keep the flowers in place, but you can make small stitches on the back for extra hold.

just for kids

Marbled Jewelry

Create your own distinctive patterns from different colors of clay and use it to make some jazzy-looking modern jewelry—a great present for your mom or sister.

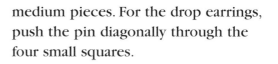

You will need:

- modeling clay in red, yellow, green, and orange
- rolling pin
- craft knife and ruler
- dressmaker's pin
- flat (matte) varnish
- old paintbrush
- 2 lengths elasticized thread, 12 in. (30 cm) each
- 2 head pins for earrings
- 2 earring findings (loops)
- round-nosed jewelry pliers
- 2 earring posts
- 2 brooch pins
- contact adhesive

1 Knead the modeling clay between your hands to make it pliable. Roll out a sheet of red, then one of yellow, green, and orange. Layer the colors and roll flat. Slice off small pieces at an angle; place together in a pattern, then roll flat to make a new marbled sheet.

2 Cut eleven $7/8$-in. (2-cm) squares, nine for a bracelet and two for earrings; four $3/8$ in. (1 cm) squares for drop earrings; and one $1^1/2$ in. (4 cm) square and one rectangle $1^1/2$ in. x 2 in. (4 cm x 5 cm) for brooches.

3 Make channels running through each small and medium piece by pushing the dressmaker's pin into the narrow edge on one side and straight out the other side. For the bracelet, push the pin horizontally through at the top and bottom of nine of the medium pieces. For the drop earrings, push the pin diagonally through the four small squares.

4 Place the pieces on a baking sheet and bake at 275°F (140°C/Gas Mark 1) for 30 minutes. Leave until cold. Brush with varnish and let dry.

5 For the bracelet, thread the pieces together with elastic thread and knot. For the drop earrings, push each head pin through two small squares; using pliers, bend the head pin at the top to form a loop. Attach to the findings and squeeze the loop to close. For the brooches and square earrings, secure the pins or the posts on the backs with adhesive.

Reindeer Potato Heads

Let your children help assemble this recipe. It's a fun way to convince them that vegetables are worthy of their attention—and not just for Christmas!

- 2 large baking potatoes
- 4 oz. (100 g) fine green beans
- 4 oz. (100 g) peas
- 4 tbsp. milk
- ½ stick (2 oz./60 g) butter
- 2 cherry tomatoes, halved
- 24 pretzel sticks

You can also use red pepper, broccoli, and other bright vegetables if you think they will be more popular

SERVES 4

1 Preheat the oven to 400°F (200°C/Gas Mark 4). Scrub the potatoes, pat dry with paper towel, and prick all over with a fork.

2 Bake the potatoes for about 1-1¼ hours or until soft when pierced with a skewer. Meanwhile, boil or steam the green beans and peas for 5 minutes or until tender. Drain. Reserve eight peas for eyes and a few beans for eyebrows, and chop the rest.

3 Cut the potatoes in half lengthwise. Taking care not to split the skins, scoop out the flesh with a spoon into a bowl.

4 In a small pan, warm the milk and butter until the butter melts. Add this mixture to the potato flesh, and mash together until smooth. Add the chopped beans and peas and spoon mixture back into the potato skins, packing firmly.

5 Cut the reserved beans into short lengths and position them on the potato halves for eyebrows. Add peas for eyes and cherry tomato halves for noses. Finally, press six pretzel sticks into the top of each head to make reindeer antlers.

Quick Tortilla Pizzas

These pizzas make a hearty snack or light lunch. You can also use pita bread as a base and sprinkle over chopped ham or chicken for a meatier meal.

- 8 6-in. (15-cm) tortillas
- 6 tbsp. tomato sauce
- 1 can (3 oz./75 g) jalapeño or green chile peppers
- 2 garlic cloves, finely chopped
- 2 tbsp. chopped fresh parsley or cilantro
- ground black pepper
- 4 tbsp. shredded cheddar cheese

SERVES 4

1 Preheat oven to 300°F (150°C/Gas Mark 2). Wrap tortillas in foil and warm in the oven for 10 minutes; then remove. Increase oven temperature to 375°F (190°C/Gas Mark 5).

2 Arrange tortillas on two nonstick baking sheets. Spread a thin layer of tomato sauce over each tortilla.

3 Sprinkle jalapeños, garlic, parsley, and black pepper over the sauce. Sprinkle cheese on top. Bake until cheese melts, about 10 minutes.

Spicy Nut Mix

Kids young and old love these tasty nibbles. You can store the mix for a week or more in an airtight jar—if it lasts that long!

- 2 tbsp. butter
- 1 tbsp. Worcestershire sauce
- 3 cups (12 oz./375 g) of mixed pecan halves, whole almonds, peanuts, wheat chex, and small pretzels, to taste
- 1 tsp. chili or curry powder
- ½ tsp. garlic salt
- ¼ tsp. cayenne pepper

1 Preheat oven to 300°F (150°C/ Gas Mark 2). In a small saucepan, melt the butter and add Worcestershire sauce. Make a mix of nuts, cereals and pretzels in desired quantities. Spread mix in a large baking pan and pour butter over. Toss well to coat.

2 Bake for half an hour, stirring occasionally. Remove from the oven and sprinkle over the dry ingredients (use less salt if some items in the mix were ready-salted). Toss until well coated. Serve warm or store at room temperature until ready to serve.

Decorated Sugar Cookies

Don't let these delicious Christmas stocking and festive figure cookies get gobbled up right away. Save a few to hang on the tree.

For the Cookies

- 1¼ sticks (5 oz./140 g) butter
- 1 cup (8 oz./230 g) granulated sugar
- 2 egg yolks
- 4 tsp. milk
- 3 cups (13 oz./375 g) all-purpose flour
- 1 tsp. baking soda
- 1 tsp. ground cinnamon
- 2 tsp. finely grated lemon rind

MAKES ABOUT 20 COOKIES

For the Sugar Paste Fondant Icing

- 1 tbsp. powdered gelatin
- 3 tbsp. cold water
- 3 tbsp. liquid glucose
- 1 tbsp edible glycerine
- 1 lb. (750g) confectioners' (icing) sugar

1 In a large bowl, beat together butter and sugar until creamy. Beat in egg yolks and milk, then sift in flour, baking soda, and cinnamon. Stir in lemon rind.

2 Press the mixture together to make a smooth dough. Place dough in plastic wrap and chill in refrigerator for 30 minutes.

3 Preheat the oven to 350°F (180°C/ Gas Mark 4). Line two–three baking sheets with baking parchment. Roll out the dough ¼ in. (5 mm) thick and cut out desired

Sugar Paste Fondant Icing

1 Sprinkle the gelatin over the water in a small bowl. Leave to stand for 5 minutes, then dissolve the gelatin by standing the bowl in a pan of warm water.

2 Stir the liquid glucose and edible glycerine into the dissolved gelatin.

3 Sift the sugar into a mixing bowl, pour in the gelatin mix and stir in.

4 Knead until you have a smooth icing. Store in a tightly sealed plastic bag. To color the icing, cut off a small section and add a few drops of desired coloring. Knead in well.

shapes using Christmas cookie cutters. Skewer holes in the top of any you want to hang on the tree. Lift the cookies onto the baking sheets and bake for 8-10 minutes until golden.

4 Cool the cookies on the baking trays for 5 minutes, then transfer to a wire rack and decorate when cold.

5 Make both the Christmas stocking and festive figure cookies in the same way, and decorate them following the directions on the opposite page.

To decorate stockings

- ready-made sugar paste fondant icing in red and white (to make your own sugar paste fondant icing, follow recipe on previous page)
- ready-to-pipe confectioners' frosting in white

1 Cut out stocking shapes and cuffs from sugar paste fondant icing as shown and fix them in place on cookie with confectioners' frosting.

2 Pipe a thin line of confectioners' frosting around the edge of the red sugar paste fondant icing. Personalize with initials in white sugar paste. Dampen with confectioners' frosting to fix.

To decorate figures

- ready-made sugar paste fondant icing (see recipe left) in assorted colors
- ready-to-pipe confectioners' frosting in assorted colors
- colored and silver dragées
- desiccated coconut

1 Cut out various shapes from suitable colors of sugar paste fondant icing—see picture—and fix in place with confectioners' frosting.

2 Pipe lines and dots on figures in various colors as desired. Decorate figures with dragées as shown, and add desiccated coconut for Santa's beard.

to make confectioners' frosting

If you are unable to find ready-made sugar paste icing or ready-to-pipe confectioners' frosting, you can make confectioners' frosting by adding icing sugar to hot water to form the right consistency: it should be thick for piping (with piping bags and nozzles) and thinner to use in place of sugar paste to frost flat areas. Add vanilla or lemon flavoring to taste, and food coloring to mix desired colors. Mix small amounts to prevent drying out in use.

Holly Cupcakes

Make it easy on yourself by using a bought cake mix in whatever flavor you like for the cupcakes, and save your creativity for the holly leaves and berries that decorate them.

- 1 package cake mix

For Buttercream Frosting

- 1 lb. (450 g) confectioners' (icing) sugar
- ½ cup (4½ oz./125 g) butter, softened
- ⅛ tsp. salt
- 1 tsp. vanilla extract
- 3–4 tbsp. milk

To Decorate

- ready-made sugar paste in red and green (see page 134 for recipe)
MAKES 12

1 Preheat the oven to 350°F (180°C/ Gas Mark 4), or as directed on cake-mix package. Line a 12-cup cupcake pan with paper liners. Make up the cake mix according to the package directions.

2 Pour the batter into the liners and bake following the cake mix directions—about 30 minutes or until golden and a skewer pushed into the center of a cake comes out clean. Cool completely on a wire rack.

3 For the frosting, cream the butter, one-third of the sugar, and salt in a large bowl. Blend the vanilla and half the milk into the mixture. Add more sugar alternating with the remaining milk until you have the desired amount and consistency.

4 Spread the top of each cupcake with frosting. Roll berries and cut leaves from red and green sugar paste (or from almond paste to which you have added food coloring). Arrange a sprig of holly on top of each cupcake and place in red liners.

Sour Cream Fruity Waffles

An old-fashioned breakfast treat that's just perfect for Christmas morning!

- 1¼ cups (5½ oz./150 g) all-purpose (plain) flour
- 3 tsp. baking powder
- ¼ tsp. baking soda
- ½ tsp. salt
- 2 large eggs

- ½ cup (4 fl oz./125 ml) sour cream
- ½ cup (4 fl oz./125 ml) milk
- 2 tbsp. melted butter
- 1 tsp. vanilla extract

MAKES ABOUT 4 WAFFLES

Ice Cream Cake Christmas Tree

This colorful dessert will be greeted with whoops of glee. Even the youngest hands will delight in helping you decorate this Christmas tree.

- plain yellow cake
- confectioners' (icing) sugar
- vanilla or lemon flavoring
- assortment of food colorings
- ready-to-pipe confectioners' frosting
- chocolate-filled candies such as M&Ms in various colors
- vanilla ice cream

1 Cut a piece of yellow cake in the shape of a tall triangle, about 1½ in. (3 cm) thick.

2 To decorate the Christmas tree, make confectioners' frosting in three colors, following the directions on page 135. Spread in broad stripes across the tree.

3 Pipe on thin lines of frosting to form scallops, and decorate with candies as shown. Set on serving plate.

4 For the trunk, cut a rectangle of solidly frozen ice cream and place at the base of the tree.

5 Work quickly to prevent melting, and serve immediately. Alternatively, assemble on a plate (or plates, if making several) and keep in the freezer until time to serve.

For Fruit Sauce
- 3 medium nectarines, thinly sliced
- 1 tbsp. butter
- ¼ cup (1½ oz./45 g) packed light brown sugar
- ½ cup (4 fl oz./125 ml) orange juice
- 1½ tbsp. cornstarch

1 Preheat a waffle iron. Sift the dry ingredients into a small bowl.

2 Whisk the eggs in a medium bowl. Blend in sour cream, milk, butter, and vanilla. Fold in the flour mixture just until combined. Let stand.

3 For the fruit sauce, melt the butter in a skillet over medium heat. Sauté the nectarines until lightly browned. Stir in brown sugar and cook until the sugar dissolves and becomes syrupy, about 2 minutes. Transfer nectarines to bowl with slotted spoon.

4 Mix orange juice and cornstarch in small bowl until smooth, then add 1 cup of cold water. Stir into the sugar mix in the pan, bring to a boil over medium-high heat, and cook for about 2 minutes, whisking, until the sauce boils and thickens. Return the nectarines to the pan and reheat.

5 Spoon the waffle batter onto the hot waffle iron and bake. When done, remove from the iron and keep warm. Repeat with the remaining batter. Separate each waffle into squares and serve topped with nectarines.

Colorful Party Smoothies

Smoothies have a deserved reputation for being full of goodness. These are easy enough for your kids to make themselves, all year long.

CHOCOLATE COCONUT SHAKES

- 2 scoops chocolate ice cream
- 1 small banana, chopped
- ½ cup (4 fl oz./125 ml) coconut milk
- ¼ cup (2 fl oz./50 ml) milk
- 1 tbsp. chopped hazelnuts

BANANA PINEAPPLE RIPPLES

- 2 medium bananas, chopped
- ½ cup (4 fl oz./125 ml) plain yogurt
- 2 tbsp. clear honey
- 1 ¼ cups (10 fl oz./300 ml) unsweetened pineapple juice

JOLLY BERRY JUICES

- ¾ cup (6 fl oz./200 ml) plain yogurt
- 14 oz. (400 g) fresh or frozen red berries, e.g. raspberries
- ½ cup (4 fl oz./125 ml) milk

STRAWBERRY ORANGE GULPS

- 10 oz. (275 g) fresh or frozen strawberries
- 1 ¼ cups (10 fl oz./300 ml) orange juice

EACH RECIPE MAKES 2 DRINKS

Reserve two of the strawberries for the Strawberry Orange Gulps, and blend all ingredients for the individual smoothies until smooth. Sprinkle the finely chopped hazelnuts over the top of the Chocolate Coconut Shakes and decorate the Strawberry Orange Gulps with the reserved strawberries.

CHAPTER FOUR

HOLIDAY ENTERTAINING

Share the joy of Christmas! From intimate gatherings to sophisticated occasions, here are six inspirational get-together ideas that will stimulate your imagination and get you into party-planning mode. From invitations to table settings to mouthwatering menu suggestions, here are entertaining ideas guaranteed to impress your friends and family.

★ have a merry christmas ★

Tree-Trimming Party

For most people, Christmas really begins with setting up the tree. Make this a relaxed, casual event where everyone can enjoy a delicious meal and participate in an enduring tradition—decorating the Christmas tree.

The time and place

This is the perfect low-key party to put you in the holiday spirit. Plan to have it about two weeks before Christmas so your tree will be fresh on the big day, and hold it in the evening so your Christmas lights will really glow. Now is also the time to "deck the hall with boughs of holly," so if you are using garlands, swags, and wreaths, have some already in place when your guests arrive to establish the holiday mood for the occasion.

If you have an eating area near your tree, this would be ideal—your guests will be able to see and admire their handiwork as they tuck into a delicious meal.

Menu

for 8 - 12 people

Appetizers

Sesame-Cheese Twists
(page 174)

Vegetable Bruschetta
(page 175)

First Course

Shrimp Bisque
(page 182)

Main Course

Chicken with Mushroom Sauce
(page 203)

Mixed Wild and Long-Grain Rice
Green Beans with Toasted Almonds
Poppyseed Rolls

Dessert

Ice Cream and Tree Cookie
(page 249)

Viennese Sachertorte
(page 238)

Assorted Beverages

The table setting

This is a family-style occasion, so don't put pressure on yourself with a formal table setting. Colorful china set off with placemats or tablecloths will lend a country feel to the evening and will tie in with your natural decorations. Place your casserole dish on the dining table, or on a buffet to the side.

The centerpiece

Make a simple arrangement of greenery, berries, richly colored flowers, and pretty ornaments around a central candle. Use florist's foam to keep flowers fresh and firmly in place. An arrangement at either end of the table would look attractive.

Napkins

Coordinate the stenciled, beaded napkins and napkin rings on page 58 with your table décor. The beads on the napkin rings will echo the shiny ornaments on your tree. Fold napkins with the stenciled corner at the top, slip into the napkin ring, and lay across each dinner plate.

The food

Serve appetizers that are hearty enough to stave off hunger pangs while your guests decorate the tree but easy to eat, so that greasy fingers won't spoil your decorations.

For the first and main courses, plan the simplest of fare—a soup and a casserole dish that will keep warm if they must wait for a break in decorating the tree are ideal. You should feel comfortable preparing the rice and vegetables at the last minute though—your guests will be happy to come into the kitchen and lend a hand.

Serving quantities are given with each recipe; increase quantities for the number of guests you are expecting. Wild and long-grain rice is sold in mixed packs. Allow 3 oz. (85g) rice and 5 oz. (140 g) beans per person.

SECRETS OF SUCCESS ❄ While trimming the tree, play a favorite Christmas CD or video and light plenty of candles to create just the right festive, sentimental atmosphere ❄ Keep your guests satisfied with Sesame-Cheese Twists, Vegetable Bruschetta, and something to drink before dinner ❄ A nice touch is to warm your dinner plates in a very low oven and put them out at the last minute. But make sure they're not too hot, especially if there are children present.

PARTY PLANNER

SEVERAL DAYS BEFORE

Buy your tree and set it up in its stand; if rooted, make sure it is well watered; keep in a cool place if possible.

Get out your ornaments and lights and check for damage.

Do most of your grocery shopping.

TWO OR MORE DAYS BEFORE

Make and fill gift bags.

THE DAY BEFORE

Bake the cookies and cake.

Prepare the chicken dish and bisque, and refrigerate.

Make Sesame-Cheese Twists.

THAT MORNING

Make the centerpiece.

JUST BEFORE GUESTS ARRIVE

Make Vegetable Bruschetta.

JUST BEFORE DINNER

Prepare rice and vegetables.

The finishing touch

End dinner with a dessert of decorated cookies that can also be hung on the Christmas tree. You may also like to serve a more substantial cake, such as Sachertorte, which guests of all ages will find hard to resist.

MORE IDEAS... ❄ Have

someone say a special prayer or grace,

or do a Christmas reading, before you

start to eat ❄ If there is room, place

the crowing glory of your tree—an

angel or star—in the center of the

dining table. When all the other

decorations are in place, nominate one

of your guests to place it on the tree.

make it a tradition

Set places with a gift bag and name tag for each of your guests. Buy or make small bags, adapting the directions on page 22, and fill with delicious chocolate or minty treats. Alternatively, give small ornaments or bonbon boxes to hang on the tree.

Some families like to build up a collection of "keepsake" ornaments year by year, as a memento of the holiday. Including your guests in this tradition would make it a very special Christmas for everyone.

Caroling Party

A caroling party is the perfect way to spread an atmosphere of fellowship and good cheer to your friends and neighbors. Invite everyone to your house for an evening of song and delicious desserts and warming drinks.

The time and place

Invite friends of all ages for an informal evening of Christmas carols. It is traditional to go outdoors and carol from house to house, and then return to a warm house and a hot drink next to a roaring fire.

Or you can stay indoors for a good old-fashioned sing-along—gathering around a piano and a willing accompanist would be a delight, though you can always sing along to a record, or even *a capella*.

This is a party that's sure to leave everyone with a happy heart and a warm glow.

Menu
for 12 – 16 people

Desserts

Chocolate Marble Cake
(page 243)

Mincemeat Bouchées
(page 256)

Oatmeal Macaroons
(page 257)

Brownie Thins
(page 253)

Drinks

Mulled Wine Punch
(page 259)

Hot Wassail
(page 260)

Irish Coffee
(page 259)

Assorted Beverages including Herbal Teas and Hot Chocolate

Christmas Carols

make it special

Ensure everyone knows the carols by photocopying the lyrics from the next pages and other suitable sources onto 11 in. x 17 in. (297 mm x 420 mm) sheets. Then bind them in a folder made from gold cardboard. Simply fold the cardboard and photocopies in half, punch holes, and thread through some gold cord. Make a decorative label for the front, and present them to your guests just before the caroling begins. Give them to take home as a memento of the evening.

"We wish you a Merry Christmas and a Happy New Year"
Traditional

Piping hot punch

Make sure your punch bowl will take hot liquids, or use an attractive pot, such as a gleaming copper cauldron. This will make it easier to reheat the punch on the stove from time to time, to ensure it doesn't cool off. Serve in heatproof glasses with insulated handles.

Tempting Irish coffee

It's fun to prepare this special drink in front of your guests and serve it with a flourish. Make a pot of strong coffee, and pour it into heatproof stemmed glasses or clear cups, each containing a large measure of Irish whiskey (or bourbon). Sweeten to taste—it's the sugar that keeps the cream floating on top of the coffee.

Then, over the back of a large spoon, gently pour thick cream so that it forms a luxurious, even coating on the surface of the coffee. Drink through the cream—and enjoy. It should be very hot, and very strong!

PARTY PLANNER

TWO DAYS BEFORE
Begin baking cakes, mincemeat bouchées, cookies, and brownies. These can be stored in airtight containers for a few days, but be sure to keep them moist.

THE DAY BEFORE
Prepare Christmas carol folders.
Make potpourri, dried flower, and candle arrangements.

A FEW HOURS BEFORE
If you have a fireplace, prepare the fire.
Make the punch and heat; allow to mull with spices, but do not add fresh fruit until nearer serving.

30 MINUTES BEFORE GUESTS ARRIVE
Place baked goods on decorative platters and cover with plastic wrap to keep fresh before serving.

The table setting

There is no need for a formal buffet. Instead, set up a sturdy table for the punch bowl and cups, and have platters of baked goods plus plates, forks, and napkins on small tables around the room. Consider including the table runner shown on page 56—it would look handsome in the glow of firelight.

Allow one piece of cake, plus two mincemeat bouchées, two macaroons, two brownies and two cups of punch plus coffee or hot drinks per person.

SECRETS OF SUCCESS ❄ If you go outdoors and the weather is cold, have on hand lots of scarves, hats, and mittens to lend to your guests to keep off the chill ❄ Shine a light... Carrying lanterns with candles would be festive, but even a flashlight will help illuminate the carols and lead the way ❄ Try to return home a little before your guests to turn on the Christmas lights, stoke up the fire, and make sure the punch is piping hot when they arrive back.

Aromatic decorations

Decorate your tables with gilded dried flowers, pine cones, and scented candles set in seasonal potpourri (see page 63).

If you use votive candles in glass holders in your displays, they will not only flicker atmospherically but heat from the glass will warm the potpourri and scent the entire room.

tip

Small individual trays would also be a gracious way to help your guests to balance their plates and cups.

Silent Night

Silent night, holy night,
All is calm, all is bright,
Round yon Virgin Mother and Child,
Holy Infant so tender and mild,
Sleep in heavenly peace; Sleep in heavenly peace.

Silent night, holy night,
Shepherds quake at the sight.
Glories stream from heaven afar,
Heav'nly hosts sing Alleluia,
Christ the Savior is born; Christ the Savior is born.

Silent night, holy night,
Son of God, love's pure light,
Radiant beams from Thy holy face,
With the dawn of redeeming grace,
Jesus, Lord, at Thy birth; Jesus, Lord, at Thy birth.

Deck the Halls

Deck the halls with boughs of holly,
Fa la la la la la la la la.
'Tis the season to be jolly,
Fa la la la la la la la la.
Don we now our gay apparel,
Fa la la la la la la la la.
Troll the ancient Yuletide carol
Fa la la la la la la la la.

See the blazing Yule before us,
Fa la la la la la la la la.
Strike the harp and join the chorus,
Fa la la la la la la la la.
Follow me in merry measure,
Fa la la la la la la la la.
While I tell of Yuletide treasure,
Fa la la la la la la la la.

Away in a Manger

Away in a manger, no crib for a bed,
The little Lord Jesus laid down His sweet head,
The stars in the sky looked down where He lay,
The little Lord Jesus asleep on the hay.

The cattle are lowing, the poor Baby wakes,
But little Lord Jesus no crying He makes.
I love Thee, Lord Jesus, look down from the sky,
And stay by my cradle till morning is nigh.

Be near me, Lord Jesus, I ask Thee to stay
Close by me forever and love me I pray.
Bless all the dear children in Thy tender care,
And take us to heaven to live with Thee there.

Jingle Bells

Dashing through the snow
In a one-horse open sleigh;
O'er the fields we go,
Laughing all the way.
Bells on bobtail ring,
Making spirits bright;
What fun it is to ride and sing
A sleighing song tonight.

Oh! Jingle bells, jingle bells,
Jingle all the way;
Oh, what fun it is to ride
In a one-horse open sleigh.
Hey! Jingle bells, jingle bells,
Jingle all the way;
Oh, what fun it is to ride
In a one-horse open sleigh!

Hark! The Herald Angels Sing

Hark! the herald angels sing,
"Glory to the newborn King!
Peace on earth and mercy mild,
God and sinners reconciled."
Joyful, all ye nations, rise,
Join the triumph of the skies;
With the angelic host proclaim,
"Christ is born in Bethlehem!"
Hark, the herald angels sing,
"Glory to the newborn King!"

Christ, by highest heav'n adored,
Christ, the everlasting Lord!
Late in time behold Him come,
Offspring of a Virgin's womb.
Veiled in flesh the Godhead see;
Hail the incarnate Deity,
Pleased as man with man to dwell,
Jesus, our Emmanuel!
Hark, the herald angels sing,
"Glory to the newborn King!"

Hail, the heav'n-born Prince of Peace!
Hail the Son of Righteousness!
Light and life to all He brings,
Ris'n with healing in His wings.
Mild He lays His glory by,
Born that man no more may die.
Born to raise the sons of earth;
Born to give them second birth.
Hark, the herald angels sing,
"Glory to the newborn King!"

We Wish You a Merry Christmas

We wish you a Merry Christmas;
We wish you a Merry Christmas;
We wish you a Merry Christmas
and a Happy New Year.
CHORUS: Good tidings we bring to you and your kin;
Good tidings for Christmas and a Happy New Year.

Oh, bring us a figgy pudding;
Oh, bring us a figgy pudding;
Oh, bring us a figgy pudding
and a cup of good cheer.
CHORUS

We won't go until we get some;
We won't go until we get some;
We won't go until we get some,
so bring some right here.
CHORUS

Angels We Have Heard on High

Angels we have heard on high
Sweetly singing o'er the plains,
And the mountains in reply
Echoing their joyous strains.
CHORUS: Gloria in excelsis Deo, Gloria in excelsis Deo.

Shepherds, why this jubilee?
Why your joyous strains prolong?
What the gladsome tidings be
Which inspire your heav'nly song?
CHORUS

Come to Bethlehem and see
Him whose birth the angels sing.
Come adore on bended knee
Christ the Lord, the newborn King.
CHORUS

Christmas Eve Open House

By the time Christmas Eve rolls around, most of us are in a state of hushed anticipation. There's no better time to open your doors wide and welcome dear friends and family to a sumptuous festive buffet.

The time and place

Invitations to this party are a must. Make your own by cutting a simple Christmas tree stencil (see template on page 283), and stencil onto folded cardstock. Stenciling instructions are found on page 58. Add a star and beads with white (PVA) glue. Send the invitations out three to four weeks in advance. State that it is an open house, where guests may come and go any time between set hours, typically for a buffet dinner between 6 p.m. and 9 p.m. This flexibility means that friends who have other family commitments can still drop in to wish you a Merry Christmas.

The table setting

Extend your dining table to its full length. Make sure there is plenty of circulation space around all sides of the table—otherwise, it may be better to push it against a wall.

Lay your best cloth over the table's protective pad and a thick sheet or thin blanket; this is an old restaurant trick that gives a really luxurious finish. If you are using a lace cloth, you will also need a colored undercloth. Place your floral arrangement in the center and add as many candles as you can muster.

Stack plates at both ends of the table to avoid perilously tall towers. Just as the first guests arrive, set out the food platters, remembering to include enough serving utensils—some always seem to get carried away on people's plates.

Menu
for 20 - 30 people
Savory Dishes

Spicy Nut Mix
(page 133)

Surprise Cocktail Meatballs
(page 210)

Sliced Baked Ham with Bourbon-Brown Sugar Glaze
(served cold)
(page 204)

Salmon En Croute
(page 189)

Broccoli and Bacon Quiche
(page 214)

Puff Pastry Sausage Rolls
(page 177)

Rosemary New Potatoes
(page 223)

Grilled Chicken Salad with Mango
(page 181)

Assortment of Rolls, Breads, Butter, and Condiments

Desserts

Chocolate Log and Cream
(page 240)

Jeweled Fruit Cake
(page 242)

Mandarins, Nuts, and After-Dinner Mints

Assorted Beverages

Perfect party fare

The trick with a large buffet is to serve food that can either be eaten at room temperature or kept warm on the table. It will then "take care of itself" and let you enjoy your guests' company.

You can expect guests to consume 4 oz.–6 oz. (110 g–170 g) of meat or fish, 1 cup (4 oz./110 g) of salad, 2 servings of rolls or potatoes, 2 portions of dessert, and 3–4 glasses of wine or other alcohol. Your guests will tend to try a small portion of everything, which shouldn't alter the overall quantities too much. However, serve dishes pre-portioned. Buffet food can be rich and guests will take more than they can eat if they portion themselves. Pre-portioning will help you to "count up" the servings.

PARTY PLANNER

WEEKS BEFORE

Make the Jeweled Fruit Cake—the longer it ages, the better, so long as it is properly stored in an airtight container.

ONE TO SEVERAL DAYS BEFORE

Make the Surprise Cocktail Meatballs, Salmon En Croute, Broccoli Quiche, Puff Pastry Sausage Rolls, and Chocolate Log; freeze if desired until needed. Make and store Spicy Nut Mix.

THE DAY BEFORE

Check your china, flatware, linens, and glassware, and begin to set up the buffet table. Thoroughly defrost all frozen items.

ON THE DAY

Make your flower arrangement.
Bake the ham; cool and slice. Prepare the Rosemary New Potatoes.
Prepare the Grilled Chicken with Mango Salad.

AN HOUR BEFORE GUESTS ARRIVE

Warm and slice the Quiche; warm the Sausage Rolls.

Napkins and napkin rings

Tuck forks and knives into your best linen napkins. If you don't have enough in all the same color, don't worry—a mixture of festive colors can look very rich. Tie everything together by decorating inexpensive metal rings with craft store embellishments. Glittering in the candlelight, they will look just as handsome as the finest silver.

Christmas baking

Happily, many holiday desserts act as table decorations in their own right. If you have room, consider putting desserts out with the savory dishes—people feast with their eyes too!

SECRETS OF SUCCESS ❄

Do not put out all the food at once. Plan to replenish the buffet table periodically so that later-arriving guests will have an appetizing choice ❄ Remember that some people will be ready for dessert while others are eating their main course.

A stunning centerpiece

Pull out all the stops for the centerpiece on your buffet table. Include richly colored flowers, either fresh (see previous page), such as carnations, chrysanthemums, and gerberas, or artificial, such as silk poinsettias. Add a touch of gold with flower ornaments and gilded pine cones. Use a creative assortment of seasonal greenery and include some berries. Rosemary adds a fragrance to your table. Fill in any space—professional florists know that the trick is to make a dense arrangement and using florist's foam makes this easy to do.

Spray a fresh arrangement and keep in a cool place until party time.

Christmas Dinner

The pleasure of seeing your family gathered expectantly around the dinner table at Christmas is a precious memory that everyone will treasure forever.

Menu

for 8 – 12 people

Appetizers

Crispy Potato Pancake & Smoked Salmon Canapés
(page 179)

First Course

Shellfish Salad
(page 180)

Main Course

Roast Turkey with Stuffing
(page 194)

Mashed Potatoes
Roasted Root Vegetables with Herbs
(page 224)

Dinner Rolls and Butter

Desserts

Plum Pudding and Brandied Cider Sauce
(page 236)

Assorted Beverages
including Espresso Coffee and
Port or Liqueurs
Chocolate Mints

The time and place

Christmas dinner is a time for families, as many generations as possible. It is traditional to sit down at the table in the late afternoon or early evening—depending on cooking times and other commitments—and to proceed through the courses at a leisurely pace for a couple of hours or so.

The table setting

Tradition and a certain formality give everyone a sense of occasion and will make this a Christmas dinner to remember. Use your best china, crystal, and silver, and lay the places according to your menu and serving method. If you plan to carve and serve formally, do not lay dinner plates at each place but stack them on a buffet table or at the host's place and pass laden plates to each person in turn.

Candles

Candles make a meal extra-special, even if it's still light outside. Silver candles are always in good taste and look elegant in matching candlesticks tied with a ribbon.

To prevent smoking and ensure even burning, trim the candle wick to ¼ in. (6 mm) before lighting.

" I will honor Christmas in my heart and try to keep it all the year "

Charles Dickens

PARTY PLANNER

THE DAY BEFORE
Make the table swag and keep moist in a cool place.
Do any last-minute shopping.

IN THE MORNING
Set the table, fold napkins, and make place cards.

MENU 1

WEEKS BEFORE
Make the Plum Pudding and store it.

THE DAY BEFORE
Make turkey stuffing and refrigerate.

ON THE DAY
Stuff the turkey and put it in the oven.
Make Brandy Butter. Prepare Shellfish Salad and Potato Pancakes.
Prepare Root Vegetables and roast 45 minutes before serving.
Boil and mash potatoes; make gravy; warm rolls.

MENU 2

THE DAY BEFORE
Make the Amaretti Delight and refrigerate.
Make the Tomato Soup and refrigerate;
prepare pastry and refrigerate.

A FEW HOURS BEFORE DINNER
Prepare the beef and put in the oven.
Make the Basil Sauce and set aside.
Prepare the Scalloped Potatoes and bake.

JUST BEFORE DINNER
Prepare Orange and Watercress Salad.

SECRETS OF SUCCESS

❄ When ordering meat, allow 1 lb. (450 g) of uncooked whole turkey weight per person to give generous serving and some for leftovers. If cooking the beef, allow 8 oz. (225 g) per uncooked whole joint

❄ Use the suggested menus as a guide but feel free to substitute your own favorite dishes ❄ Go over your recipes in advance and visualize preparation procedures. Plan to allow roast time to sit before carving

❄ Get older children to help serve food and clear dishes ❄ If your timing is a little off and your guests have to wait, do not worry. This is a family occasion to be enjoyed by everyone—yourself included.

Floral arrangement

A swag running down the center of the table is a sumptuous and theatrical reminder of an age of grand entertaining. Adapting the instructions for the mantel swag on page 36, twist together traditional mixed greenery, including ivy, juniper, and St. John's wort (hypericum) berries, along with rich red chrysanthemums and organza bows. If you are not setting places at the ends of the table, make the swag long enough to hang over the edges.

Napkins and place cards

Fold crisply starched linen napkins into a fan shape following the instructions shown below. Lay them at each place with a name card tied with a glass ornament and a gold ribbon.

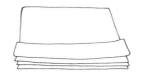

1 Fold the napkin in half lengthwise and make 1 in. (2.5 cm) accordian pleats along one edge up to the halfway point.

2 Fold right side in half, underneath.

3 Fold the top left corner down at an angle which will form an overlap on the right hand side. Fold this under for a stand. Release the pleats to form the fan.

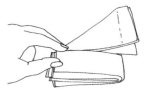

Menu 1

This is a traditional meal in five courses. It should be savored slowly.

APPETIZER: Serve your appetizer on a tray with fore-dinner drinks in the living room.

FIRST COURSE: Place plates of Seafood Salad on the table before guests come into the dining room. Have water glasses already filled, and either pour wine or invite someone to take over for you.

MAIN COURSE: When plates for the first course have been removed, carve the turkey at the table and serve it to your guests with some stuffing. Pass dishes of vegetables, potatoes, gravy, and rolls around the table.

DESSERT: Clear the table of anything not needed for dessert. Bring the plum pudding to the table with dessert plates. Serve individual portions and pass the brandied cider sauce.

COFFEE: After dessert, serve coffee in demitasse cups with port or liqueurs and chocolate mints.

MORE IDEAS... ❄ If you come from an ethnic background, have at least one dish from the Old Country to keep family traditions alive ❄ The same goes for decorations and other customs. By combining various elements of your different heritages, your family will develop its own unique celebration of Christmas ❄ While adults linger over coffee, the children can be excused from the table to get ready to put on the Rudolph Puppet Show outlined on pages 120-125 ❄ Remember to take plenty of photographs, and make a collage of the best shots to copy and send to everyone.

Menu 2
This is a less formal meal but just as special.

FIRST COURSE: Have the tomato soup on the table before you call everyone to the dining table—the crust will keep it warm for a few minutes. Either pour water and wine for your guests, or pass bottles around the table throughout the meal.

MAIN COURSE: While the soup bowls are being cleared, slice and serve the Horseradish Beef. Pass serving dishes of potatoes, vegetables, salad, sauce, and rolls around the table.

DESSERT: Bring the Amaretti Delight to the table in individual dishes. Serve coffee or tea with dessert, or afterward.

Alternative Menu
for 6 - 12 people

First Course
Pastry-Crowned Tomato Soup
(page 183)

Main Course
Horseradish Beef
(page 207)

Scalloped Potatoes
Sautéed Brussels Sprouts
(page 225)

Orange and Watercress Salad

Dinner Rolls and Butter

Desserts
Amaretti Delight
(page 235)

Assorted Beverages

New Year's Eve Cocktail Party

An effervescent party with a sophisticated silver theme is the perfect way to make the coming year feel exciting and special. Prepare well, and then let the magic take over.

The time and place

Each year, there are lots of New Year's parties, so invite guests early to make sure your celebration is well attended. Send out invitations weeks in advance. Make your own by using a snowflake punch on squares of gold paper, then glue the squares in a vertical panel down the center of folded cardstock.

The table setting

Set out serving tables that positively glow with light. Keeping colors to a minimum will enhance the effect, as will lots of candles and glass bowls of silver

ornaments. Use a good white damask cloth, which will subtly reflect the light, and strew it with glittering confetti and decorative tree lights. A silver clock on the table is a fun way to make sure everyone is set for midnight.

Try to have one table for food and another for drinks. If possible, serve drinks from a separate room that is accessible from many sides—a large hall would be ideal. In addition, serve drinks from trays taken around the room from time to time.

Menu

for 30 – 40 people

Hors d'Oeuvres

Party Nibbles
(page 170-171)

Mini Puff Pastry Tartlets
(page 176)

Tuna Diamonds
(page 173)

Red Onion Pissaladière
(page 172)

Shrimp, Scallop and Mango Skewers
(page 178)

Beef, Scallion and Asparagus Roll-Ups
(page 178)

Desserts

Rich Chocolate Tart
(page 234)

Drinks

Rose Sparkle
(page 263)

Alcoholic and Nonalcoholic Cocktails
(page 260-263)

Assorted Beverages including Champagne, Soft Drinks, Coffee, and Mocha Magic
(page 258-263)

❄ Premix cocktails in large glass jugs so you don't have to play bartender all night ❄ Make sure you have enough chilled champagne, soft drinks, and ice ❄ Allow about 3–4 alcoholic drinks per person.

Festive glassware

Don't be tempted to use your good crystal—let the rest of your decorations lend sparkle to a mixture of less expensive glasses. Plan on two glasses per person to allow for ones that are broken or abandoned.

Decorated cocktail glasses are available, but you can easily make decorations with silver wire and shiny plastic motifs sold by the bagful in craft stores.

Plates and napkins

There is no reason why you should not use paper plates and napkins, decorated in silver. But show off with china coffee cups and the most glamorous serving plates you can find. Small mirrors would look great as serving trays or platters. Bring out the silver forks (or borrow some—you will need up to 80) and remember to count them before throwing out the garbage!

Did you know?

Making noise at New Year is believed to scare off evil spirits. In South America, a dummy burned on a bonfire is meant to symbolize an event of the past year. It burns, the old year is forgotten, and the New Year begins.

PARTY PLANNER

SEVERAL DAYS BEFORE

Do food shopping and buy alcohol and cocktail ingredients.

Buy and make decorations.

THE DAY BEFORE

Make Rich Chocolate Tart and chill.

Chill champagne.

ON THE DAY

Make all canapés and hors d'oeuvres, and cover.

Set tables and put out glasses.

BEFORE GUESTS ARRIVE

Premix pitchers of cocktails and make punch.

Prepare and cover trays of cold hors d'oeuvres.

Heat warm hors d'oeuvres.

Silver centerpieces

You can create an impressive display with sparkling gilded "trees" placed strategically on your serving tables and mantel. Simply wind strings of gold and silver metallic beads around tall Styrofoam cones, and secure in place with white (PVA) glue and T-pins. Attach white flowers, set trees on raised stands, and surround with candles so they will catch the light.

Serving your guests

Plan to serve hors d'oeuvres for about two hours. Guests will help themselves, but it is gracious to circulate with trays, constantly replenishing them to keep food fresh. Most people will eat 6–10 canapés and four larger hors d'oeuvres.

Prepare enough plates with wedges of dessert and a sparkler in each. Get help to light the sparklers all at once, and bring them in with panache. Coffee can be served with dessert before midnight, but a treat like Mocha Magic (page 260) would be a memorable way to round out the night.

AULD LANG SYNE

❄ Should auld acquaintance be forgot and never brought to mind? Should auld acquaintance be forgot and days of auld lang syne?

❄ For auld lang syne, my dear, for auld lang syne, we'll take a cup o' kindness yet, for auld lang syne.

❄ Should auld acquaintance be forgot and never brought to mind? Should auld acquaintance be forgot and days of auld lang syne?

❄ And here's a hand, my trusty friend, and gie's a hand o' thine, we'll take a cup o' kindness yet, for auld lang syne.

New Year's Day Brunch

Out with the old, and in with the new! Get the New Year off to a fresh start by replacing your now-jaded Christmas decorations with soft, cheerful colors and serving a brunch designed to comfort and soothe a fuzzy head.

The time and place

Invite your guests for around 11 a.m. and welcome them with mimosas (orange juice with champagne), or plain orange juice. A Bloody Caesar (see page 263) is reputed to be good for a hangover, or try the alternative of a Bloody Mary, made with plain tomato juice. Plan to eat in the kitchen—as this is the most intimate room in your house, it will create a warm, inviting atmosphere.

Menu
for 6 – 12 people

Cocktails

Bloody Caesar or Bloody Mary
(page 263)

Mimosa (Buck's Fizz)

Orange Juice

First Course

Fresh Fruit Compote
Sweet Rolls and Doughnuts
or
Blueberry Popovers and Berry Salad
(page 187)

Second Course

Eggs Benedict
(page 185)

Smoked Salmon Scramble
(page 184)

Choice of Milk, Coffee, or Tea

The table setting

Keep your table arrangement simple and let the food do the talking. Put a dish of fresh fruit at each place, along with a starched napkin tied with bear grass with a sprig of flowers tucked into the loops. Sparkling glassware and traditional china complete the natural look.

Fragrant baking

It is well worth making the effort to bake something fresh, for the aroma from the oven will permeate the house. Even if you opt for store bought sweet rolls, heating them in a low-temperature oven just before your guests arrive will have the same effect.

The aroma of freshly brewed coffee is also hard to beat—simply smelling it is invigorating.

The centerpiece

Fresh blossoms evoke a promise of the year to come and will enhance the casual charm of your breakfast table. We show freesias, carnations, and baby's breath, but forced hyacinths or daffodils in small decorative pots would be delightful.

PARTY PLANNER

THE DAY BEFORE
Buy sweet rolls and doughnuts.
Buy fresh fruit. Chill champagne.

AN HOUR OR TWO BEFORE
Make centerpiece and individual arrangements.
Make Blueberry Popovers.
Make melba toast or Hollandaise sauce.
Prepare Fruit Compote.

JUST BEFORE GUESTS ARRIVE
Prepare pitchers of cocktails and orange juice, ready to serve.

A mini flower arrangement at each place creates an extra-special touch for very little effort.

Make it easy

Two of the most impressive egg dishes you can serve are Eggs Benedict and smoked salmon with scrambled egg, but both are best enjoyed hot off the stove.

If your guest numbers are small and you are happy to put your cooking skills on the line, go for Eggs Benedict. Otherwise, Smoked Salmon Scramble is very quick to make, practically foolproof, and every bit as delicious.

first-footing

In Scotland, the first person who crosses your threshold after midnight of the New Year is said to bring either good or bad luck for the year. A tall dark-haired man is particularly lucky, especially if he carries a gift such as bread, coal, or money. (Invite someone like this to your brunch—and make sure he arrives first!) On the other hand, first-footing from a blond or redhead, or from a woman, is said to bring bad luck, so be warned.

SECRETS OF SUCCESS ❄ Be prepared to cocoon your guests—some may be feeling a little fragile. Rehydration is essential for a hangover, so supply plenty of liquid—watch alcohol or coffee, however, as both are diuretics. The vitamin C and vitamin B in your menu, and a couple of aspirin, should do the rest ❄ Round off the meal with a group walk in the fresh air ❄ Count your blessings, and your friends!

Christmas Cooking

★have a merry christmas★

CHAPTER FIVE

APPETIZERS AND BRUNCH

With all the entertaining at Christmas, it seems we never stop eating—and the demand is high for snacks, appetizers, first courses for formal meals, and treats for a special brunch. These recipes will make sure you rise to the occasion every time.

Party Nibbles

Olive tapenade spread on toasted bread, Spanish tapas—anchovy and olive banderillos, impressive-sounding caviar potatoes, tasty hummus croustades. One taste will have your guests asking for the recipes before the festivities are over.

Olive Crostini

- 12 slices of small baguette
- olive oil for baking
- 1/3 cup (60 g) tapenade (black olive paste)
- 36 small capers

MAKES 12

1 Preheat the oven to 400°F (200°C/Gas Mark 6).

2 Brush the slices of baguette with olive oil and place them on a baking sheet. Bake for 10 minutes or until lightly browned.

3 Spread each slice with tapenade, top with the capers, and serve warm.

tip

Instead of capers, you could top the slices with cherry tomato quarters or cucumber slices.

Vodka Cherry Tomato Shots

- 12 cherry tomatoes
- unflavored vodka, chilled

MAKES 12

1 Put a bottle of unflavored vodka into the refrigerator to chill overnight.

2 Cut a slit into the skins of the cherry tomatoes.

Place one tomato into each 1½ fl oz. (40 ml) straight-sided shot glass.

3 Pour over the ice-cold vodka and serve.

Caviar Potatoes

- 12 small new potatoes, unpeeled
- 5 tbsp. crème fraiche or sour cream
- 2 tbsp. caviar
- 12 chives, snipped diagonally

MAKES 12

1 Cook the potatoes in a pan of boiling salted water for 10 minutes or until tender.

2 Drain the potatoes and, when cool enough to handle, slice off both ends so they stand up.

3 With a small teaspoon, scoop out a little flesh from

the center of each potato and carefully fill with crème fraiche or sour cream.

4 Top with a little caviar and garnish with a few chives.

tip

You can prepare the potatoes the day before and fill an hour before serving.

Hummus Croustades

- 15 oz. (425 g) can chickpeas, drained and rinsed
- 2 tbsp. olive oil
- squeeze of lemon juice
- 12 pastry shells
- 12 marinated cherry tomatoes

MAKES 12

1 Blend the chickpeas with the oil and lemon juice until smooth. You won't need all the hummus for the pastry shells but the rest can be served as a dip with bread sticks or chips.

2 Season the hummus to taste and then spoon or pipe it into the pastry shells.

3 Top each filled shell with a cherry tomato and arrange on a serving platter.

ALTERNATIVE FILLING
Fill the shells with cream cheese with added dill weed, then top with a chopped black olive and a sprig of parsley.

Banderillos

- 12 marinated flat anchovies
- 12 stuffed green olives
- 12 toothpicks

MAKES 12

1 Roll an anchovy filet around each olive.

2 Thread a toothpick through the center of the anchovy and olive to fix securely together.

Party Bites

This assortment of bite-size finger foods offers a colorful focus and a variety of textures. Impressive looking, they are easy to prepare. A pissaladière is a classic recipe from Provence for an onion and anchovy pizza.

Crostini with Toppings

For the Crostini

- 2 thin baguettes
- olive oil

Each topping will cover 20 slices

1 Preheat the oven to 400°F (200°C/Gas Mark 6). Slice each baguette thinly into 10 slices. Lay the slices out on a baking sheet and brush the tops lightly with olive oil. Bake the crostini until crisp, and a pale gold color, about 6–8 minutes.

SUN-DRIED TOMATO, PESTO & MOZZARELLA TOPPING
Cut a 4½ oz. (125 g) mozzarella into 20 pieces. Spread the crostini with ¼ cup (2 oz./60 g) pesto, top with finely chopped sun-dried tomatoes, and mozzarella. Season.

ROASTED PEPPER, GOATS' CHEESE & OLIVE TOPPING
Roast and peel one red and one yellow bell pepper. Slice finely. Cut 5 oz. (150 g) goats' cheese into 20 pieces and toss in olive oil with thyme leaves. Quarter five pitted black olives. Pile onto the crostini and season.

ARTICHOKE & MINT TOPPING
Cut five artichoke hearts into quarters. Add one quarter to each crostini with chopped mint leaves, and a drizzle of olive oil.

PATÉ TOPPING
Slice 3 oz. (75 g) of firm paté and place on the crostini. Top with a caper or a sliced pickle.

Red Onion Pissaladière

- 1 lb. (450 g) red onions, thinly sliced
- 2 tbsp. olive oil
- 3 cloves garlic, chopped
- 5 plum (Roma) tomatoes, skinned and chopped
- sprig of thyme, stripped
- 2 x 2 oz. (56 g) cans flat anchovy filets, drained, rinsed and chopped
- extra anchovy filets, to garnish (optional)
- 20 blinis or cocktail bread rounds

1 In a large, heavy-based pan, gently stew the sliced onion in olive oil for about 40 minutes until very soft. Preheat the oven to 375°F (190°C/Gas Mark 5).

2 Add the garlic, tomatoes and thyme to the pan. Simmer, stirring occasionally, until the tomato juice has evaporated and the mixture has thickened.

3 Mash down and add the anchovies. Spread the topping evenly over the blinis or bread rounds and heat in the oven for 5 minutes. Season and garnish with extra anchovies.

Roasted Vegetable Wedges

- ²/₃ cup (6 fl oz./175 ml) olive oil
- 3 sprigs of fresh rosemary
- 4–5 whole garlic cloves, unpeeled
- 1 lb. (450 g) each of raw beets, Yukon Gold potatoes, parsnips, carrots, and celeriac

SERVES 20

1 Preheat the oven to 425°F (220°C/Gas Mark 7). Heat the oil with the rosemary sprigs and unpeeled garlic cloves. As soon as the oil is hot (don't let it boil), remove the pan from the heat and set it aside to let the flavors infuse.

2 Peel all the vegetables and cut into wedges. (Make the beet wedges thinner as they take longer to cook.) Spread the vegetables out in a single layer in two large roasting pans and pour the infused oil over them, turning them to make sure they are well coated with the oil.

3 Roast the vegetables in the oven for 1 hour, turning them over after 30 minutes. Reverse the position of the pans if they are on different shelves so the vegetables become evenly golden and caramelized. When they are tender, turn them into a large bowl, season, and serve warm with a selection of dips.

tip

Shallow roasting pans will help the vegetables brown and caramelize more easily.

Tuna Diamonds

- 2 tbsp. olive oil
- 7 oz. (200 g) tuna steak, skinned and cut through the middle to give two steaks

For the Guacamole

- flesh of 1 ripe avocado
- 3 scallions, white part only
- 2 tbsp. chopped cilantro (coriander) leaves
- 1–2 jalapeno peppers, cored and seeded
- juice of ¹/₂ lime
- extra cilantro (coriander) leaves, to garnish

MAKES 18–20

1 Brush a heavy griddle pan with half the olive oil and heat it until just smoking. Brush the tuna on both sides with oil.

2 Griddle the steaks for about 1 minute on each side, until the surfaces are opaque but the tuna is still rare in the middle. Remove the steaks from the pan.

3 Place all the guacamole ingredients in a blender and whizz until the mixture is very smooth. Taste and season.

4 Up to 2 hours before serving, cut each tuna steak into nine or ten bite-size diamond shapes. Up to an hour before serving, spoon or pipe some guacamole onto each piece of tuna. Garnish each diamond with a torn leaf of cilantro.

Party Fare

This selection of nibbles is great for snacking on while sipping a Christmas drink and catching up with loved ones.

Crudités with Three Dips

For the Pesto-Yogurt Dip

- 1 cup (1½ oz./42 g) fresh basil leaves
- 1 garlic clove (crushed)
- 1 tbsp. pine nuts
- 1 cup (9 oz./250 g) plus 2 tbsp. plain low-fat yogurt

For the Fresh Herb Dip

- ¾ cup (6 fl oz./170 ml) sour cream
- 1 scallion, minced
- 2 tbsp. chopped parsley
- 1 tbsp. fresh chives, finely snipped
- 1 tsp. tarragon vinegar

For the Italian-Style Tomato Dip

- ¾ cup (2 oz./56 g) sun-dried tomatoes (dry-packed)
- ⅓ cup (2½ oz./75 g) cottage cheese
- ⅓ cup (2½ oz./75 g) plain low-fat yogurt
- ½ cup (¾ oz./21 g) fresh basil leaves

To Serve

- 1 lb. (450 g) mixed vegetable crudités, such as baby carrots, zucchini sticks, baby sweetcorn, green beans (blanched in boiling water for 1 minute), bell pepper strips, Belgian endive, and broccoli florets

SERVES 8

1 For the Pesto-Yogurt Dip, crush the basil, garlic, and pine nuts into a paste with a mortar and pestle. Work in the yogurt a little at a time, until mixed. Season to taste. Transfer to a bowl, cover, and chill.

2 For the Fresh Herb Dip, stir all ingredients together in a bowl until blended. Cover tightly and chill.

3 For the Italian-Style Tomato Dip, place the sun-dried tomatoes in a heatproof bowl and pour over boiling water to cover. Leave to soak until the tomatoes are tender, about 30 minutes. Drain the tomatoes, pat dry, then finely chop. Purée the cottage cheese with the yogurt in food processor. Transfer to a bowl and stir in the tomatoes. Cover and chill.

Sesame-Cheese Twists

- ½ cup (2 oz./50 g) whole-wheat flour
- ¾ cup (3¼ oz./90 g) all-purpose (plain) flour
- ¼ tsp. salt
- 3 tbsp. butter
- ½ cup (2 oz./60 g) freshly grated Parmesan cheese
- 1 extra large egg
- 2 tbsp. low-fat (2%) milk
- 1 tsp. paprika
- 1 tbsp. sesame seeds

MAKES 20 Sticks

Vegetable Bruschetta

- 1 medium red pepper
- 1 medium yellow pepper
- 2 small zucchini
- 1 medium head fennel
- 1 red onion
- 5 tbsp. olive oil
- 2 garlic cloves
- 1 small tomato
- 1 loaf of ciabatta bread, or 1 baguette
- 6 large basil leaves

SERVES 4

1 Preheat the broiler to high. Rinse and dry the peppers, zucchini, and fennel. Cut the peppers lengthwise into eight, and remove the stems and seeds. Trim the zucchini and slice diagonally. Trim the fennel, cut it lengthwise into thin slices. Peel the onion and slice into rings.

2 Cover the grill rack with a single layer of vegetables, laying the peppers skin-sides down. Brush with olive oil and grill, on one side only, until they are lightly browned but still slightly firm. If necessary, cook them in batches and keep the first batch warm in the oven.

3 Peel and halve the cloves of garlic and rinse, dry, and halve the tomato. Cut the loaf down and then across into quarters and toast on both sides.

4 Rub the top of each slice with the cut garlic and tomato, then pile the grilled vegetables on top. Drizzle over the remaining oil and season the bruschetta to taste. Rinse, dry, and tear the basil leaves and scatter them over the top.

1 Preheat the oven to 350°F (180°C/Gas Mark 4). Line a cookie sheet with parchment paper. Sift the flours and salt into a bowl, tipping in the bran left in the sifter. Rub in the butter until the mixture resembles fine bread crumbs. Stir in the Parmesan cheese.

2 Beat the egg and milk together. Reserve a teaspoon of the mixture, and stir the rest into the dry ingredients to make a dough. Knead on a lightly floured surface until smooth.

3 Sprinkle the paprika over the floured surface, then roll out the dough on it to form an 8-in. (20-cm) square; trim the edges to make them straight. Brush the dough with the reserved egg mixture and sprinkle with the sesame seeds. Cut the square of dough in half, then cut into 40 sticks that are 4-in. (10-cm) long and about ½-in. (1½-cm) wide.

4 Twist the sticks and place on the cookie sheet. Lightly press the ends of the sticks down so they do not untwist during baking. Bake until lightly brown and crisp, about 15 minutes. Cool on the cookie sheet for a few minutes, then serve warm, or transfer to a wire rack to cool completely. The sticks will keep in an airtight container for up to five days.

Mini Puff-Pastry Tartlets

- 3 lb. (1.3 kg) puff pastry
- 1 large yellow bell pepper, seeded and cut into thin strips
- 3 oz. (75 g) Parmesan cheese, grated
- 4 tomatoes, sliced
- 6 oz. (175 g) goats' cheese, crumbled
- 6 thin slices prosciutto, cut in half
- 2 mozzarella cheeses, (10 oz./280 g), each cut into 6 slices
- chopped fresh herbs, e.g. parsley, chives, basil, to garnish

MAKES 36

These mouth-watering mini tartlets have three different toppings, so every guest should find something to their taste. The steam created by the damp baking sheets helps the pastry to rise quickly and evenly.

1 Cut the pastry into six equal pieces and roll each to a rectangle measuring 9 in. x 6 in. (23 cm x 15 cm). Cut each rectangle into six 3-in. (7.5-cm) squares, to make 36 squares.

2 Preheat the oven to 425°F (220°C/Gas Mark 7). Dampen enough baking sheets to lay out the pastry squares.

3 Place the pastry squares on the baking sheets, leaving a space between them, and divide the pepper slices and Parmesan between 12 of them. Top another 12 with the tomato slices and goats' cheese, and the final 12 with the prosciutto and mozzarella.

4 Bake in the oven until the pastry is puffed and golden brown, about 10–15 minutes.

5 Serve the mini tartlets warm, sprinkled with chopped fresh herbs of your choice.

Spicy Morsels

Served warm from the oven, these spicy chicken skewers and crisp puff pastry sausage rolls will be favorites with adults and children.

Spiced Chicken Skewers

- 1 lb. (450 g) boneless chicken breasts, skinned and cut into thin strips
- ½ tsp. coriander seeds, coarsely crushed
- ½ tsp. cumin seeds
- 1 tsp. curry paste
- 1 garlic clove, crushed
- 1¼ cups (11 oz./320 g) plain yogurt

MAKES ABOUT 16

1 Put the chicken in a bowl, add the spices, garlic, and yogurt, and season to taste. Stir well until the chicken is coated in the yogurt mixture.

2 Cover the bowl and leave the chicken to marinate in the fridge overnight. If you like things hot, add finely chopped chili pepper to the marinade.

3 Leave 16 wooden skewers to soak in water for 30 minutes. Thread the chicken on to the skewers and arrange in a single layer on a baking sheet or a foil-lined broiler pan.

4 Grill for 6–10 minutes until the chicken is cooked, turning the skewers over once or twice. Serve hot.

Puff Pastry Sausage Rolls

- 8 pork or chicken sausages, each about 3 in.-4 in. (7.5 cm-10 cm) long
- 8 oz. (250 g) puff pastry
- 2 tbsp. jellied cranberry sauce
- beaten egg, to glaze

MAKES 32

1 Broil or fry the sausages in a skillet for about 10 minutes, turning them over regularly until they are evenly browned. Set aside and leave until cold.

2 Roll out the pastry to a rectangle measuring about 20 in. x 10 in. (50 cm x 25 cm) and cut into eight 5 in. (13 cm) squares. Spread each square with a little jellied cranberry sauce.

3 Brush the edges of the squares with a little water, place a sausage along one side and roll up, pressing the pastry edges together to seal.

4 Place the rolls on a baking sheet, seam side down, and chill for 30 minutes in the fridge.

5 Preheat the oven to 425°F (220°C/Gas Mark 7). Brush each sausage roll with beaten egg and bake for 15–20 minutes or until golden brown. When cool enough to handle, cut each roll into four equal-size pieces and serve warm.

Tasty Wraps

Prepare these elegant appetizers ahead of time and then serve them freshly cooked to savor the delicious combination of flavors.

Shrimp, Scallop, and Mango Skewers

- 32 raw shrimp
- 8 large raw scallops, cut in half
- 3 tbsp. sweet chili sauce
- 1 tbsp. chopped fresh parsley
- 8 rashers of bacon, cut in half
- 1 medium mango, peeled and flesh chopped

SERVES 4

1 Soak 16 wooden skewers for 30 minutes in cold water to prevent them from burning when under the grill.

2 Peel the shrimp and devein. Mix the shrimp and scallops with the chili sauce and parsley and leave to marinate for 20 minutes.

3 Wrap each half scallop in a piece of bacon and thread on to the skewers, alternating with the shrimps and mango.

4 Broil for 6–8 minutes, turning once. Serve with a little extra chili sauce for a real spicy kick.

Beef, Scallion, and Asparagus Roll-Ups

- 8 asparagus stalks, trimmed to 6-in. (15-cm) lengths
- 8 thin slices sirloin steak (4 oz./115 g)
- 4 scallions, trimmed to 6-in. (15-cm) lengths
- 2 tsp. vegetable oil
- 3 tbsp. bottled teriyaki sauce
- 1 tbsp. sesame seeds, toasted
- 1 tbsp. chopped cilantro (coriander)

SERVES 4 (2 roll-ups per serving)

1 Boil a saucepan of water. Cut each asparagus stalk in half. Blanch in boiling water for 1 minute, and drain. Pound the sirloin slices to 1/8-in. (3-mm) thickness. Cut each scallion into two pieces, 3-in. (7.5-cm) thick.

2 Place two pieces of asparagus and one piece of scallion at one end of each beef strip. Roll the beef around the middle of the vegetables.

3 Heat the oil in a large nonstick skillet over a medium-high heat. Add the beef rolls, brown for 2 minutes, turning the rolls frequently. Add the teriyaki sauce, lower heat to medium, and cook for 3 minutes.

4 Transfer the rolls to a serving platter. Sprinkle with sesame seeds and cilantro.

Crispy Potato Pancake & Smoked Salmon Canapés

- 1 lb. (450 g) floury potatoes such as Idaho
- 1 medium onion
- 1 large egg
- 2 tbsp. whole-wheat flour
- sunflower oil for frying
- 7 oz. (200 g) smoked salmon
- ⅔ cup (6½ oz./180 g) thick sour cream
- sprigs of fresh dill or flat-leaf parsley, to garnish

MAKES 12 PANCAKES

Potatoes make a sophisticated appetizer when transformed into these deliciously crisp pancakes. Top them with sour cream and succulent strips of smoked salmon for a taste sensation.

1 Preheat the oven to 270°F (140°C/Gas Mark 1). Peel and grate the potatoes and finely chop the onion; put them both in a sieve. Press with a spoon to squeeze out as much starchy liquid as possible.

2 Transfer the mixture to a bowl, add the egg, flour, salt, and pepper to taste, and mix well.

3 Pour the oil into a frying pan to a depth of about ⅜ in. (2 cm) and heat until it shows a haze.

4 Put a tablespoon of the potato mixture into the oil, flattening it to a small pancake about 2 in. (5 cm) in diameter. Keep adding more tablespoons of the mixture to the pan, cooking four to six at a time. Fry for about 1 minute or until they are golden on the bottom, then turn them over and cook the other side until crisp and golden but still soft in the center.

5 Remove the pancakes from the pan, drain them on paper towels, and keep them warm in the oven while you cook the remainder.

6 Cut the salmon into small strips. Rinse and dry the dill or parsley. Serve each pancake topped with a spoonful of sour cream and a few strips of salmon, and garnished with some dill or parsley.

Elegant Shellfish Salad

Traditional shrimp cocktail with a designer label! The succulent lobster meat, crab claws, and tiger shrimp are drizzled with a lighter than light dressing, making this a colorful Christmas appetizer.

For the Dressing

- 1 cup (8 fl oz./225 ml) buttermilk
- 1 tbsp. Dijon mustard
- 4 tbsp. snipped fresh dill
- finely grated zest and juice of 1 lemon

For the Salad

- ½ head frisee lettuce, or mesclun mix
- ½ cucumber, cut into fine ribbons
- 7 oz. (200 g) cooked and peeled tiger shrimp
- 4 cooked lobster tails, halved lengthwise
- 16 cooked crab claws (shelled)

SERVES 8

tip

Use a vegetable peeler to slice the cucumber into long, thin ribbons.

1 Combine all of the dressing ingredients and season with salt and pepper to taste.

2 Arrange the lettuce and cucumber onto eight plates, top with the tiger shrimp, lobster and crab claws.

3 At this stage, either store in the fridge until ready to serve, or drizzle the salads with the dressing and serve right away.

Grilled Chicken Salad with Mango

Infused with the delicate flavors of lime and garlic, and served on a tropical Christmas salad which includes coconut, raisins, cashews, and mango, this refreshing dish makes an excellent light lunch or supper.

- 2 whole skinless, boneless chicken breasts (about 1½ lb./675 g)
- 2 tbsp. lime juice
- 2 tbsp. vegetable oil
- 2 tsp. minced garlic
- ½ cup (1½ oz./40 g) flaked coconut
- 2 cups (3½ oz./100 g) shredded romaine lettuce
- 1 medium-size mango, peeled, pitted, and cut into ½-in. (0.5-cm) cubes
- ¼ cup (1 oz./30 g) light seedless raisins
- ⅓ cup (1 oz./30 g) coarsely chopped toasted cashews
- 1 cup (8 oz./225 g) julienned carrots
- 2 tbsp. chopped cilantro (coriander)

SERVES 4

1 Place the chicken, one tablespoon each of the lime juice and oil, and the garlic in a glass bowl and marinate, covered, in the refrigerator for 5 hours.

2 Preheat the oven to 350°F (180°C/Gas Mark 4). Spread the coconut in an ungreased shallow baking pan and toast, stirring often, until golden brown, about 10 minutes.

3 Preheat the broiler and broil the chicken 5 in. (12 cm) from the heat until dark brown, about 10 minutes on each side.

4 In a large bowl, toss the remaining tablespoon of lime juice and oil, toasted coconut, romaine, mango, raisins, cashews, carrots, and cilantro together.

5 Slice the chicken into strips about ¼-in. (0.5-cm) thick.

6 Divide the salad equally among four serving plates, top with the chicken slices, and serve immediately.

Sumptuous Soups

On a cold winter day, nothing warms the soul like a piping hot bowl of soup. Treat your holiday guests to this yummy selection of recipes.

Shrimp Bisque

- 1 lb. (400 g) raw, headlesss jumbo shrimp
- 4 tbsp. dry white wine
- 4 lemon slices
- 4 black peppercorns, lightly crushed
- 2 sprigs fresh parsley, stems bruised
- 1 fennel bulb
- 1 tsp. fresh lemon juice
- 1 tbsp. butter
- 1 tbsp. sunflower oil
- 1 shallot, minced
- ⅓ cup (35 g) fine, white bread crumbs, made from day-old bread slices
- pinch paprika
- 1 red bell pepper, seeded and finely diced
- chopped leaves from the fennel bulb, or herb fennel

SERVES 6

1 Shell the shrimp and set aside. Place the shells in a large saucepan. Pour in 5 cups (40 fl oz./1125 ml) cold water and add the white wine, lemon slices, peppercorns, and parsley. Bring to a boil over a high heat. Reduce the heat and simmer 20 minutes, skimming off any scum.

2 Use a small, sharp knife to devein each shrimp. Cover and chill the shrimp until needed.

3 Leave the broth to cool slightly, then pick out and discard the lemon slices. Line a sieve with cheesecloth and place it over a large bowl. Process the broth in a food processor until the shells are finely ground, then strain through the cheesecloth-lined sieve; discard the residue from the shells.

4 Coarsely chop ⅔ cup of the fennel, then finely chop the remainder of the bulb. Place the finely chopped fennel in a medium bowl, add the lemon juice, and toss well; cover closely with plastic wrap and set aside.

5 Melt the butter with the oil in the washed saucepan over a medium heat. Add the chopped fennel and the shallot and sauté, stirring frequently, until the vegetables are soft, but not brown, 5–8 minutes. Stir in the bread crumbs, paprika, and stock. Bring slowly to a boil, then reduce the heat

so the soup simmers. Add the shrimp and continue simmering for 3 minutes.

6 Use a slotted spoon to remove six shrimps for garnishing the soup; set them aside. Season the soup with salt and pepper to taste, and simmer for 15 minutes longer.

7 Purée the soup in a food processor until smooth. Return to the saucepan and add the finely chopped fennel and the red bell pepper. Reheat the soup until piping hot. Serve with the reserved shrimp and chopped fennel leaves.

Pastry-Crowned Tomato Soup

- 2 tbsp. vegetable oil
- 3 medium onions, chopped
- 3 celery sticks, chopped
- 2 tbsp. chopped fresh basil
- 3 cups (27 fl oz./800 ml) drained canned tomatoes
- 2 tbsp. tomato paste (purée)
- 2 cups (17 fl oz./500 ml) vegetable stock
- 2/3 cup (5 fl oz./250 ml) heavy (double) cream
- 1 package (17.3 oz./490 g) chilled ready-rolled puff pastry
- 1 egg, beaten

SERVES 6

1 In a large saucepan, heat the oil and cook the onions and celery over a low heat until the onions are soft; add the tomatoes and tomato paste and simmer, covered, for 10 minutes. Uncover, add the stock, bring to a boil; reduce the heat and simmer for 20 minutes.

2 Transfer the mixture to the food processor and purée. Stir in the cream and season to taste. Refrigerate until the pastry top is ready.

3 Divide the soup between six deep, ovenproof soup bowls. Leave a 1 in. (2.5 cm) gap at the top of each bowl.

4 Roll the pastry to 1/8-in. (3-mm) thickness and cut out six circles about 1 in. (2.5 cm) larger than the top of the bowls. Place a circle of pastry over each bowl, sealing the pastry to the outside of the bowl. Chill for at least half an hour. Preheat the oven to 350°F (180°C/Gas Mark 4).

5 Brush the pastry with beaten egg and place the soup bowls in the lower third of the oven and bake for 15–20 minutes or until the pastry is puffed and golden.

Classic Onion Soup

- 2 tbsp. butter or margarine
- 5 medium-size yellow onions, thinly sliced
- 2 tbsp. sugar
- 3 1/2 cups (28 fl oz./790 ml) browned beef stock or canned reduced-sodium beef broth
- 5 cups (40 fl oz./1125 ml) water
- 1/4 cup (2 fl oz./56 ml) brandy (optional)
- 4 1/2-in. (11 1/2-cm) thick slices French bread, toasted
- 4 tbsp. grated Gruyère cheese

SERVES 4

1 Preheat the oven to 400°F (200°C/Gas Mark 6). In a 5-quart Dutch oven (heavy-based casserole dish), over a moderately high heat, melt the butter. Add the onions and sugar and sauté over a high heat until the onions are golden, about 10 minutes. Reduce the heat to low and sauté for 10 minutes, stirring occasionally.

2 Add the stock and water and boil over a high heat. Reduce the heat to moderately low and simmer, uncovered, for 20 minutes. Add brandy, if using, salt and pepper to taste, and return to a boil over a high heat.

3 Ladle the soup into four deep, ovenproof soup bowls and place on a heavy-duty baking sheet. Top with the toasted French bread and sprinkle with one tablespoon grated Gruyère cheese.

4 Bake, uncovered, until the cheese has melted, about 5 minutes.

Exceptional Eggs

Eggs make an ideal brunch or light lunch and these classic recipes are quick to prepare and are sure to become firm family favorites.

Vegetable Frittata

- 4 oz. (115 g) white or cremini mushrooms, thinly sliced
- 1/3 cup (1 1/2 oz./42 g) thinly sliced red onion
- 2 cups (16 fl oz./480ml) fat-free egg substitute
- 1 large egg
- 1/2 tsp. chopped fresh oregano
- 1/4 tsp. fresh thyme leaves
- 4 small plum (Roma) tomatoes, thinly sliced
- 2 tbsp. shredded part-skim mozzarella cheese

SERVES 4

1 Preheat the broiler. Coat a 9- or 10-in. ovenproof nonstick skillet with nonstick cooking spray and set over a medium-high heat. Sauté the mushrooms and onion until tender, about 5 minutes. Transfer to a plate. Wipe out the skillet, coat again with the cooking spray, and place over a medium heat.

2 Whisk the egg substitute, egg, oregano, thyme, salt, and black pepper to taste in a medium bowl; pour into a hot skillet. Cook, without stirring,

until the eggs begin to set, about 2 minutes, lifting up the edge with a spatula while tilting skillet and letting the uncooked portion flow underneath.

3 Arrange the tomato slices and sautéed vegetables in concentric circles on top. Continue cooking the frittata until the eggs are golden brown on the bottom and almost set on top, 2–3 minutes longer.

4 Sprinkle the mozzarella around the edge of the frittata. Transfer the skillet to the broiler and broil until the cheese melts and begins to brown, about 2 minutes. Cut the frittata into quarters, and serve.

Eggs Benedict

- 1 tbsp. white wine vinegar
- pinch of sea salt
- 2 large eggs
- 2 slices ham
- 1 English muffin

For the Hollandaise sauce

- 1 tbsp. vinegar
- 6 black peppercorns, crushed
- 2 bay leaves
- a squeeze of lemon juice
- 2 egg yolks
- 1³/₄ sticks (7 oz./200 g) butter, cut into small pieces

SERVES 2

1 To make the sauce, boil the vinegar, peppercorns, bay leaves, and lemon juice in a small pan until reduced by two-thirds. Add one tablespoon cold water and whisk in the egg yolks until fluffy. Transfer to a bowl set over a pan of hot water and whisk until the yolks have thickened to the consistency of unwhipped heavy (double) cream. Remove from the heat and gradually whisk in the butter. Season, strain, and keep warm.

2 Bring a shallow pan of water to the boil, add the vinegar and salt. Turn off the heat. Crack in the eggs, cover, and

leave to stand until the whites are opaque, about 3–4 minutes. Grill the ham, split the muffin and toast it. Top the muffin halves with ham, eggs, and sauce.

Smoked Salmon Scramble

- 10 large eggs
- ¹/₂ cup (4 fl oz./100 ml) half and half (half milk and half single cream)
- 5 oz. (150 g) smoked salmon, cut into bite-size pieces
- 2 medium tomatoes, finely chopped
- 1 medium chili pepper, seeded and chopped (optional)
- 12 slices white bread to make melba toast
- 1 tbsp. chopped parsley

SERVES 6

1 Whisk together the eggs and add the half and half. Pour the mixture into a non-stick pan and cook over a gentle heat, stirring constantly until the eggs begin to scramble.

2 Stir the salmon pieces into the eggs with the tomatoes and chili pepper, if using.

3 Toast six thin-cut slices of white bread on both sides for the melba toast. Trim off the crusts and cut

each slice horizontally in half to give 12 very thin slices. Lightly toast the untoasted sides of the bread until light golden. Serve the salmon and egg mixture on melba toast, sprinkled with a little parsley as a garnish.

Apricot-Nut Loaf

Years ago, this fruit bread was often served at afternoon teas. With its dried
fruit, orange zest, and nuts, it will give a festive flavor to any Christmas spread.

- boiling water
- 1 package (6 oz./165 g) dried apricots, chopped
- 2 cups all-purpose (plain) flour
- 3/4 cup (5 3/4 oz./165 g) granulated (white) sugar
- 1 tbsp. baking powder
- 1/4 tsp. salt
- 2 large egg whites
- 2/3 cup (5 fl oz./150 ml) apricot nectar or orange juice
- 3 tbsp. vegetable oil
- 2 tsp. grated orange zest
- 1/2 cup (2 oz./55 g) finely chopped pecans or walnuts
- 3-4 tsp. orange juice
- 1/2 cup confectioners' (icing) sugar

MAKES 1 LOAF (16 SERVINGS)

1 Preheat the oven to 350°F (180°C/Gas Mark 4). In a small bowl, pour enough boiling water over the apricots to cover; let stand for 5 minutes. Drain and set aside.

2 Meanwhile, in a large bowl, stir together the flour, granulated sugar, baking powder, and salt. In a medium-size bowl, combine the egg whites, apricot nectar, oil, and orange zest. Add to the flour mixture all at once and stir just until combined. Fold in the apricots and chopped pecans.

3 Spoon the mixture into a lightly greased 8-in. x 4-in. x 2-in. (20-cm x 10-cm x 4-cm) loaf pan. Bake for 50–55 minutes or until a toothpick inserted in the center comes out clean. Cool the bread in the pan on a wire rack for 5 minutes; then remove from the pan.

4 In a small bowl, gradually stir the orange juice into the confectioners' sugar until the mixture is thin enough to drizzle. Drizzle over the loaf. Cool completely.

tip

For even slices that don't crumble, make sure the bread is completely cool before you cut it.

Blueberry Popovers & Berry Salad

For the Popovers

- 1 tsp. butter
- 1 cup (4 oz./100 g) all-purpose (plain) flour
- pinch salt
- 1 tsp. sugar
- 2 large eggs
- 1 cup (8 fl oz./225 ml) low-fat (2%) milk
- ½ cup (2 oz./50 g) blueberries
- 1 tbsp. confectioners' (icing) sugar

For the Mixed Berry Salad

- 1 heaped cup (6 oz./175 g) raspberries
- ⅔ cup (3 oz./75 g) blueberries
- 1½ cups (6 oz./150 g) strawberries, hulled and thickly sliced
- 1 tbsp. confectioners' (icing) sugar

SERVES 4

This sweet version of a North American classic is perfect for breakfast or for a tasty brunch. Serve the popovers with plump fresh berries for an extra burst of flavor.

1 Preheat the oven to 425°F (220°C/Gas Mark 7). Using a piece of crumpled paper towel and the butter, lightly grease eight of the cups in a nonstick muffin tray.

2 To make the popovers, sift the flour, salt, and sugar into a large mixing bowl and make a well in the middle. Break the eggs into the well, add the milk, and beat together thoroughly with a fork.

3 Using a wire whisk, gradually work the flour into the liquid to make a smooth batter that has the consistency of light (single) cream. Pour the batter into a measuring jug.

4 Divide the batter evenly between the prepared muffin cups—they should each be about two-thirds full. Drop a few of the blueberries into the batter in each cup, dividing the berries equally between the popovers.

5 Bake in the middle of the oven until the popovers are golden brown, well risen, and crisp around the edges, about 25–30 minutes.

6 Meanwhile, make the berry salad. Purée two-thirds of the raspberries by pressing them through a nylon sifter into a bowl. Add the remainder of the raspberries to the bowl, together with the blueberries and strawberries. Sift the confectioners' sugar over the fruit and fold gently together so all the ingredients are mixed.

7 Remove the popovers using a round-bladed knife, and dust with the confectioners' sugar. Serve hot, with the berry salad.

CHAPTER SIX

MAIN MEALS

Choose the perfect main course for every meal—
from family get-togethers to formal dinner parties;
from intimate suppers to a buffet for thirty. Dip
into these pages for memorable dishes that are
sure to please any crowd.

★ have a merry christmas ★

Salmon En Croute

An excellent party dish as it can be prepared ahead and just popped in the oven when your guests arrive. If there are any small bones still lodged in the salmon fillets, the easiest way to pull them out is with a pair of tweezers.

- 2 tbsp. oil
- ½ red bell pepper, seeded and finely chopped
- 1 leek, trimmed and thinly sliced
- 6 oz. (175 g) peas, cooked and mashed
- juice of ½ lemon
- 4 lb. (1.8 kg) salmon, filleted and skinned, giving two long fillets
- 1¼ lb. (550 g) store-bought puff pastry
- 1 egg, lightly beaten, to glaze

SERVES 8

1 Heat the oil in a skillet and sauté the pepper and leek until softened. Stir in the mashed peas and lemon juice, then remove from the heat and leave to cool.

2 Season the salmon with salt and pepper and lay one fillet on a board, skinned side down. Spread with the mashed pea mixture and top with the second fillet, skinned side up.

3 Roll out one-third of the pastry to a rectangle ¾ in. (2 cm) larger all around than the salmon. Lift the pastry on to a nonstick or greased baking sheet and place the salmon in the center.

4 Gather up any pastry trimmings and roll out with the rest of the pastry to a rectangle large enough to cover the salmon. Dampen the pastry edges with the egg mixture and press them together to seal. Cut a

hole in the top for steam to escape and decorate with pastry leaves cut from the trimmings. Chill for 30 minutes.

5 Preheat the oven to 425°F (220°C/Gas Mark 7). Brush the pastry with beaten egg and bake for 20 minutes. Turn the oven down to 375°F (190°C/Gas Mark 5) and bake for a further 20–25 minutes until the pastry is golden brown.

Festive Fish

Baked fresh cod with a herby pesto crust, and a zesty salmon fillet, make fine family supper dishes for any special occasion.

Cod Baked with Pesto

- 1½ lb. (680 g) starchy potatoes, such as Idaho
- 4 thick pieces of cod fillet, or cod steaks, about 6 oz. (170 g) each
- 1 tbsp. green or red pesto
- 1 tbsp. olive oil
- 1 clove garlic
- 3 tbsp. (50 g) butter
- ¼ cup (50 ml) light (single) cream
- 4 sprigs of basil to garnish

SERVES 4

1 Preheat the oven to 400°F (200°C/Gas Mark 6) and put a kettle of water on to boil.

2 Scrub the potatoes and cut them into ¾ in. (2 cm) cubes. Put the cubes into a saucepan, cover with boiling water, and add salt to taste. Cover, bring back to the boil, and boil for 10–15 minutes, until cooked.

3 Meanwhile, line a small roasting pan with aluminum foil. Wipe the cod with paper towels and lay the fillets in the pan. Spread the pesto evenly over each and season to taste. Drizzle with olive oil and bake on the top shelf of the oven for 15–20 minutes or until the flesh flakes easily.

4 Drain the potatoes and return them to the pan. Peel the garlic, crush it into the potatoes, and mash. Stir in the butter and cream and reheat gently. Serve with the fish and garnish with the basil.

Salmon on a Bed of Greens

- ¼ cup (2 fl oz./56 ml) grapefruit juice
- 1½ tbsp. mustard
- 1½ tbsp. honey
- ¼ tsp. red pepper flakes
- 4 salmon fillets (6 oz./ 168 g) each
- 1½ lb. (2.5 kg) kale, large stems removed and leaves chopped
- 3 tbsp. olive oil
- ½ red bell pepper, seeded and finely chopped
- ½ yellow pepper, seeded and finely chopped

SERVES 4

1 In a baking dish large enough to hold fish fillets in a single layer, combine the grapefruit juice, mustard, honey, and pepper flakes. Add the salmon, turning it to coat both sides with the marinade. Cover and refrigerate for 30 minutes. Heat broiler.

2 In a large pot, bring 2 quarts (2 liters) of water to a boil. Add the kale and boil for 5 minutes. Drain well. Squeeze out any excess water.

3 Heat the olive oil in large skillet over a medium heat. Add the red and yellow bell peppers and sauté for 1 minute, then add the kale. Sauté until the peppers and kale are tender, about 3 minutes. Remove from the heat and keep warm.

4 Place the salmon, skin side down, on a rack in a foil-lined broiler pan. Reserve the marinade.

5 Broil the salmon 4 in. (10 cm) from heat for 3 minutes. Brush on the remaining marinade. Broil until fish is opaque and flakes when touched, 3–4 minutes. (If the fish browns too quickly, drop to a lower rack in broiler.) Serve on a bed of kale and peppers.

Deliciously Seasoned Seafood Cakes

These rich crab and shrimp cakes are spiced with mustard, Worcestershire sauce, and a little cayenne pepper, then coated in bread crumbs and fried until the outside is a crunchy golden brown, perfect for a light supper.

- 2 slices dry bread, about 2 oz. (50 g)
- ½ cup (4 fl oz./110 ml) milk
- 2 cans (4oz./120 g) fresh crab meat
- 8 oz. (230 g) peeled, cooked shrimp
- 2 large eggs
- 2 tsp. Dijon mustard
- 1 tbsp. Worcestershire sauce
- ½ cup (60 g) ground almonds
- a large pinch of cayenne pepper
- 1 tbsp. thick mayonnaise
- a handful of fresh parsley

For the Coating
- ⅓ cup (40 g) all-purpose (plain) flour
- 1½ cups (168 g) dried bread crumbs
- sunflower oil for frying

SERVES 4

1 Soak both slices of bread in the milk for 5 minutes. Flake the crab meat, put it into a bowl, chop the shrimp and add them to the crab.

2 Separate the eggs and set the whites aside. Add the yolks, mustard, Worcestershire sauce, almonds, cayenne pepper, and mayonnaise to the crab. Rinse, dry, and chop enough parsley to give 1 tbsp. and add it to the bowl.

3 Squeeze the bread dry, add it to the crab mixture, and stir until soft but not sloppy. Add some bread crumbs if the mixture is too moist.

4 To make the coating, put the flour onto one plate and the bread crumbs onto another. Whisk 1 tbsp. of water into the egg whites. Divide the crab mixture into eight portions and shape them into cakes.

Dip the crab cakes into the flour, shake off the excess, then dip them into the egg whites, and coat with the bread crumbs.

5 Heat ½ in. (1 cm) of oil in a large skillet over a fairly high heat. Fry the fish cakes for 2–3 minutes on each side until they are crisp and golden, then drain them on paper towels and serve two per person.

Lobster Newburg

This recipe's luxurious richness is cleverly achieved by using chicken broth and nonfat half-and-half instead of the egg yolks, cream, and butter typically used in the sauce. Lemon peel, tarragon, and sherry liven up the flavor.

- 1 cup (7 oz./200 g) long-grain white rice
- 2 live lobsters (1¼ to 1½ lb. each)
- 1 cup (8 fl oz./240 ml) reduced-sodium chicken broth
- 3 tbsp. all-purpose (plain) flour
- 1 cup (8 fl oz./240 ml) nonfat half-and-half (or half milk; half single cream)
- 2 tbsp. dry sherry
- 2 tbsp. chopped fresh tarragon and sprigs for garnish
- 1 tsp. grated lemon zest
- 3 cups (12 oz./300 g) small white or cremini mushrooms, sliced

SERVES 4

1 Prepare the rice according to package directions, adding ⅛ tsp. salt and ¼ tsp. black pepper to cooking water. Let stand 5 minutes, covered.

2 Meanwhile, bring 2 in. (5 cm) of water to a vigorous boil in a large stockpot fitted with a rack over high heat. Add the live lobsters, head first. Cover and steam until the shells turn bright red and the meat is opaque throughout, 12–15 minutes. Remove the lobsters from the pot and rinse with cold water to stop the cooking. Remove the lobster meat from the shells and cut into 1½-in. (4 cm) chunks.

3 Put the broth and flour in a jar with a tight-fitting lid and shake until blended and smooth. Pour into a small saucepan. Bring to a boil, stirring constantly, and then add the half-and-half. Reduce heat to medium-low and simmer the sauce until smooth and thickened, about 5 minutes. Stir in the sherry, 1 tbsp. chopped tarragon, lemon zest, and salt and black pepper; remove from the heat. Lightly coat a large nonstick skillet with nonstick cooking spray and set over a medium-high heat. Sauté the mushrooms until tender, about 5 minutes; stir in the sauce and lobster. Cook over a medium heat just until heated through, about 4 minutes.

4 Generously coat six timbales with cooking spray and pack in the rice with a spoon. Turn out each timbale of rice onto a dinner plate. Spoon on the lobster mixture. Garnish with tarragon sprigs.

Shrimp Gumbo

A bowl of steaming gumbo—a thick and spicy cross between a soup and a stew, full of bell peppers, tomatoes, okra, herbs, and shrimp—brings you the good tastes of the Louisiana bayou. Serve with steamed rice or crusty bread.

- 1 tbsp. extra-virgin olive oil
- 2 onions, chopped
- 1 red bell pepper, seeded and chopped
- 2 celery stalks, chopped
- 3 garlic cloves, chopped
- 2 oz. (60 g) lean smoked Canadian bacon, diced
- 1 tbsp. all-purpose (plain) flour
- 1 tbsp. paprika
- 1 quart (35 fl oz./1 liter) fish stock, preferably homemade
- 1 tsp. chopped fresh thyme
- ½ can (14 oz./400 g) crushed tomatoes
- 2 tbsp. chopped parsley
- 2 bay leaves
- 2 tsp. Worcestershire sauce
- hot red pepper sauce to taste
- 3 oz. (80 g) okra, sliced crosswise
- 12 oz. (350 g) shelled raw large shrimp, with tails left
- ⅓ cup (2 oz./56 g) thin green beans, cut into bite-size pieces
- 3 scallions, thinly sliced

SERVES 4

1 Heat the oil in a large saucepan. Add the onions, bell pepper, and celery and sauté until light brown, 5–6 minutes. Stir in the garlic and bacon and cook 3–4 minutes longer. Stir in the flour, increase the heat slightly, and stir 2 minutes. Stir in the paprika and continue stirring 2 minutes longer. Gradually add the stock, stirring well to dissolve the flour mixture.

2 Add the thyme, tomatoes, parsley, bay leaves, and Worcestershire sauce. Bring to a boil, then reduce the heat to low, and add hot red pepper sauce to taste. Add the okra and simmer until the okra is tender and the gumbo mixture is thick, about 15 minutes.

3 Add the shrimp and green beans and cook until the shrimp turn pink and the beans are crisp-tender, about 3 minutes. Remove the bay leaves and season the gumbo with salt and pepper to taste. Serve in bowls, sprinkled with the sliced scallions.

tip

To vary the recipe, use a mixture of 6 oz. (170 g) shrimp and 6 oz. (170 g) crabmeat, adding the crab at the end, with the final seasoning.

Roast Turkey with Stuffing

Sausage meat, cranberries, dried figs, and chestnuts combine to produce a delicious stuffing that will keep the turkey flesh moist and flavorful when roasting.

Did you know?
Benjamin Franklin suggested the turkey to become the official bird of the United States. He was very disappointed when the bald eagle was chosen instead, because he believed the eagle had a bad moral character. He thought the turkey was a more respectable bird and ideal as it was also native to North America.

main meals

For the stuffing

- ½ stick (2 oz./50 g) butter
- 1 onion, finely chopped
- 10 oz. (275 g) pork sausage meat
- 7 oz. (200 g) canned chestnuts, drained and chopped
- ½ cup (3 oz./75 g) dried cranberries
- 3 oz. (75 g) ready-to-eat dried figs
- ¾ cup (2¼ oz./60 g) fresh white bread crumbs
- 2 tbsp. chopped thyme and extra sprigs, to garnish

For the turkey

- 10 lb. (4.5 kg) oven-ready turkey
- ½ stick (2 oz./50 g) butter
- 1 onion, quartered
- 1 lemon, quartered
- 2 bay leaves
- dried figs, to serve

SERVES 10

1 Before you begin preparations check that the turkey is completely thawed and that there are no remaining ice crystals in the body cavity. To make the stuffing, melt the butter in a skillet over a low heat. Add the onion and cook gently for 10 minutes until softened. Allow to cool. In a bowl, mix together the sausage meat (break it up first with a fork), chestnuts, cranberries, figs, bread crumbs, and thyme.

2 Rinse the turkey inside and out and pat dry with paper towels. Preheat the oven to 375°F (190°C/ Gas Mark 5).

3 Carefully push your hand under the skin covering the breast and smear the flesh with butter. Place the onion, lemon, and bay leaves in the body cavity and tie the legs together with string. Pack as much stuffing into the neck end as you can (without overfilling it or the skin will split), tuck the flap of skin under the bird and secure with a small skewer. Shape the remaining stuffing into small balls, place in a single layer in an ovenproof dish, cover and set aside.

tip

When buying a turkey allow about 1 lb. (450 g) per person for generous servings and some leftovers for sandwiches.

4 Season the turkey and lift into a large roasting pan. Pour one cup (225 ml) water into the pan and cover tightly with a double thickness of foil. Roast the turkey for 2½ hours, then remove the foil, scatter with a handful of fresh thyme sprigs and roast for a further 45 minutes, putting the dish of stuffing balls in the oven underneath the turkey. Check to see if the bird is cooked by piercing the thickest part of the thigh with a small skewer—the juices should run clear, not pink. If necessary, return to the oven for 20 minutes and then test again.

5 Transfer the turkey to a carving platter and cover with foil. Leave to rest in a warm place for 30 minutes to allow the juices to flow back into the bird, making it more tender and easier to carve. Serve the turkey with the stuffing, dried figs, gravy, and a selection of vegetables.

TURKEY TIMETABLE

* Ensure the turkey is completely thawed before cooking.

Oven-ready weight (including stuffing)	Number of servings	Approx. thawing time in the fridge for frozen turkey	Cooking time at 375°F/190°C/ Gas Mark 5	Resting time before carving
3–5 lb. (1.4–2.3 kg)	4–6	24 hours	2–2½ hours	15 minutes
6–8 lb. (2.7–3.6 kg)	7–10	36 hours	2½–3½ hours	20 minutes
9–11 lb. (4–5 kg)	11–15	48 hours	3½–4 hours	30 minutes
12–16 lb. (5.4–7.2kg)	16–20	72 hours	4½–5 hours	30 minutes

Stuffed Turkey Roll

- 1½ lb. (675 g) boneless turkey breast, skinned
- ½ stick (2 oz./50 g) butter
- 1 large onion, chopped
- 4 cloves garlic, crushed
- 1 large sweet potato (1 lb./450 g), peeled and cubed
- 1 tsp. grated fresh ginger (or ½ tsp. ground ginger)
- 1 tbsp. red pepper flakes (or to taste)
- finely grated zest of 1 lemon
- 4 tbsp. chopped parsley
- 1 cup (4 oz./115 g) chopped pecans
- 2½ cups (7 oz./200 g) fresh white bread crumbs
- 2 large egg yolks, lightly beaten
- 1 lb. (450 g) bacon rashers
- cranberry or apple jelly, to serve

SERVES 8

Fill a succulent turkey breast with a spicy stuffing made from red pepper flakes, ginger, pecans and sweet potato, then roll it in bacon. This versatile dish is wonderful for a sit-down meal or a buffet-style dinner.

1 Remove the skin from the turkey breast. Place the turkey on a board and slice through the center horizontally, without cutting all the way through. Open the meat out, place between two sheets of plastic food wrap, and pound with a meat mallet or rolling pin to a thickness of ½ in. (1.5 cm).

2 Melt the butter in a saucepan, add the onion and sauté over a medium heat for 5 minutes until soft. Add the garlic and sauté for a further 1 minute. Stir in the sweet potato, ginger and red pepper flakes. Cover and cook gently for 15 minutes, or until the sweet potato is just tender, stirring occasionally to prevent it from sticking to the pan.

3 Remove the saucepan from the heat and set aside to cool. Stir in the lemon zest, parsley, pecans, bread crumbs and egg yolks. Season with salt and pepper.

4 Spread the mixture over the meat and then roll it up like a jelly roll. Place in a greased roasting pan and wrap the bacon rashers over the roll, tucking the ends of the rashers underneath. Tie up the roll with thin string at 1-in. (2.5-cm) intervals. Preheat the oven to 350°F (180°C/Gas Mark 4) and roast for about 1 hour or until cooked through.

5 Remove the meat from the oven, cover loosely with foil and set aside for 10 minutes to rest. Uncover the turkey roll, cut off the string and carve into slices. Serve with cranberry or apple jelly.

Turkey and Black Bean Enchiladas

Make way for the Mexican Express! Fifteen minutes in the oven, and these hearty, easy-to-fix enchiladas, packed with left-over turkey, black beans, and melted cheese, are bubbling hot and ready to serve.

- 2 cups (16 oz./448 g) medium salsa
- 1 cup (2 oz./56 g) chopped cilantro (coriander)
- 1 tsp. ground cumin
- 8-in. x 6-in. (15-cm) corn tortillas
- 8 oz. (225 g) cooked turkey breast, shredded
- I cup (9 oz./252 g) canned black beans, rinsed and drained
- 1 small red onion, finely chopped
- 1 cup (4 oz./115 g) shredded reduced-fat cheddar cheese

1 Preheat the oven to 350°F (180°C/Gas Mark 4). Spray a 7-in. x 11-in. (18 cm x 28 cm) baking dish with nonstick cooking spray, making a light but even coating.

2 Combine the salsa, cilantro (coriander), and cumin in a shallow bowl at least 6 in. (15 cm) in diameter.

3 Working with one at a time, dip each tortilla in the salsa mixture, coating it completely.

4 Place on a plate or sheet of wax paper. Top each tortilla with 2 tbsp. salsa mixture. Top with turkey, beans, and red onion. Sprinkle with 1 tbsp. cheese. Roll the tortilla up and place it seam-side down in a baking dish. Repeat the filling and rolling with the remaining tortillas.

5 Spoon the remaining salsa mixture over the enchiladas and sprinkle with the remaining cheese. Bake until bubbling, about 15 minutes.

Pot-Roasted Partridge with Sage

Partridge is perfect for pot-roasting and makes an ideal alternative to chicken or turkey.

- 4 partridges
- ½ oz. (10 g) fresh sage
- 1 tbsp. butter
- 1 tbsp. extra-virgin olive oil
- 1 onion, finely chopped
- 1 tbsp. all-purpose (plain) flour
- 1¼ cups (10 fl oz./360 ml) hard cider or apple juice
- ⅔ cup (5 fl oz./150 ml) chicken stock
- 2 tsp. German or whole-grain mustard
- 3 walnut halves, thinly sliced
- 1 red-skinned dessert apple, cored and cut into thick slices

SERVES 4

tip

The recipe for Cinnamon & Maple Mashed Sweet Potato on page 223 makes a perfect partner for this delicious dish.

1 Preheat the oven to 325°F (170°C/Gas Mark 3). Tuck some sage sprigs into the body cavity of each bird. Reserve a few sprigs to garnish.

2 Melt the butter with the oil in a Dutch oven, or heavy-based casserole dish with tight-fitting lid, (large enough to hold the birds), over medium heat. Add the partridges and fry over a moderately high heat, turning until evenly brown, 3–4 minutes. Lift the birds from the oven and set aside.

3 Add the onion to the Dutch oven and sauté until light brown, about 3 minutes. Sprinkle in the flour and stir into the onion. Add the cider, stock, and mustard, and season with salt and pepper. Bring to the boil, stirring constantly. Add the walnut halves.

4 Return the partridges to the Dutch oven, breasts side down. Cover and transfer to the oven and cook until the partridges are tender, about 1 hour.

5 Lift the partridges out of the Dutch oven and place on a warm serving plate, cover and keep hot.

6 Set the Dutch oven on the stovetop over a high heat. Bring to the boil and boil until the cooking liquid has reduced by a third, about 5 minutes. Add the apple slices for the last 2 minutes of cooking time.

7 Spoon the apple around the birds and garnish with sage sprigs. Serve with the sauce.

Sun-Dried Tomato Chicken

This stuffed chicken dish provides a colorful focus to brighten any party table. Garnish the serving platter with basil leaves and plump cherry tomatoes sliced in half for a Christmassy feel.

- 4 boneless chicken breasts
- 3 oz. (75 g) baby spinach leaves
- 5 oz. (150 g) feta cheese, crumbled
- 8 sun-dried dry tomatoes, chopped
- 2 garlic cloves, crushed
- 4 tbsp. olive oil

For the Sauce

- 1 cup (8 fl oz./225 ml) dry white wine
- 2 tbsp. tomato paste

SERVES 4

1 Skin the chicken breasts if necessary. Make a sideways cut into the center of each one and open out to form a pocket.

2 Rinse the spinach and place in a pan with just the droplets of rinsing water on the leaves. Cover the pan and cook over a low heat until the leaves wilt. Transfer to a board and chop, then mix with the feta cheese, sun-dried tomatoes and garlic. Divide the filling into four and use to stuff the pocket of each chicken breast. Reshape the breasts and secure with tooth picks.

3 Heat the oil in a large skillet, add the chicken breasts and fry over a low heat until cooked through (about 10–15 minutes), turning occasionally.

4 To make the sauce, mix together the wine and tomato paste. Season with salt and pepper and simmer in a pan until reduced by half.

5 Spoon the sauce over the chicken and serve with rice and salad, or vegetables of your choice.

tip

Leave the skin on the chicken if preferred, but brown the breasts over high heat first, before reducing the heat to finish cooking the meat.

French-Style Chicken in Wine

Accompany this classic bistro dish with boiled potatoes and some fresh-from-the-bakery bread for a real feast.

- 12 shallots or pearl onions
- 1½ tbsp. garlic-flavored olive oil
- 2 oz. (56 g) Canadian bacon, cut into thin strips
- 12 cremini or white mushrooms
- 4 chicken pieces such as breast halves, (6 oz./168 g)
- several sprigs of parsley, stems bruised
- several sprigs fresh thyme
- 1 bay leaf
- ⅔ cup (5 fl oz./150 ml) chicken stock
- 1½ cups (12 fl oz./335 ml) full-bodied red wine, such as Shiraz
- 2 carrots, about 10 oz. (275 g), cut into chunks
- pinch of sugar
- 1 tbsp. cornstarch
- chopped parsley

SERVES 4

1 Put the shallots or onions in a heatproof bowl and pour over enough boiling water to cover. Leave for 30 seconds, then drain. When cool enough to handle, peel and set aside.

2 Heat 1 tbsp. of the oil in a Dutch oven, or heavy-based casserole dish with a tight-fitting lid, over a medium heat. Add the bacon and sauté, stirring often, until crisp, about 3 minutes. Remove the bacon with a slotted spoon and set aside.

3 Add the shallots to the Dutch oven and sauté until brown all over, 5–8 minutes. Remove with a slotted spoon and set aside.

4 Add the mushrooms to the Dutch oven, with the remaining ½ tbsp. of oil, if needed, and sauté until golden, 3–4 minutes.

5 Return half of the bacon and shallots to the Dutch oven. Place the chicken pieces on top and sprinkle with the remaining bacon and shallots. Tie the herbs into a bouquet garni and add to the Dutch oven with the stock and wine. Season generously with salt and pepper.

6 Bring to a boil, then reduce the heat to very low. Cover, and simmer for 15 minutes. Add the carrots and continue simmering over a low heat until the chicken is cooked and the juices run clear when pierced, and the carrots are fork-tender.

7 Remove the chicken and arrange on a warm serving platter. Strain the liquid into a saucepan. Add the bacon, mushrooms, shallots and carrots to the chicken, and keep warm.

8 Put the bouquet garni back in the strained liquid, add the sugar, and bring to a boil. Boil until the sauce is reduced to about 1½ cups. Meanwhile, mix the cornstarch with a little water until a smooth paste forms. Stir into the sauce, and simmer until thicker. Adjust the seasoning to taste and discard the bouquet garni. Spoon the sauce over the chicken and vegetables and sprinkle with the parsley.

Tangy Crusted Chicken

You'll love the zing of the marmalade-mustard marinade. Serve this dish with fresh sugar snap peas and ripe cherry tomatoes for a colorful combination.

- 4 tbsp. orange juice

- 4 tbsp. orange marmalade

- 6 tsp. Dijon mustard

- 4 small skinless, boneless chicken breast halves (about 1¼ lb./1.25 kg), pounded to ¼-in. (0.5-cm) thickness

For the Coating

- 2 slices firm-textured white bread (2 oz./56 g)

- I cup (5½ oz./150 g) unblanched almonds

- ¼ cup (⅓ oz./11 g) packed parsley leaves

- 4 tbsp. olive oil

SERVES 4

1 In a shallow glass or ceramic baking dish, stir together 2 tbsp. of orange juice, 2 tbsp. of marmalade, and 4 tsp. of mustard. Place the chicken in the orange mixture and coat well. Let sit while you prepare the coating.

2 In a food processor, combine the bread, almonds, and parsley. Process to a fine crumb consistency. Transfer to a shallow plate or sheet of waxed paper. Lift the chicken from the orange mixture (discard any mixture remaining in dish). Dip the chicken in the almond-crumb mixture, pressing it into the chicken. Transfer to a baking

sheet or platter large enough to hold the chicken breasts in a single layer and refrigerate, uncovered, for at least 1 hour or a maximum of 8 hours.

3 In a small bowl, stir together the remaining 2 tbsp. orange juice, 2 tbsp. marmalade, and 2 tsp. mustard. In a large nonstick skillet, heat 2 tbsp. of oil over a medium heat. Add two chicken breasts to the pan and cook for 1½ minutes per side or until golden brown and cooked through. Repeat with all the remaining chicken breasts and oil. Slice each of the chicken breasts across to serve.

Chicken Pot Pie

This pot pie recipe is a great way to use up any left-over chicken or turkey, or you can use fresh chicken cubes instead. The classic flaky crust has been replaced by store-bought puff pastry. Bacon has been added for a surprising smoky flavor.

- 6 slices bacon, cut crosswise into 1-in. (2.5-cm) pieces
- 3 carrots, thinly sliced
- 3 tbsp. flour
- $^2/_3$ cup (5 fl oz./150 ml) milk
- 12 oz. (340 g) skinless, boneless chicken breast, cut into 1-in (2.5-cm) cubes
- 1 cup (3.5 oz./100 g) frozen peas
- 1 sheet 10 in. x 9 in. (25.5 cm x 23 cm) store bought puff pastry
- 1 large egg, lightly beaten with 1 tsp. water

SERVES 4

1 In a large saucepan, cook the bacon over a medium-low heat for 7 minutes or until crisp. Transfer the bacon to paper towels to drain. Add the carrots to the pan and cook, stirring frequently, for 7 minutes or until crisp-tender. Sprinkle the flour over the carrots and stir until they are all well coated.

2 Gradually whisk the milk into the pan. Season and cook until lightly thickened. Stir in the chicken and the peas, and cook for 10 minutes or until the chicken is cooked through. Crumble the cooked bacon and stir into the mixture to combine.

3 Preheat the oven to 400°F (200°C/Gas Mark 6). Spoon the chicken mixture into a 9-in. (23-cm) deep-dish pie plate. Cool the mixture to room temperature.

tip

If you already have cooked chicken to use up, don't cook the chicken as shown in step 2. Stir the chicken into the pan after the white sauce has cooked, and remove from the heat.

4 Using the pie plate as a pattern, cut the puff pastry into a 9-in. (23-cm) shell. With a sharp paring knife, cut scallops into the edge of the shell. Place the pastry shell on top of the chicken mixture. Brush with the egg mixture (being careful not to let any drip down the sides of the pastry.) Place the pie plate on a baking sheet and bake for 30 minutes or until piping hot and the pastry has risen.

Chicken with Mushroom Sauce

Tender, pan-fried breast of chicken is simmered gently in a smooth sauce of white mushrooms and green onions, laced with cream, to produce a luxurious and satisfying dish.

- 1 tbsp. olive oil
- 1½ tbsp. (25 g) butter
- 4 boneless, skinless chicken breasts, about 6 oz. (170 g) each
- 4 scallions
- ¾ lb. (335 g) white mushrooms
- 1 tbsp. all-purpose (plain) flour
- ⅔ cup (5 fl oz./150 ml) chicken stock
- ⅔ cup (5 fl oz./150 ml) light (single) cream

SERVES 4

tip

The recipe for Irish Mashed Potatoes with Cabbage & Leeks on page 222, or a refreshing salad would make a good accompaniment to the chicken.

1 Preheat the oven to a low setting to keep the chicken warm later. Put the olive oil and butter into a frying pan and heat until sizzling hot. Season the chicken breasts on both sides with salt and black pepper.

2 Add the chicken to the pan and cook for 2–3 minutes on each side until golden, then reduce the heat to low, cover, and continue cooking for 8–10 minutes, turning once.

3 Meanwhile, trim, rinse, and thinly slice the scallions. Clean and thinly slice the mushrooms.

4 When the juices of the chicken run clear, put the chicken breasts on a plate, cover with foil, and keep warm.

5 Add the scallions and the white mushrooms to the pan, spread them out, and fry them over a moderate heat for 3–4 minutes, or until softened.

6 Stir the flour into the pan and cook for 1 minute, then add the stock, and bring to the boil, stirring constantly. Cook the mushroom sauce for 2–3 minutes, then reduce the heat and stir in the cream. Return the chicken breasts, and any juices, to the pan and heat through for 2–3 minutes.

7 Put the cooked chicken breasts onto warmed plates, spoon over the mushroom sauce, and serve them immediately sprinkled with a few scallions as a garnish.

Baked Ham with Bourbon-Brown Sugar Glaze

A sweet and tasty twist on the traditional baked ham, this recipe makes a superb centerpiece to a special holiday meal.

- 8½ lb. (3.8 kg) cooked, bone-in shank portion of smoked ham
- ½ cup (100 g) firmly packed light brown sugar
- 2 tbsp. bourbon or beef stock
- 1¼ tsp. black pepper

SERVES 16

1 Preheat the oven to 325°F (170°C/Gas Mark 3). Remove any skin from the ham and trim fat to a ¼-in. (6-mm) thickness.

2 Place the ham, cut side down, on a rack in a shallow roasting pan. Insert a meat thermometer in the center of the ham making sure it does not touch the bone (or test later with an instant-read thermometer).

3 Bake the ham, uncovered, until the thermometer reads 130°F–135°F (55°C–60°C), about 2–2¾ hours.

If the ham browns too fast, cover it loosely with foil. Meanwhile, combine the sugar, bourbon, and pepper in a small bowl.

4 Remove the ham from the oven and increase the oven temperature to 375°F (190°C/Gas Mark 5). Using a sharp paring knife, score the fat on the surface of the ham in a diamond pattern. Brush the sugar mixture over the ham.

5 Return the ham to the oven and bake, uncovered, until the thermometer reads 140°F (60°C), about 15–20 minutes. Let the ham stand for at least 15 minutes before carving.

Pork Tenderloin with Honey-Mustard Sauce

Although rosemary is usually associated with chicken or lamb, it goes just as well with pork. Here, the honey-mustard sauce provides a sweet and hot kick to delight your holiday guests.

- 1 tbsp. chopped fresh rosemary or 1 tsp. dried
- 2 garlic cloves, minced
- 1 tsp. grated lemon zest
- ½ tsp. salt
- 1 pork tenderloin (about 1 lb./450 g), trimmed
- ⅓ cup (2½ fl oz./80 ml) fresh lemon juice
- ¼ cup (2 fl oz./56 ml) honey
- 3 tbsp. coarse Dijon mustard
- ½ cup (4 fl oz./125 ml) half-and-half (or half milk; half single cream)
- 1 tbsp. all-purpose (plain) flour

SERVES 4

1 Preheat the oven to 400°F (200°C/Gas Mark 6). Line a small roasting pan with foil. Combine the rosemary, garlic, lemon zest, and salt in a small bowl and rub evenly over the pork tenderloin; transfer the pork to a pan. Mix the lemon juice, honey, and mustard in a small bowl. Transfer half to a small saucepan and set aside.

2 Brush the pork with 2 tbsp. of the honey-mustard sauce. Roast the pork until glazed and golden brown or until an instant-read thermometer shows 160°F (75°C), about 25 minutes, basting two or three times with the remaining sauce.

3 Meanwhile, put the half-and-half in a small bowl and whisk in the flour until smooth. Warm the reserved honey-mustard sauce in a small saucepan over a low heat. Gradually whisk in the half-and-half mixture and cook, whisking constantly, until the sauce thickens, about 3 minutes. Serve with the pork.

tip

A serving of Roasted Root Vegetables with Herbs from page 225, will complement this meal perfectly. For a lighter alternative, try the Spinach, White Bean & Bacon Salad from page 226.

Did you know?

Pork tenderloin is one of the leanest cuts of meat you can buy. A plain 3 oz. (75 g) cooked portion has around 4 g of fat, that's almost as low as a skinless chicken breast. So not only is it a low-fat meat, it tastes great and makes a healthy yet impressive Christmas meal.

Garlic Roast Pork

This tender loin of pork is infused with garlic and a mix of fragrant herbs. Served with a spiced pear chutney made with white wine and cider vinegar, it makes a great alternative to traditional Christmas dishes.

- 4½ lb. (2 kg) pork loin, on the bone
- 3 garlic cloves, cut into slivers
- 4 sprigs oregano
- 4 sprigs thyme

For the Pear Chutney

- 6 pears, peeled, cored, and roughly chopped
- ⅔ cup (¼ pint/150 ml) dry white wine
- ½ cup (4 fl oz./125 ml) cider vinegar
- 1 cup (4½ oz./125 g) light brown sugar
- 2 cinnamon sticks
- 5 cloves

SERVES 8

1 Preheat the oven to 425°F (220°C/Gas Mark 7). Cut the skin off the pork and trim the fat and sinew away from the top of each rib bone, scraping the bones clean.

2 Make slashes all over the joint and push the garlic slivers and herb sprigs into them.

3 Place the pork in a roasting pan and cover with a sheet of foil, shiny side down. Roast for 25 minutes, then reduce the oven temperature to 350°F (180°C/Gas Mark 4) and cook for 20 minutes per 1 lb. (450 g), removing the foil for the last 20 minutes of cooking time.

4 Meanwhile, place the pears, wine, vinegar, sugar, and spices in a pan and bring to the boil. Reduce the heat, cover and simmer until the pears have softened, about 30 minutes. Uncover, remove the whole spices and continue to cook the pear chutney until most of the liquid has evaporated.

5 Leave the pork to rest in a warm place for 15 minutes, loosely covered with foil. Carve and serve with the chutney.

tip

The pear chutney would also go well with roasted ham or a selection of cooked meats.

Horseradish Beef

Melt-in-the-mouth beef roasted with a sweet and spicy glaze gives a new twist to an old favorite. The peppery pesto complements the horseradish crust perfectly.

Did you know?

The root and leaves from horseradish were used medicinally during the Middle Ages. It was taken internally to help fight fever and used externally to help fight infection.

- 6 tbsp. creamed horseradish
- 1 tbsp. light brown sugar
- 4 lb. (1.8 kg) sirloin tip roast

For the Pesto

- 3 oz. (75 g) watercress
- 2 tbsp. pine nuts
- 2 garlic cloves, crushed
- 2 tbsp. grated Parmesan cheese
- 6 tbsp. olive oil

SERVES 8

1 To cook the beef, preheat the oven to 400°F (200°C/Gas Mark 6). Mix together the creamed horseradish and brown sugar. Spread this over the outside of the beef roast.

2 Season well with salt and pepper and lift the roast into a roasting pan. Roast in the oven for 20 minutes, then reduce the oven temperature to 350°F (180°C/Gas Mark 4) and continue to roast for a further 20 minutes per 1 lb. (450 g) for medium.

3 To make the pesto, wash the watercress thoroughly and discard any yellow leaves or coarse stalks. Process in a blender or food processor with the pine nuts, garlic, cheese, and olive oil. Season to taste.

4 When the beef is cooked, remove it from the oven, cover the roast loosely with foil, and let stand in a warm place for 15 minutes. This will allow time for the juices to flow back into the meat, making it easier to carve.

5 Carve the beef into slices and serve with the pesto. Accompany with roast or boiled potatoes and vegetables of your choice.

tip

Add or subtract 5 minutes per 1 lb. (450 g) to the roasting time for well-done or rare beef.

Beef Tenderloin in Red Wine Sauce

For a really impressive meal with a minimum of effort, try this beef tenderloin recipe. Your dinner guests will be glad you did.

- 1 beef tenderloin roast (4 lb/1.8 kg), trimmed
- 2 tsp. salt
- 1½ tsp. coarsely ground black pepper
- 2 cups (17 fl oz./500 ml) dry red wine
- 2 lb. (900 g) onions, chopped
- 3 garlic cloves, crushed
- 6 sprigs fresh thyme
- 10 oz. (285 g) white mushrooms, trimmed
- 1 tbsp. sugar
- 12 oz. (340 g) baby carrots
- 1 pint (450 g) red or yellow cherry tomatoes
- 16 oz. (450 g) wide egg noodles

SERVES 4

1 Preheat the oven to 450°F (230°C/Gas Mark 8). Rub the roast with salt and pepper. Tuck the ends under and tie with string. Mix the wine with 1¼ cups of water.

2 Coat a large heavy skillet with nonstick cooking spray and set over a medium-high heat. Add the beef, one-third of the onions, and garlic and sear the meat until browned on all sides, about 10 minutes. Discard the garlic and onion and transfer to a roasting pan. Pour in half of the wine mixture. Add three thyme sprigs and put the pan in the oven.

3 Meanwhile, set aside five mushrooms and slice the remaining ones. Sauté the sliced mushrooms, the remaining onions, and sugar in a skillet until brown, about 7 minutes. Cook the carrots in boiling water in a saucepan until crisp-tender, 5–7 minutes. Drain.

4 After the meat roasts for 20 minutes, add the carrots and sautéed vegetables to the pan. Pour in the remaining wine mixture. Continue to roast until it is done to taste, about 25 minutes, or longer for medium. Transfer meat to a cutting board and let stand for 10 minutes. Add the tomatoes to the pan, cover, and let stand.

5 Meanwhile, cook the noodles according to the package directions. Drain. Trim the reserved mushrooms and cut thin slivers out of the caps with a paring knife. Coat a skillet with cooking spray and sauté the mushrooms over a medium heat until golden, about 5 minutes. Arrange the noodles and vegetables on a platter. Slice the beef and add to the platter. Garnish with mushrooms and thyme. Serve with pan juices.

Beef Fillets with Creamy Mushroom & Leek Sauce

A prime cut of beef pairs perfectly with the creamy mushroom and leek sauce, and makes a wonderful meal for any special occasion.

- 1 tbsp. olive or vegetable oil

- 4 beef tenderloin steaks or 2 sirloin steaks (1½ lb./680 g), 1-in. (2.5-cm) thick and trimmed

For the Sauce

- 1½ cups (5½ oz./150 g) sliced fresh mushrooms

- ½ cup (100 g) sliced leek

- ½ cup (4 fl oz./110 ml) dry white wine or lower-sodium chicken broth

- ½ cup (2 oz./110 ml) sour cream

- 1 tbsp. all-purpose (plain) flour

For the Garnish

With a small, very sharp knife or vegetable peeler, carefully peel a continuous strip of tomato skin and curl it into the shape of a rose

SERVES 4

1 In a 12-in. (30-cm) nonstick skillet, heat the oil over a moderately high heat. Add the steaks. Reduce the heat to medium. Cook the steaks for 8–10 minutes for medium-rare or until the steaks are the way you like them, turning them often. Transfer to a platter and cover with foil.

2 To prepare the sauce, add the mushrooms, leek, wine, salt, and pepper to the drippings in the skillet.

Bring to a boil. Reduce the heat and simmer, uncovered, for 3 minutes or until the mushrooms are tender.

3 In a small bowl, stir together the sour cream and flour. Stir into the mushroom mixture. Cook over a medium heat, stirring constantly, for 2 minutes or until thickened (do not boil). Serve the sauce over the steaks.

Surprise Cocktail Meatballs

When this sweet and sour dish first became popular, the surprise inside was a cube of cheese. Today, water chestnuts, green pepper, or pineapple make more healthful fillings.

For the Meatballs

- 12 oz. (350 g) lean ground beef
- ½ cup (2 oz./50 g) fresh bread crumbs (1 slice)
- ¼ cup (1½ oz./42 g) finely chopped yellow onion
- ¼ shredded carrot
- 2 tbsp. minced parsley
- 2 tbsp. low-fat (1%) milk
- ½ tsp. dried marjoram leaves
- ⅛ tsp. ground sage
- 1 large egg white, lightly beaten
- 18 water chestnut halves, pecan halves, pineapple tidbits, and/or small sweet green pepper squares

For the Sauce

- ¼ cup (2 fl oz./60 ml) apple juice
- ⅓ cup (2 oz./60 g) firmly packed dark brown sugar
- ¼ cup (2 fl oz./60 ml) red wine vinegar or cider vinegar
- 4 tsp. cornstarch
- 1 tbsp. low-sodium soy sauce
- ¼ tsp. garlic powder

MAKES 18 MEATBALLS

1 Preheat the oven to 350°F (180°C/Gas Mark 4). To prepare the meatballs, in a large bowl, mix the beef, bread crumbs, onion, carrot, parsley, milk, marjoram, sage, egg white, and season to taste. Divide into 18 pieces. Wrap each piece around a water chestnut half. Place the meatballs in a 13 in. x 9 in. x 2 in. (33 cm x 23 cm x 5 cm) baking pan. Bake for 15–20 minutes or until the meatballs are no longer pink. Transfer to paper towels and drain well.

2 Meanwhile, to prepare the sauce, in a medium-size saucepan, whisk together the apple juice, brown sugar, vinegar, cornstarch, soy sauce, and garlic powder. Bring to a boil and cook for 2 minutes or until thickened, stirring often. Stir the meatballs into the apple juice mixture and simmer for 3 minutes or until the meatballs are heated through. Place in a small shallow serving dish. Use cocktail forks or toothpicks to serve.

Spinach-Stuffed Meat Loaf

Meat loaf never looked or tasted this great—and was certainly never this good for you! This is a low-fat version of a perennial favorite meal. If you have any leftover turkey, you can make use of it in this tasty recipe.

- 1 lb. (450 g) lean ground beef
- 8 oz. (225 g) lean ground turkey
- 1 small onion, finely chopped
- 1 cup (4 oz./100 g) fresh bread crumbs
- 1 tsp. garlic salt
- 1 tbsp. tomato paste
- 1 egg white
- 1 cup (8 oz./225 g) part-skim ricotta cheese
- 1 package (10 oz./280 g) frozen chopped spinach, thawed and drained
- 2 large onions, thinly sliced
- 2 carrots, coarsely chopped
- 1 can (28 oz./800 g) crushed tomatoes

SERVES 6

1 In a bowl, mix the beef, turkey, chopped onion, bread crumbs, garlic salt, and tomato paste. In another bowl, mix together the egg white, ricotta, spinach, and season.

2 Preheat the oven to 350°F (180°C/Gas Mark 4). Turn out the beef mixture onto a large sheet of wax paper, and form into 9 in. x 10 in. (23 cm x 25 cm) rectangle.

3 Spoon the spinach stuffing lengthwise down center of the meat, leaving about 1 in. (2.5 cm) uncovered at each short end.

4 With wax paper, lift the long edges of meat. Fold the meat over the stuffing to enclose it. Using your fingers, pinch the edges of the meat together. Place the loaf seam side down in a nonstick roasting pan. Add the onions, carrots, and tomatoes to the pan.

5 Bake until the meat and vegetables are cooked, about 1½ hours. Transfer the meat to a platter. Purée the vegetables in a blender or food processor and serve as sauce with the meat loaf.

Lamb Chops with Red Currants

Coated with cumin seeds and ground spices, and served in a red wine sauce, these broiled lamb chops make a great main meal. The red currant sauce lends the dish a real festive look.

- 4 well-trimmed lamb chops, about 4½ oz. (125 g each)
- a bunch of watercress to garnish

For the Sauce

- 2 tsp. cumin seeds
- 1 tsp. ground coriander
- 1 tsp. cinnamon
- 1 tsp. paprika
- ¾ cup (6 fl oz./175 ml) red wine
- 3 tbsp. (50 g) sugar
- 7 oz. (200 g) fresh red currants

SERVES 4

tip

Fresh or frozen cranberries can be used instead of red currants.

1 Preheat the broiler to high. To make the sauce, mix the spices with a good grinding of black pepper. Put half of the mixture into a small saucepan with the wine and sugar, and set the rest aside.

2 Rinse the red currants and reserve a few sprigs for the garnish. Run a fork down the other sprigs to remove the red currants; add them to the wine. Bring to the boil over a moderate heat, stirring gently, then lower the heat and simmer for 12–15 minutes, or until the liquid is slightly syrupy.

3 Rub the reserved spice mixture into both sides of the chops and broil for 6–8 minutes, turning once. Meanwhile, rinse, dry, and trim the watercress, discarding any coarse stems.

4 Pour some sauce onto each plate and place a chop on top. Garnish with the watercress and red currants.

Asian Lamb Medallions

Succulent and tender lamb medallions are served with an assembly of
crisp, stir-fried green vegetables and baby corn. Together, they provide a
a wonderfully surprising contrast in textures.

- ½ in. (1 cm) piece fresh ginger
- 4 oz. (112 g) broccoli florets
- 4 oz. (112 g) leek
- 1 bunch of watercress
- 4 oz. (112 g) snow peas
- 4 oz. (112 g) baby corn
- 1 lb. (450 g) lamb fillet, or 8 lamb noisettes
- 1–2 tbsp. olive oil
- 2 tbsp. peanut oil
- 3 tbsp. lamb or chicken stock
- 1–2 tbsp. light soy sauce

SERVES 4

1 Peel and chop the ginger and set it aside. Rinse the vegetables. Cut the broccoli into pieces, and the leek into matchstick-thin strips. Chop the watercress, top and stem the snow peas, leave the baby corn whole. Set them all to one side.

2 If using lamb fillet, cut it into eight 1-in. (2.5-cm) thick medallions. Brush noisettes with the olive oil and season with a little salt and pepper.

3 Warm a frying pan over a moderate heat, add the lamb, and dry fry it for 2 minutes, or until browned underneath. Turn and fry for

another 3–4 minutes until cooked but slightly pink in the center. Cover the pan and keep warm.

4 Meanwhile, heat the peanut oil in a wok or large frying pan. Add the ginger and the vegetables and stir-fry for 3–4 minutes, until just tender.

5 Add the stock and soy sauce to the vegetables and season to taste, then cover and cook for a further 2 minutes, stirring occasionally.

6 Lay two lamb medallions on each plate and spoon the vegetables over and alongside them.

Tasty Tarts

These delicious tarts can be made ahead and frozen for up to three months. Simply defrost and reheat for an instant supper whenever you need one. Perfect with tossed green salad.

Mushroom and Leek Tart

- 8 oz. (250 g) store-bought pie pastry
- ½ stick (2 oz./50 g) butter
- 10 oz. (325 g) sliced mushrooms
- 1 tbsp. olive oil
- 1 large leek, thickly sliced
- 1 garlic clove, crushed
- ½ tsp. chopped thyme
- 4 tbsp. dry white wine
- 2 eggs, lightly beaten
- ½ cup (100 ml) heavy (double) cream
- 4 tbsp. full-fat milk
- 1 tsp. mustard powder
- 4 tbsp. grated Parmesan cheese

SERVES 6

1 Preheat the oven to 400°F (200°C/Gas Mark 6.) Roll out the pastry and use it to line a 4 in. x 13 in. (10 cm x 34 cm) loose-based fluted tart tin. Chill for 10 minutes then line with waxed paper and fill with pie weights (or dried beans).

2 Bake blind for 10 minutes then remove the paper and weights and bake for a further 5 minutes. Reduce the oven temperature to 325°F (160°C/Gas Mark 3).

3 Melt the butter in a skillet and fry the mushrooms for 5 minutes until softened. Drain on a plate lined with paper towels.

4 Wipe out the skillet, add the oil and cook the leek over a medium heat for 10 minutes until softened. Add the garlic, thyme, and wine and cook for a further 2 minutes. Spoon into the pastry shell, then spoon the mushrooms on top, spreading them out evenly.

5 Whisk together the eggs, cream, milk, mustard, and Parmesan cheese until evenly combined. Pour into the pastry shell over the vegetables and bake for 15 minutes or until just set.

Broccoli & Bacon Quiche

- 8 oz. (250 g) store-bought pie pastry
- 3 rashers of bacon
- 8 oz. (250 g) broccoli
- 4 oz. (100 g) blue Stilton, or a similar blue cheese, crumbled
- 4 oz. (100 g) garlic cream cheese
- 1¼ cups (300 ml) milk
- 2 eggs, beaten

SERVES 6

1 Roll out the pastry and line into a 9-in. (23-cm) tart pan. Chill for 30 minutes. Meanwhile, grill the bacon until brown. Chop into small pieces and leave to cool.

2 Divide the broccoli into small florets and slice the stalks. Steam for 5 minutes or until tender. Put broccoli in a colander and run cold water over it to cool. Dry with paper towels. Arrange the broccoli in the shell and add the bacon. Sprinkle with blue cheese.

3 Preheat the oven to 375°F (190°C/Gas Mark 5). Beat the cream cheese, milk, eggs, and seasoning together until smooth.

4 Pour into the pastry shell and bake for about 40 minutes or until the filling is set. Cut into wedges and serve warm.

Roasted Vegetable Tart

Vegetarians... enjoy this! Rich and hearty butternut squash, zucchini, red onion, and peppers combine to provide a colorful burst of flavor.

- 1 unbaked store-bought pie pastry (9 in./22.5 cm)
- 1 small (12 oz./350 g) butternut squash, peeled
- 1 large zucchini, cut into ¼-in. (0.5-cm)-thick slices
- 1 medium red onion, cut into ¼-in. (0.5-cm)-thick slices
- 1 tbsp. plus 1 tsp. olive oil
- ½ tsp. salt
- ¼ cup (25 g) grated Parmesan cheese
- 3 tbsp. chopped basil
- 1 jar (6 oz./150 g) roasted red peppers, drained and cut into strips

SERVES 6

tip

Serve a delicious salad, such as the Shredded Beets and Red Cabbage with Cranberries, found on page 226. This will make a colorful and festive side dish for the tart

1 Heat the oven to 400°F (200°C/Gas Mark 6). With a rolling pin, reshape the round crust into a square and place it in an 8-in. (20-cm) baking pan. Fold over the edges and crimp to make a decorative edge. Prick the bottom with a fork. Line the pie crust with waxed paper and fill with pie weights or dried beans. Bake for 15 minutes. Remove the waxed paper and weights. Bake until golden, 5–10 minutes. Leave the oven on.

2 Meanwhile, slice the long neck of squash crosswise into ¼-in. (0.5-cm)-thick rounds until you reach the seeded end. Scoop out the seeds from the rest of the squash. Slice the squash into rings. In a large bowl, combine the squash, zucchini, onion, 1 tbsp. oil, and season.

3 Arrange the squash and half of the onion in a single layer on a baking sheet. Arrange the zucchini and the remaining onion in a single layer on a second baking sheet. Roast until the zucchini is tender, 10–12 minutes. Remove the zucchini from the baking sheet. Continue roasting the squash and onion until they are just tender,

about 5 minutes longer. Reduce the oven temperature to 250°F (130°C/Gas Mark 2).

4 Just before serving, assemble the tart. Sprinkle the bottom of the pie shell with 1 tbsp. cheese. Top with an even layer of zucchini, half of the onion, 1 tbsp. of cheese, and 1 tbsp. of basil. Next, layer the squash, remaining onion, 1 tbsp. of cheese, and 1 tbsp. of basil. Arrange the roasted pepper on top. Brush with the remaining 1 tsp. of oil. Sprinkle with the remaining 1 tbsp. of cheese. Heat the tart in the oven for 10 minutes. Sprinkle with the remaining basil and serve warm.

Mushroom Lasagna

This is the ideal party food since it can be made in advance and frozen for up to one month. The recipe is so tasty it will prove popular with vegetarians and non-vegetarians alike.

tip

No-cook lasagna pasta saves time since it needs no pre-cooking and can be used straight from the box.

- ½ stick (2 oz./50 g) butter)
- 1 tbsp. olive oil
- 7 oz. (200 g) white mushrooms
- 5 oz. (150 g) shiitake mushrooms, torn in half
- 5 oz. (150 g) oyster mushrooms, torn in half
- 3 garlic cloves, crushed
- 1¼ cups (½ pint/300 ml) red wine
- 5 oz. (150 g) no-cook lasagna
- 2 balls (10 oz./280 g) mozzarella cheese, sliced

For the Bechamel Sauce

- 2½ cups (1 pint/625 ml) milk
- 1 bay leaf
- 1 blade mace
- ¾ stick (3 oz./75 g) butter
- ½ cup (2¼ oz./60 g) all-purpose (plain) flour
- 6 oz. (175 g) fresh Parmesan cheese, grated

SERVES 6

1 Melt the butter and oil in a large skillet; cook the mushrooms for 10 minutes. Add the garlic and red wine, boil then simmer for 20 minutes.

2 Meanwhile, make the bechamel sauce. Heat the milk with the bay leaf and mace, then leave to infuse for 20 minutes. Strain the sauce and return it to the pan.

3 In a separate pan over a low heat, melt the butter and add the flour, stirring until browned. Add the milk gradually, stirring all the time. Once thickened, season. Reserve 1 tbsp. of the Parmesan, add the rest to the sauce, stir well and set aside.

4 Assemble the lasagna in a large ovenproof dish. Put a third of the mushrooms in the base, cover with a layer of

pasta, then a third of the bechamel, then half the mozzarella. Repeat the layers, then top with the remaining mushrooms, cover with pasta, and pour over the rest of the sauce. Scatter the remaining Parmesan over the top.

5 Preheat the oven to 400°F (200°C/Gas Mark 6). Bake the lasagna until browned and bubbling, about 45 minutes. Serve with a green salad on the side.

tip

To freeze, prepare to the end of step 4, cool, then double-wrap in freezer-proof foil. Thaw overnight in the fridge. Bake as described in Step 5.

Chicken-Stuffed Manicotti with Provolone Cheese

Pasta casseroles, such as this irresistible manicotti dish, are always a big hit at parties, since guests can dig in and help themselves.

- 8 manicotti (about 6 oz./168 g)
- 2 tbsp. olive oil
- 2 large onions, finely chopped
- 1 lb. (450 g) ground chicken
- 3 cups (12 oz./350 g) Provolone cheese, shredded
- 2/3 cup (1 oz./30 g) chopped fresh basil leaves
- 3 tbsp. grated Parmesan cheese
- 1 large egg yolk
- 1 can (35 oz./700 g) tomatoes, chopped with their juice
- 1 tsp. sugar
- 1/4 tsp. crushed red pepper flakes

SERVES 4

1 In a large pot of boiling water, cook the manicotti according to the package directions. Drain and rinse under cold running water.

2 Meanwhile, in a large skillet, heat the oil over a medium heat. Add the onions and cook, stirring, for 10 minutes or until they are golden brown and tender. Transfer half of the onions to a large bowl. Set the skillet with the remaining onions aside.

3 Let the onions in the bowl cool to room temperature, then stir in the ground chicken, half the Provolone, half the basil, the Parmesan cheese, salt and pepper, and the egg yolk. Fill a pastry bag or large sturdy plastic zipper bag with the chicken filling. Pipe the filling into the cooked manicotti.

4 Preheat the oven to 375°F (190°C/Gas Mark 5). Add the tomatoes, remaining basil, salt, sugar,

and red pepper flakes to the onions in the skillet. Bring to a boil, reduce to a simmer, and cook for 5 minutes or until slightly thickened.

5 Spoon 1/2 cup (4 fl oz./120 ml) of the tomato sauce into the bottom of a large glass baking dish. Arrange the stuffed manicotti on top of the sauce. Spoon the remaining sauce over the manicotti and bake for 20 minutes. Sprinkle the remaining Provolone cheese on top and bake for 5 minutes until the cheese is bubbly.

tip

You can use 3 cups (25 fl oz./ 775 ml) of bottled basil-flavored pasta sauce if you're in a hurry. Add to the sautéed onions in step 4, and leave out the rest of the sauce-making step.

Pasta with a Hearty Sauce

When friends call last minute for the holidays, don't fret.
Invite them to enjoy this quick-to-make meal of penne,
peas, tomatoes, and pork sausage.

main meals

- 1 medium onion
- 1 clove garlic
- 1 tbsp. olive oil
- 1 lb. (450 g) lean pork sausages
- 3 tbsp. brandy, white wine, or chicken stock
- 1 can (19 oz./540 ml) chopped tomatoes
- 1 lb. (450 g) fresh penne or 12 oz. (335 g) dried
- 5 oz. (140 g) frozen peas
- a small bunch of chives, to garnish
- Parmesan cheese, for serving

SERVES 4

Did you know?

In parts of Italy, the Christmas meal includes seven different fish dishes, to commemorate the Seven Sacraments. The fish is accompanied by pasta, salads, fruits, and breads, as well as Italian wine. Desserts usually include salads, the panettone fruit cake, spicy cookies, nougat, and nuts.

tip

The choice of sausage is crucial to the success of this dish. Use a really meaty, coarse-cut variety of sausage, or a very high quality sausage meat.

1 Bring a large saucepan of water to the boil for the pasta. Peel and coarsely chop the onion; and peel and crush the garlic. Fry the onion and garlic in the oil over a moderate heat for about 4 minutes, until the onion is soft, stirring occasionally.

2 Coarsely chop the sausages, or remove their skins and break them up with a fork. Add the sausages to the pan containing the onion and garlic and stir over a high heat for 7 minutes, or until browned.

3 Add the brandy, wine, or stock, and the tomatoes, and season with salt and pepper to taste. Bring to the boil, reduce the heat and simmer for 10 minutes, stirring occasionally.

4 When the water boils, add the fresh pasta, peas, and some salt, bring back to the boil and cook for 4-5 minutes, or until the pasta is al dente. If using dried pasta, cook for 6-7 minutes before adding the peas.

5 Meanwhile, prepare the chives as a garnish by trimming, rinsing, and chopping them.

6 Drain the pasta and peas and toss them in the tomato sauce. Taste and adjust the seasoning, garnish with the chives, and serve with freshly grated Parmesan cheese.

Rice Recipes

Rice dishes are excellent as main meals, side dishes, or as colorful offerings at a holiday buffet table.

Vegetarian Paella

- 3 tbsp. olive oil
- 2 garlic cloves, crushed
- 1 medium onion, sliced
- 1 red bell pepper, diced
- 1 green bell pepper, diced
- 1 large carrot, sliced
- 1⅓ cups (8 oz./225 g) long grain rice
- 14 oz. (400 g) can chopped tomatoes
- 2½ cups (20 fl oz./ 600 ml) vegetable stock
- 6 oz. (175 g) green beans, sliced
- 1 tbsp. chopped fresh oregano
- 1 tsp. paprika

SERVES 4

1 Heat the oil in a large pan and cook the garlic and onion for 2 minutes over a medium heat. Add the pepper and carrot to the pan and stir fry for 3 minutes.

2 Add the rice and cook for 3-4 minutes. Pour in the tomatoes and 1 cup (8 fl oz./225 ml) of the stock. Cook for 5 minutes or until the liquid is absorbed.

3 Add the beans to the pan with another half cup of the stock. Cover and cook for 5 minutes, then add the remaining stock, salt, pepper, oregano, and paprika. Cover and simmer gently until the stock is absorbed and the rice and vegetables are tender. Serve immediately.

tip

You can use any seasonal vegetables for this dish. Just make sure they are colorful and as fresh as possible.

main meals

Herb and Saffron Risotto

- 1 tbsp. butter
- 1 tbsp. extra-virgin olive oil
- 1 small onion, chopped
- 1 3/4 cups (12 1/2 oz./365 g) risotto rice
- 2/3 cup (5 fl oz./150 ml) dry white wine
- small pinch saffron strands
- 1 3/4 quarts (1 2/3 liters) vegetable stock, hot
- fresh-grated zest of 1 lemon
- 2 tbsp. lemon juice
- 2 tbsp. snipped fresh chives
- 2 tbsp. chopped parsley
- 1/2 oz. (15 g) piece Parmesan cheese
- snipped fresh chives

SERVES 6

1 Melt the butter with the oil in a large saucepan over a medium heat. Add the onion and sauté until soft, stirring occasionally, 4–5 minutes.

2 Add the rice and stir for 1 minute, to coat all the grains with the butter and oil. Stir in the wine and boil until almost evaporated.

3 Stir the saffron into the hot stock. Add a ladleful of the stock to the saucepan and slowly boil until it is absorbed, stirring frequently. Continue adding the stock a ladleful at a time, letting each be almost absorbed before adding the next, and stirring frequently. Total cooking time will be 15–20 minutes. The risotto is ready when the rice is tender, but the grains are still whole and firm, and the overall texture is moist and creamy.

4 Remove the saucepan from the heat and stir in the lemon zest and juice, chives, and parsley. Season with salt and pepper to taste.

5 Using a swivel-bladed vegetable peeler, pare thin shavings from the parmesan and scatter them over the risotto together with the chives.

Did you know?

Fresh parsley is a great breath freshener, as well as being a rich source of vitamin C and iron. If it is chewed after a meal, it can neutralize the aftertaste of strongly flavored ingredients such as garlic.

Vegetable Dishes

This collection of vegetable side dishes will complement any meat, fish, or poultry meal, and will put the finishing touch to your Christmas dinner.

Irish Mashed Potatoes with Cabbage and Leeks

- 2 lb. (900 g) Yukon Gold potatoes, unpeeled and quartered
- 2 cans (14½ oz./435 g each) fat-free chicken broth, plus cold water as needed
- 1 lb. (450 g) leeks, trimmed, thinly sliced, and rinsed
- 1 cup (8 fl oz./240 ml) low fat (1%) milk
- 3 cloves garlic, crushed
- 1 bay leaf
- 1 lb. (450 g) green cabbage, cored and thinly sliced
- ¼ cup (2 fl oz./62 ml) cold water
- ¼ tsp. ground nutmeg
- ¼ tsp. white pepper
- 2 tbsp. unsalted butter
- ¼ cup (½ oz./11 g) minced chives

SERVES 8

1 In a large saucepan, combine the potatoes, broth, and water as needed to cover the potatoes with liquid. Boil the potatoes until tender, 20–25 minutes.

2 In a second large saucepan, combine the leeks, milk, garlic, and bay leaf. Cover and bring to the boil and simmer until the leeks are softened, 15–20 minutes. Drain, reserving the leeks, milk, and garlic separately. Discard the bay leaf.

3 In the same saucepan, combine the cabbage and the ¼ cup (56 ml) of water. Cover and gently boil until tender, 10–15 minutes. Drain, squeeze the cabbage dry and finely chop.

4 Drain the potatoes and transfer to a large bowl. Add the milk and garlic to the potatoes, then mash. Stir in the leeks, cabbage, nutmeg, salt, pepper, and butter. Top the mound of potatoes with the chives.

Cinnamon and Maple Syrup Mashed Sweet Potatoes

- 2 lb. (900 g) sweet potatoes, peeled and chopped
- 1 cinnamon stick
- 2 tbsp. maple syrup
- 1½ tbsp. butter or vegetable oil

SERVES 6

1 In a medium saucepan, combine the sweet potatoes, salt to taste, cinnamon stick, and just enough water to cover the potatoes. Boil, uncovered, stirring occasionally, until the potatoes are tender, about 20 minutes. Drain and discard the cinnamon stick.

2 Transfer the potatoes back to the saucepan. Add 1½ tbsp. of the maple syrup and the butter, then mash. Serve, drizzled with the remaining maple syrup.

Rosemary New Potatoes

- 1¼ lb. (560 g) even-sized baby new potatoes
- 2 tbsp. olive oil
- 1 lemon
- 2–3 large sprigs of fresh rosemary

SERVES 4

1 Preheat the oven to 450°F (230°C/Gas Mark 8) and boil a kettle of water.

2 Scrub the potatoes and put in a large saucepan. Cover with boiling water, and boil gently for 5 minutes.

3 Pour the olive oil into a large, shallow roasting pan and put it into the oven to heat.

4 Wash the lemon and finely grate the rind. Rinse the rosemary leaves.

5 Drain the potatoes well. Remove roasting pan from oven and place potatoes into the hot oil and stir well to coat evenly. Make sure the oil is really hot before you begin roasting—the potatoes should start to sizzle as soon as you put them into the pan. Sprinkle the lemon rind, rosemary leaves, and some salt and black pepper over them.

6 Roast the potatoes on the top rack of the oven for 20 minutes, until golden.

Twice-Baked Stuffed Sweet Potatoes

- 2 large sweet potatoes (1½ lb./675 g total)
- 1 can (8 oz./225 g) crushed pineapple, drained
- 1 tbsp. vegetable oil
- 1 tbsp. butter
- 1 tbsp. light- or dark-brown sugar
- 1 tsp. grated orange zest
- 2 tbsp. chopped pecans

SERVES 4

1 Preheat the oven to 350°F 180°C/Gas Mark 4). Pierce each sweet potato twice with the tip of a knife and place on a baking sheet.

2 Bake the sweet potatoes until soft, about 50 minutes. Set aside until cool enough to handle but still very warm. Reduce the oven heat to 325°F (170°C/Gas Mark 3).

3 Cut the potatoes in half lengthwise. Being careful not to tear the skin, scoop out the flesh and place in a medium bowl. Reserve the skins. Add the pineapple, oil, butter, sugar, zest, and salt, to taste, to the flesh. Whip with an electric mixer or whisk until slightly fluffy.

4 Place the skin shells on a baking sheet. Fill with the potato mixture, mounding each. Bake for 15 minutes. Sprinkle with the pecans. Bake for 5 minutes to warm through.

Roasted Root Vegetables with Herbs

A nutritious and colorful combination of carrots, potatoes, parsnips, rutabaga, sweet potatoes, are roasted together and are delicious served with poultry, meat, or fish.

- 2¼ lb. (2.4 kg) mixed root vegetables, such as potatoes, sweet potatoes, carrots, parsnips, and rutabaga or turnips
- 8 oz. (240 g) shallots or pearl onions
- 2 tbsp. extra-virgin olive oil
- 1 tsp. coarse sea salt
- 1 tsp. cracked black peppercorns
- few sprigs fresh thyme, plus extra to garnish
- few sprigs fresh rosemary, plus extra to garnish

SERVES 4

1 Preheat the oven to 425°F (220°C/Gas Mark 7). Scrub or peel the vegetables, according to type and taste. Halve or quarter any large potatoes. Cut any large carrots or parsnips in half lengthwise, then cut the pieces crosswise in half again. Cut the rutabaga into large chunks (about the same size as the potatoes). Leave the shallots or the pearl onions whole.

2 Place the vegetables in a large saucepan over a high heat and cover with boiling water. Bring back to a boil, then reduce the heat and simmer until the vegetables are lightly cooked, but not yet tender, 5–7 minutes.

3 Drain the vegetables and place them in a roasting pan. Brush with the oil and sprinkle with salt and peppercorns. Add the herb sprigs to the pan and place in the oven.

4 Roast until the vegetables are golden brown, crisp, and tender, 30–35 minutes, turning them over after 15 minutes. Serve the vegetables hot, garnished with sprigs of thyme or rosemary, if liked.

Sautéed Brussels Sprouts

The smoky flavor of bacon, the citrus zing of the orange, and the crunchy texture of water chestnuts in this recipe give new life to a traditional Christmas vegetable.

- 1 tbsp. corn oil
- 5 slices smoked bacon
- 1 lb. (450 g) fresh Brussels sprouts
- 1 orange
- 3 tbsp. butter
- 2 tsp. whole grain mustard
- 1 can (5 oz./140 g) whole water chestnuts in water

1 Heat the corn oil in a skillet, then dice the smoked bacon and fry it for 2–3 minutes until it turns golden brown.

2 Rinse the Brussels sprouts, trim them if necessary, and cut in half. Wash any wax off the orange and grate the zest into the skillet with the bacon and add the butter, mustard, and sprouts. Cook over a moderate heat for 5 minutes, stirring, until the sprouts are crisp.

3 Meanwhile, drain and roughly chop the water chestnuts, stir them into the sprouts, and cook them for 3–4 minutes until the sprouts are golden and the chestnuts are heated through. Add salt and black pepper to taste and serve.

Simple Salads

Healthy salads and side dishes work well with any main meal. As a light meal on their own, they help to keep those extra Christmas calories at bay.

- 1 tbsp. olive oil
- 3 slices turkey bacon, cut crosswise into 1/2-in. (0.5-cm) wide strips
- 12 oz. (340 g) fresh shiitake mushrooms, stems removed and caps thinly sliced
- 1 can (19 oz./540 g) white beans, rinsed and drained
- 1/2 cup (4 fl oz./125 ml) low-sodium mixed vegetable juice
- 2 tbsp. red wine vinegar
- 1 tbsp. Dijon mustard
- 12 cups (1 lb./450 g) spinach leaves
- 1 yellow bell pepper, cut into small cubes
- 1 large red onion, halved and thinly sliced

SERVES 4

Spinach, White Bean, and Bacon Salad

1 Heat the oil in a large skillet over a medium heat. Add the bacon and cook until crisp, about 5 minutes. Transfer the bacon to paper towels to drain.

2 Add the shiitake mushrooms to the skillet and cook until tender, about 5 minutes. Add the beans and cook until heated through, about 3 minutes.

3 In a bowl, whisk the vegetable juice, vinegar, mustard, and salt and black pepper. Add to the mushrooms and bring to the boil.

4 Combine the spinach, bell pepper, red onion, and bacon in a large bowl. Add the mushroom mixture to the bowl, toss to combine, and serve the salad immediately.

Shredded Beets and Red Cabbage with Cranberries

- 2 tbsp. olive oil
- 1 1/2 cups (6 oz./170 g) coarsely shredded red cabbage
- 1 1/2 cups (9 oz./250 g) peeled, coarsely shredded cooked fresh or canned whole baby beets
- 1/3 cup (1 3/4 oz./45 g) fresh or canned whole berry cranberry sauce
- 1 tbsp. balsamic vinegar
- 1/8 tsp. ground allspice
- 1/8 tsp. ground cloves

SERVES 4

1 In a 10-in. (25.5-cm) skillet or Dutch oven, (a casserole dish with a tight-fitting lid), heat the oil for 1 minute over a moderate heat. Add the cabbage and sauté, stirring occasionally, for 5 minutes.

2 Stir in the beets, cranberry sauce, vinegar, allspice, and cloves, and season to taste. Cook, covered, until tender, about 10 minutes.

Updated Caesar Salad

- 3 cloves garlic, peeled and halved
- 4 x ½-in. (0.5-cm) thick slices Italian or French bread
- 5 tbsp. olive oil
- 3 tbsp. mayonnaise
- 3 tbsp. lemon juice
- 6 anchovies, mashed, or 2 tsp. anchovy paste
- 1 medium-size head romaine lettuce, torn into bite-size pieces
- ¼ cup (1 oz./25 g) grated Parmesan cheese

SERVES 4

1 Preheat the oven to 400°F (200°C/Gas Mark 6). Using two cloves of the garlic, rub the slices of bread on both sides. Brush with 2 tbsp. of the oil and cut into ½-in.(0.5-cm) cubes. Spread out on an ungreased baking sheet and bake, uncovered, tossing occasionally, until golden brown and crisp, about 10 minutes.

2 Meanwhile, rub a large chilled bowl with the remaining garlic. Add the mayonnaise, lemon juice, anchovies, salt and pepper to taste, and the remaining 3 tbsp. oil and whisk until creamy. Add the romaine, Parmesan, and croutons and toss until well coated. Divide evenly among four chilled plates and serve.

Goats' Cheese and Arugula

- ½ lb. (230 g) smoked back bacon
- 1 tbsp. vegetable oil
- 2 small, round, soft goats' cheeses, about ¼ lb. (110 g) each
- 3 oz. (85 g) arugula or watercress

For the Dressing
- 1 clove garlic
- 1 tsp. wholegrain mustard
- 2 tsp. white wine vinegar
- 2 tbsp. extra virgin olive oil

SERVES 4

1 Preheat the oven to 475°F (240°C/Gas Mark 9). Derind and dice the bacon. Heat the oil and fry the bacon until crisp then drain it on paper towels.

2 To make the dressing, peel the garlic, crush it into a small bowl, then whisk in the mustard, vinegar, and extra virgin olive oil. Season to taste.

3 Line a baking sheet with baking parchment. Cut the goats' cheeses in half horizontally and lay the pieces on the paper. Bake for 5 minutes or until they begin to melt and turn a toasty brown on top.

4 Meanwhile, trim, rinse, and dry the arugula or watercress and put it into a mixing bowl with the bacon.

Pour the dressing over and toss lightly, then arrange in circles on individual plates.

5 Remove the cheese from the oven, place one piece in the center of each salad and serve immediately.

CHAPTER SEVEN

SWEET TREATS

Nothing surpasses the spicy scents and delightful
flavors of traditional seasonal desserts. So indulge
your friends and family with delicious cakes,
cookies, pies, and candies—after all, Christmas
comes but once a year.

★have a merry christmas★

Chocolate Truffles

There's nothing nicer than a delicious homemade gift that shows you took the time to care. A pretty box of chocolate truffles is certain to be a hit with the special people on your list.

- 5 oz. (150 g) dark chocolate
- ¼ stick (1 oz./30 g) butter
- 2 tbsp. brandy, rum, or whisky, or a liqueur such as Cointreau, Tia Maria, or Malibu
- 1 tbsp. cocoa powder
- 1 tsp. confectioners' (icing) sugar

MAKES 12

1 Chop the chocolate into small pieces and place in a heatproof bowl with the butter. Stand the bowl over a pan of steaming (not boiling) water, without letting the bottom of the bowl touch the water. Leave until the chocolate and butter have melted. Stir until smooth and evenly mixed.

2 Remove the bowl from the pan and leave to cool before stirring in the brandy or liqueur.

3 Leave the bowl in a cool place (not the refrigerator) until the mixture is thick and firm, stirring occasionally to ensure it sets evenly.

4 Measure the cocoa powder and confectioners' sugar into a sieve and sift together onto a plate.

5 Check that the mixture is firm then divide it into 12 equal pieces and roll each one into a ball. Roll the balls in the cocoa powder and sugar until well coated.

6 Place the truffles in candy paper cases and pack in a rigid box tied with a colorful ribbon. To make this pretty star-shaped box, turn to page 110 for instructions.

tip

Use chocolate with a high percentage of cocoa solids, ideally 70 percent.

Gingerbread House

This whimsical gingerbread house may be lit from the inside by an electric candle. When the gingerbread pieces are baked, assemble them on a cake board around the candle, cutting a hole in the back wall section for the cord before baking.

For the Dough

- 3 tbsp. molasses (golden syrup)
- 1½ sticks (6 oz./175 g) butter
- 1½ cups (6 oz./175 g) light brown sugar
- 3 egg yolks
- 6 cups (1½ lb./700 g) all-purpose (plain) flour
- 1½ tsp. baking soda
- 1 tbsp. ground ginger
- about ½ cup (4 fl oz./125 ml) milk

To Decorate

- a few colored hard candies, broken up
- white confectioners' (icing) sugar
- selection of brightly colored small candies
- 14 in. x 20 in. (35 cm x 50 cm) cake board

1 Preheat the oven to 350°F (180°C/Gas Mark 4). Line several baking sheets with nonstick baking parchment. Using the measurements below, draw patterns for the house on thin cardboard and cut out.

2 Heat the molasses until melted. In a bowl, cream the butter and sugar, beat in the egg yolks, and sift in the flour, baking soda, and ginger. Add the molasses and milk and mix to a soft dough. Knead until smooth and roll out ¼-in. (6-mm) thick.

3 Using a small, sharp knife and the pattern measurements (right), cut out two end walls, two side walls, two roof panels and four chimney panels. Cut two windows from each side panel and a door from one end wall, reserving the "door."

4 Lift the shapes onto the baking sheets, and bake for 10 minutes. Remove from the oven and place a few pieces of broken hard candy in the window spaces. Return to the oven for a further 5 minutes so the candies melt.

5 Cool on the baking sheets and allow the windows to harden before lifting. Leave in a cool, dry place for 24 hours to harden.

tip

After baking, check the shapes against the patterns and trim them if necessary while still warm, before they harden.

6 In a bowl, combine the confectioners' sugar with a little water to make a thick icing. Assemble the walls on a cake board by sticking them together with the icing. Leave them to set supported with food cans. Stick on the roof panels and chimney with icing and leave to set.

7 Decorate the house with small candies, fixing them in place with icing, and spread more icing over the board for snow. Arrange a path and fence in the snow if liked. Leave to set for at least 24 hours.

Did you know?

The Germans call gingerbread houses "Hexenhaüsle" or "witches' houses" after the witch's house that featured in Grimm's fairytale "Hansel and Gretel."

PATTERN MEASUREMENTS
End walls: draw a rectangle 7 in. (18 cm) wide x 7½ in. (19 cm) tall, then remove the two top corners to give an apex and side walls 5 in. (12 cm) tall
Side walls: 7½ in. (19 cm) wide x 5 in. (12 cm) tall
Roof panel: 8 in. (20 cm) wide x 5½ in. (14 cm) tall
Chimney panel: 1¼ in. (3 cm) wide x 4½ in. (4 cm) tall

Meringue Snowmen

These jolly little fellows will be a hit with children of all ages. If you're feeling particularly creative, add bright scarves, carrot noses, or colorful hats molded out of almond paste and fixed in place with icing.

For the Meringue

- 4 large egg whites
- 2/3 cup (5 oz./140 g) granulated sugar
- 3/4 cup (3 1/4 oz./90 g) confectioners' (icing) sugar
- 1 tbsp. cornstarch

To Decorate

- 1 2/3 cups (7 oz/200 g) confectioners' (icing) sugar
- 1 tube each of black, and red decorating icing
- licorice candies (thin circles for base of hats, thicker ones for tops)

MAKES 12

1 Preheat the oven to 225°F (110°C/Gas Mark 1/4). Line two large baking sheets with baking parchment.

2 Put the egg whites in a large bowl and whisk until soft peaks form. Gradually whisk in the sugars, a little at a time, until the whites are thick and shiny. Whisk in the cornstarch with the last addition of sugar.

3 Spoon the meringue into a large pastry bag fitted with a 1/4-in. (5-mm) plain nozzle and pipe 48 small mounds onto the baking sheets. Smooth down any "points" of meringue with a small brush.

4 Bake the meringues in the oven until crisp, about 1 1/2 hours. Turn off the oven and leave the meringues inside to cool.

5 Sift the confectioners' sugar into a bowl and mix with 4–5 tbsp. water to make a thick icing. Sandwich the flat sides of 24 meringues together with the icing and leave to set. Fix 12 meringues, rounded side to rounded side, to the top of each for the snowmen's heads and leave to set. Fix the remaining 12 to the base of each, rounded side to rounded side, so the snowmen stand up.

6 Make hats from licorice and fix in place with white icing. Pipe on eyes and buttons using a tube of black decorating icing. Finally, pipe on smiling mouths with the red decorating icing.

tip

When making the meringues, whisk in the sugar a spoonful at a time so it combines with the whites and doesn't leak out when baking.

Rich Chocolate Tart

A generous amount of good-quality semisweet chocolate makes this European-style cake moist and rich—just a small slice will satisfy even the sweetest tooth. Serve warm with a spoonful of sour cream.

For the Dough

- 6 oz. (175 g) good-quality semisweet chocolate (at least 70 percent cocoa solids)
- 1/3 cup (3 oz./80 g) unsalted butter
- 4 large eggs
- 1/2 cup (4 oz./115 g) soft light brown sugar
- 3 1/2 tbsp. all-purpose (plain) flour

To Decorate

- cape gooseberries, papery skins folded back (optional)
- confectioners' (icing) sugar
- unsweetened cocoa powder

SERVES 10

1 Preheat the oven to 350°F (180°C/Gas Mark 4). Grease a 9-in (23-cm) springform cake pan and line with waxed paper.

2 Chop the chocolate and put it in a heatproof bowl with the butter. Set the bowl over a pan of almost-boiling water, making sure the water does not touch the bottom of the bowl. Melt the chocolate and butter, then remove the bowl from the heat and stir the mixture until smooth.

3 Put the eggs and sugar in a large bowl. Beat with an electric mixer until the mixture increases in volume and leaves a trail on the surface when the beaters are lifted out.

4 Add the chocolate mixture to the whisked egg mixture and fold it in with a large metal spoon. Gradually sift the flour over the top then fold it in until just combined.

5 Pour the batter into the cake pan, gently smoothing the surface. Bake until the top of the cake feels just firm to the touch, 15–20 minutes. Leave to cool on a wire rack in the pan.

6 Remove the cake from the pan and peel away the lining paper. Cut into thin wedges for serving, decorating each piece with a cape gooseberry, and dusting the plates and tart with sifted confectioners' sugar and cocoa powder.

tip

Fold the flour in carefully until it is just incorporated with the other ingredients. If you beat it in, the finished cake will be heavy rather than light and airy.

Amaretti Delight

Homemade desserts always add a welcoming touch to a holiday meal. Here contrasting layers of crunchy amaretti crumb and creamy amaretti egg whisk make this a delightfully light but flavorsome dessert. Top each serving with chocolate stars sprinkled with cinnamon.

- 1¼ sticks (5 oz./140 g) butter
- 2 cups (6 oz./115 g) soft bread crumbs
- 3 oz. (75 g) amaretti cookies, crushed
- 2 tbsp. light brown sugar
- 4 large egg yolks
- ⅓ cup (2½ oz./75 g) superfine (caster) sugar
- 4 tbsp. amaretto liqueur
- 1 tsp. ground cinnamon
- chocolate stars, to decorate (see tip box)

SERVES 4

1 Melt ½ stick (2 oz./60 g) butter in a skillet, stir in the bread crumbs, crushed amaretti cookies and brown sugar and cook until crisp. Remove from the skillet and leave to cool.

2 Melt the remaining butter in a small pan and set aside to cool. In a large heatproof bowl, beat together the egg yolks, superfine sugar, and amaretto liqueur until smooth.

3 Stand the bowl over a pan of boiling water, making sure the bottom of the bowl does not touch the water. Whisk for about 10 minutes until the mixture is thick and creamy, and holding its shape. Then gradually whisk in the melted butter until combined. Allow to cool.

4 Layer up the whisked egg mixture and amaretti crumb mixture in serving glasses, finishing with a layer of the whisked egg mixture. Sprinkle the cinnamon over the top of each serving and decorate with chocolate stars.

tip

To make chocolate stars, melt dark chocolate in a bowl over a pan of hot water. Spoon melted chocolate into a paper pastry bag, snip off the end, and pipe star shapes onto a sheet of baking parchment. Leave the stars to harden before carefully lifting off.

" *He that is of a merry heart hath a continual feast.* "

Proverbs 15:15

Plum Pudding

This versatile Christmas dessert tastes more like a spiced cake than a fruit dessert. Made with butter instead of the traditional suet, you can add your favorite candied fruits, currants or raisins—whatever you like best.

- 1¼ cups (5½ oz./155 g) all-purpose (plain) flour
- 1 tsp. grated orange rind
- 1 tsp. ground cinnamon
- ¾ tsp. baking powder
- ½ tsp. ground ginger
- ⅛ tsp. ground cloves
- ½ cup (3½ oz./100 g) firmly packed light-brown sugar
- ¼ cup (2 oz./60 g) butter or margarine, at room temperature
- 4 large egg whites
- ¼ cup (4 fl oz./125 ml) cider or apple juice
- ½ cup (4 oz./112 g) shredded carrot
- ¾ cup (3¼ oz./90 g) raisins
- ⅓ cup (3 oz./85 g) candied (glacé) cherries, halved, or currants or raisins
- ⅓ cup (1½ oz./45 g) chopped candied (glacé) pineapple, currants, or raisins
- ⅓ cup (1½ oz./40 g) pecan halves

Brandied Cider Sauce

(recipe, opposite)

SERVES 8

1 Lightly grease a 1½-quart (1.4 liter) steamed pudding mold or casserole. In a medium-size bowl, stir together the flour, orange rind, cinnamon, baking powder, ginger, and cloves.

2 In a large bowl, with an electric mixer on medium, cream the brown sugar and butter until light and fluffy, scraping the side of the bowl often. Add the egg whites and beat well. Using a wooden spoon, stir in one-third of the flour mixture, then half of the apple cider or juice. Repeat, then stir in the remaining mixture. Stir in the carrot, fruits, and nuts.

3 Spoon the batter evenly into the prepared mold. Cover the mold with foil. Tie the foil in place with string.

4 Place the mold on a rack in a Dutch oven, (a heavy-based casserole dish with tight-fitting lid). Pour boiling water into the Dutch oven until the water is halfway up the side of the mold. Cook, covered, over a low heat for 2–2½ hours or until a toothpick inserted in the center comes out clean.

5 Place the mold upright on a wire rack and let stand for 10 minutes. Using a narrow metal spatula, loosen the side of the plum pudding from the mold, then invert the pudding onto a serving plate. Serve warm, with brandied cider sauce.

Did you know?

Charms were often dropped into the pudding mix before it was cooked. Tradition states that a ring, a button, a thimble, and a coin should be added. The lucky (or unlucky), person to find one of these objects can expect marriage, spinsterhood, bachelorhood, or wealth respectively, during the following year.

Brandied Cider Sauce

1 In a small saucepan, whisk together ¾ cup (6 fl oz./170 ml) cider or apple juice, ¼ cup (2 oz./56 g) firmly packed light brown sugar, and one tablespoon cornstarch. Bring to a boil over a moderate heat, whisking constantly. Cook for 2 minutes or until the mixture is thickened, whisking all the time. Stir in 2 tbsp. of brandy or apple juice and 1 tsp. of butter or margarine. Makes about ¾ cup (6 fl oz./170 ml).

tip

You can make this dessert up to a week in advance. Simply cover and refrigerate the pudding. To reheat it, steam as directed in Step 4 for 1 hour or until heated through.

Viennese Sachertorte

Use the best-quality dark chocolate you can afford to make this cake really chocolatey. Store the cake for a day, if possible, to allow the full depth of the flavor to develop.

- 1 cup (5½ oz./150 g) dark (semisweet) chocolate
- ⅔ cup (5½ oz./150 g) butter
- 1¼ cups (5½ oz./150 g) confectioners' (icing) sugar
- few drops of vanilla extract (essence)
- 6 eggs, separated
- 1 cup (4½ oz./125 g) all-purpose (plain) flour
- ¼ tsp. baking powder
- 3–4 tbsp. apricot jam
- 1⅓ cups (7 oz./200 g) dark (semisweet) chocolate

Serves 8

1 Use a 23-cm (9-in) springform pan. Line the base of the tin with baking parchment. Preheat the oven to 300°F (150°C/Gas Mark 2).

2 Break up the chocolate and melt in a bowl placed over simmering water. Using an electric mixer, beat the chocolate, butter, confectioners' sugar, vanilla extract, and egg yolks in a medium bowl until well combined.

3 Sift the flour and baking powder and stir gently into the batter. Beat the egg whites in a separate bowl until stiff and fold into the batter with a metal spoon.

4 Place the batter in the pan and smooth the top, building the mixture up a little higher toward the edge. Bake for 60–70 minutes. Remove from the oven; let stand for 5 minutes. Remove the outer ring of the pan.

5 Cover cake with baking parchment. Weigh down with a small board and leave to cool completely. Turn onto a wire rack and remove the pan base.

6 Sieve the jam into a pan, add a little water and heat gently. Spread evenly over the cake and allow to set. Melt the chocolate in a bowl placed over simmering water and spread over the cake. To prevent cracking, lift the cake onto a serving platter before the chocolate hardens.

Did you know?

The "Original Sachertorte" recipe, invented by Franz Sacher in 1832, has become a trademark. Hotel Sacher in Vienna, built by Sacher's son, has registered the trademark. The original recipe is a well-guarded secret. Although there are many variations of this chocolate cake, there is only one authentic sachertorte.

Mocha and Ginger Log

A festive dessert that's perfect for those pleasurable moments when friends call unexpectedly. It is quick and requires no cooking.

- 2 tbsp. instant coffee
- 2 cup (16 fl oz./450 ml) heavy (double) cream
- ¼ cup (2 fl oz./50 ml) sweet sherry
- 1 package (8 oz./227 g) ginger cookies
- silver and gold balls, to decorate

For the Spun Sugar

- ½ cup (4 oz./100 g) granulated sugar
- ⅓ cup (3 fl. oz/90 ml) corn syrup

SERVES 6-8

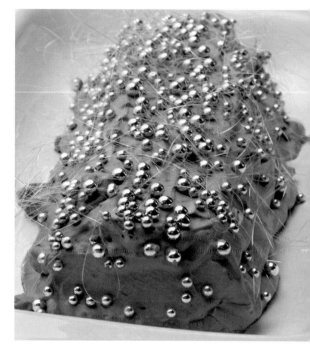

1 Put the instant coffee granules in a cup, then add 1 tbsp. of hot water. Stir continuously until the coffee dissolves.

2 Spoon the cream into a bowl. Add the dissolved coffee and whisk until the cream is stiff and holds its shape.

3 Pour the sherry into a saucer. Dip the cookies briefly in the sherry, one at a time, and sandwich them together with a little of the whipped cream mixture. Do not use all of the cream as you will need the remainder later. Arrange the cookie sandwiches in a long roll on a plate.

4 Spread the remaining cream over the outside of the roll in an even layer. Draw lines in the cream with a fork, so the dessert resembles a log.

5 Decorate the log with silver and gold balls or spun sugar (see above). Chill for several hours before serving.

Spun Sugar

1 Cover the floor in front of the work surface with newspaper. Oil the handles of 2 long wooden spoons and tape them to the counter 12 in. (30.5 cm) apart. Position them so the handles extend over the floor.

2 Combine the granulated sugar and the corn syrup in a heavy saucepan and bring to the boil, stirring constantly. When the sugar dissolves, boil until a candy thermometer registers 320°F–338°F (160°C–170°C).

3 Remove the mixture and pour into a metal bowl. Let cool for 2 minutes.

4 Hold two forks side by side and dip into the mixture. Wave the forks back and forth quickly over the spoon handles so sugar strands fall on them. Drape the strands over the back of an oiled bowl before they set. Store airtight at low humidity.

tip

Don't dip the cookies in the sherry for too long, or they'll go soggy and fall apart when you try to sandwich them with the cream.

Chocolate Log

Based on a chocolate sponge cake, the filling of this dessert is flavored with mouthwatering Bailey's Irish Cream liqueur and lightly set with gelatin. Whatever your Christmas meal, this cake will provide the perfect ending.

- 4 eggs
- 4 tsp. tepid water
- ½ cup (4 oz./115 g) superfine (caster) sugar
- ½ cup (2 ¼ oz./60 g) all-purpose (plain) flour
- ¼ cup (1 oz./25 g) cocoa
- 1 level tsp. baking powder
- butter for greasing
- confectioners' (icing) sugar for dusting

For the Filling
- 3 tsp. unflavored gelatin
- ½ cup (4 fl. oz./115 ml) Bailey's Irish Cream
- ¼ cup (2 oz./55 g) superfine (caster) sugar
- ½ tsp. vanilla extract
- 1 cup (8 fl oz./225 ml) whipping cream

SERVES 8

1 Preheat the oven to 400°F (200°C/Gas Mark 6). Whip the eggs and water together until frothy. Gradually add the sugar a little at a time, lightly beating the mixture. In a separate bowl, mix together the flour, cocoa, and baking powder. Fold gradually into the egg mixture.

2 Line a jelly roll pan measuring approximately 14 in. x 16 in. (35 cm x 40 cm) with greased baking paper, and spread the runny mixture evenly on the paper. Bake until firm, about 12–15 minutes.

3 Carefully turn out, face down, onto a clean tea towel that has been dusted with confectioners' sugar and peel off the baking paper. Roll up the sponge with the tea towel inside, starting at one long side. Lift onto a wire rack and allow to cool.

4 Sprinkle the gelatin over 2 tbsp. of water in a small bowl and leave for 5 minutes. Dissolve the gelatin by standing the bowl in a pan of warm water. Mix together the Bailey's Irish Cream, sugar, and vanilla. Stir in the dissolved gelatin and chill until starting to thicken, about 20 minutes. Whip the cream until stiff and fold into the setting mixture.

5 Unroll the sponge and spread the Bailey's Irish Cream evenly over it. Roll up again and chill for about 1 hour. Decorate with rosemary and red currants if desired.

tip

Sprinkle the top of the yule log with some confectioners' sugar to create a fresh and festive snow-covered appearance.

Did you know?

A yule log is a popular dessert in many countries. It has its origins in the belief that when a log was burned in an open fire at Christmas, the ashes had miraculous powers. The first mention of this custom can be traced back to Germany in 1184.

Festive Cupcakes

Even if your guests are full after Christmas dinner, they won't be able to resist one of these delectable cupcakes. Decorate in whatever way you wish with piped icing and small candies.

- 1½ cups (6¾ oz./185 g) all-purpose (plain) flour
- 1 cup (4 oz./100 g) fine granulated sugar
- 3 tbsp. cocoa
- 1 tsp. baking soda
- 1 tsp. baking powder
- ½ cup (4 fl oz./125 ml) buttermilk
- 1 large egg
- ½ cup (4 fl oz./125 ml) warm water
- ¼ cup (2 fl oz./56 ml) oil
- ½ tsp. vanilla
- chocolate and vanilla icings, decorating icing, small candies, silver balls

MAKES 20–24

1 Put the flour, sugar, cocoa, baking soda, baking powder, buttermilk, egg, water, oil, and vanilla in a mixing bowl and whisk together until they are all well blended.

2 Preheat the oven to 350°F (180°C/Gas Mark 4). Line muffin cups with cupcake paper liners.

3 Spoon the mixture into the liners until three-quarters full. Bake for about 20 minutes or until a tooth pick pushed into the center of a cupcake comes out clean. Transfer the cupcakes to a wire rack to cool.

4 Ice half the cupcakes with chocolate confectioners' sugar and half with vanilla. Decorate lavishly with piped colored decorating icing, small candies, silver balls, and cake decorations such as mimosa balls.

tip

For extra chocolaty cupcakes, add 4 oz. (100 g) semisweet chocolate chips to the mixture.

Jeweled Fruit Cake

Delectable mouthfuls of glistening glazed dried fruits and nuts make this cake a hit for the holidays. Tie a colorful ribbon around the side to complete the effect.

tip

Hollowing out the top of the cake mixture helps the cake to rise evenly. Avoid over-beating the mixture or the cake will peak and crack.

For the Dough

- 2¼ cups (12 oz./350 g) currants
- 2 cups (9 oz./250 g) dark raisins
- 1⅓ cup (6 oz./170 g) golden raisins
- ½ cup (2 oz./60 g) candied (glacé) orange peel, chopped
- ½ cup (2 oz./60 g) candied (glacé) cherries, chopped
- 4 tbsp. brandy
- 1¾ cups (8 oz./225 g) all-purpose (plain) flour
- 1 tsp. ground cinnamon
- 2 sticks (8 oz./225 g) butter
- 1 cup (8 oz./230 g) light soft brown sugar
- 4 large eggs, beaten
- 1 tbsp. black strap molasses
- grated zest of 1 lemon

For the Topping

- 6 tbsp. apricot jam
- about 16 walnut halves
- 7 pitted prunes
- 8 candied (glacé) cherries
- 4 dried apricots
- 4 whole blanched almonds

SERVES 14

1 Put the dried fruits, candied peel and chopped cherries in a bowl. Pour over the brandy, cover, and leave to steep overnight.

2 Preheat the oven to 275°F (140°C/Gas Mark 1). Grease an 8-in. (20-cm) deep round cake pan and line with baking parchment.

3 Sift together the flour and cinnamon. In a large mixing bowl, beat the butter and sugar together until creamy. Beat in the eggs a little at a time, and then fold in the flour and cinnamon. Finally stir in the molasses and lemon zest.

4 Spoon the mixture into the pan and spread it level, hollowing out the center a little. Bake the cake for about 4½ hours or until a skewer inserted into the center comes out clean. If the top of the cake is sufficiently browned before it is cooked, cover it with a sheet of foil for the remaining cooking time.

5 Leave the cake to cool completely in the pan, then turn out onto a wire rack to cool, and peel off the lining paper.

6 Warm the apricot jam, strain, and brush half over the top of the cake. Arrange the walnut halves, prunes, cherries, apricots, and almonds in circles over the cake and brush with the remaining jam.

Chocolate Marble Cake

There is a magic ingredient that makes this cake moist and flavorful—canned yams. The yams sweeten the batter and give a golden color that makes this cake perfect for any special occasion.

For the Dough

- 3 cups (13 oz./375 g) all-purpose (plain) flour
- 1¼ cups (10 oz./335 g) granulated sugar
- 2 tsp. baking powder
- 2 tsp. baking soda
- 2 tsp. cinnamon
- ¼ tsp. ground cloves
- 1 tsp. salt
- 2 cans (15¾ oz./440 g each) yams in syrup, drained or canned carrots
- 1½ cups (12 fl oz./340 ml) vegetable oil
- 4 large eggs
- 4 oz. (115 g) semisweet chocolate, melted
- 1 tsp. vanilla extract

For the Glaze

- 1 cup (4¼ oz./125 g) confectioners' (icing) sugar
- 1 tbsp. unsweetened cocoa powder
- ½ tsp. vanilla extract
- 2–3 tbsp. boiling water

SERVES 8–10

1 Preheat the oven to 350°F (180°C/Gas Mark 4). Coat a 10-in. (25.5-cm) Bundt or tube pan with nonstick cooking spray. Dust with flour.

2 In a medium bowl, stir together the flour, sugar, baking powder, baking soda, cinnamon, cloves, and salt.

3 In a large bowl, beat the yams and vegetable oil with an electric mixer until blended. Beat in the eggs, one at a time. Beat in the flour mixture until smooth. Spoon one-third of the batter into a small bowl. Stir in the melted chocolate and vanilla.

4 Spoon the batters alternately into the pan and swirl together with a knife for a marble effect.

5 Bake until a toothpick inserted in the center comes out clean and the side of the cake shrinks from the side of the pan, 50–60 minutes. Transfer the pan to a wire rack and let cool for 10 minutes. Turn the cake out onto the rack. Let cool completely.

6 For the glaze, in a small bowl, whisk together the confectioners' sugar and cocoa powder. Whisk in the vanilla extract and add 2–3 tbsp. of boiling water until you get good glazing consistency (like thick syrup). Drizzle the glaze over the cooled cake.

Christmas Cake

This rich fruit cake looks impressive, covered with delicious almond paste and iced in a simple style. It can be prepared a month ahead to allow the flavors to develop.

- 1 cup (9 oz./250 g) butter
- 1½ cups (10 oz./280 g) dark-brown sugar
- 6 eggs
- 2 cups (9 oz./250 g) all-purpose flour, sifted
- 3 cups (13 oz./375 g) golden raisins (sultanas)
- 2 cups (10 ½ oz./300 g) currants
- 3 cups (13 oz./375 g) seedless raisins, roughly chopped
- 2 cups (15 oz./420 g) candied (glacé) cherries, cut in halves
- ¾ cup (5 oz./140 g) mixed candied peel, chopped
- ¾ cup (2¾ oz./80 g) ground almonds
- finely grated zest of 1 large orange and 1 large lemon
- ⅓ cup (2½ fl oz./80 ml) rum, whisky, or brandy, for sprinkling over the cake before icing

SERVES 12

1 To make the cake, use a 9-in. (23-cm) cake pan; line the base and side with a double layer of baking parchment.

2 Preheat the oven to 300°F (150°C/Gas Mark 2). Place the butter and sugar in a large mixing bowl; beat until very light and fluffy. Add the eggs one at a time; beat well after each addition. (The mixture will curdle a little at this point, but it will come together when the dry ingredients are added.)

3 Fold in the flour. Stir in the dried fruit, candied cherries, chopped peel, ground almonds, and zests.

4 Spoon the mixture into the pan and smooth the top. Bake in the center of the oven for 3½–4 hours or until a skewer inserted in the center comes out clean.

5 Remove the cake from the oven; leave to cool in the pan for 1 hour. Carefully turn the cake out onto a wire rack and leave to cool completely. Do not remove the baking parchment.

6 Wrap the cold cake, still in the parchment paper, in plastic and wrap it again in foil. Place the cake in an airtight container and store in a cool, dry, airy cupboard until ready to ice it (see almond paste recipe right.)

Almond Paste (Marzipan)

- 4½ cups (1 lb./450 g) ground almonds
- 1½ cups (6½ oz./180 g) confectioners' (icing) sugar, sifted
- 1½ cups (12 oz./350 g) superfine (caster) sugar
- 8 egg yolks
- 1 tsp. almond or vanilla extract (essence)
- 3 tbsp. apricot jam, heated and sieved

1 Mix the ground almonds with the sugars. Add the egg yolks and the almond or vanilla essence, and mix to form a soft, but not sticky, paste. Smooth by kneading very briefly on a work surface lightly dusted with confectioners' sugar.

2 Remove the cake from its wrappings and place upside-down in the center of a 12-in. (30-cm) round gold or silver cake board, or on a cake stand, if preferred.

3 Using a fine skewer, make several holes in the base of the cake; insert the skewer to a depth of about 1½ in. (4 cm). Spoon the rum, whisky, or brandy over the base of the cake and allow it to seep into the holes.

4 Roll out the almond paste to a neat round about 13-in. (33-cm) diameter. Turn the cake the right side up and brush all over with the warm, sieved apricot jam.

5 Carefully lift the paste onto the cake; smooth it evenly over the top and down the side, pressing it gently but firmly into position. Trim off any excess paste from the base. Smooth the paste with a palette knife.

6 Leave the cake, uncovered, in a cool, dry place for 24 hours to allow the paste to dry completely before adding the icing.

Royal Icing

- 3 cups (13 oz./375 g) confectioners' (icing) sugar, sifted
- 4 egg whites
- 2 tsp. lemon juice

1 Place the sifted confectioners' sugar and egg whites in a large mixing bowl and beat until smooth and fluffy. Beat in the lemon juice.

2 Spoon 3 tbsp. of icing mixture onto the cake; spread evenly over the top only. Using a metal ruler, smooth the icing by pulling the ruler across the cake top. Trim any excess icing. Leave overnight to dry.

3 Put the remaining icing in a clean bowl, cover the surface closely with plastic wrap and refrigerate overnight. On the next day, beat the icing and coat the top of the cake again; smooth the icing as before.

4 Spread the remaining icing around the side of the cake; let a little come up onto the top. Use a palette knife to work the icing up into peaks and swirls.

5 Leave the icing to dry overnight. Decorate with your choice of Christmas ornaments.

tip

Adding lemon juice to royal icing makes it harder, which is ideal for this cake topping. Add a little more juice if you're making decorations too and you want them to hold their shape.

Epiphany Cake

Traditionally eaten on Twelfth Night in France, this delicious cake is made from two layers of crisp puff pastry sandwiched with a creamy almond paste. It makes a dramatic ending for a special meal and your guests are sure to be impressed.

- 1¼ sticks (5 oz./150 g) butter
- ⅔ cup (5½ oz./150 g) superfine (caster) sugar
- 1 cup (4 oz./110 g) ground almonds
- 1 tsp. vanilla extract (essence)
- 2 large eggs, beaten
- 1 lb. (450 g) puff pastry
- 1 fava bean
- milk or beaten egg, to glaze

SERVES 8

1 In a bowl, beat the butter until creamy. If the butter is very hard, put it in a microwave for 8-10 seconds, or as necessary, to soften. Stir in the sugar and almonds until evenly mixed. Add the vanilla to the eggs and gradually beat into the almond mixture.

2 Roll out half the pastry to a 12-in. (30-cm) circle. Lift onto a greased baking sheet and spoon the filling onto the pastry, spreading it to within 1 in. (2.5 cm) of the edges. Press the fava bean into the filling and brush the pastry border with water to dampen.

3 Roll out the remaining pastry to a 12-in. (30-cm) circle, lift over the filling and press the edges firmly together to seal. Flute the edges with the back of a knife pressing the knife fairly deeply, and score a swirly pattern on the top with the tip of the knife blade. Cut a small hole in the center to allow steam to escape. Chill in the fridge for 30 minutes.

4 Preheat the oven to 400°F (200°C/ Gas Mark 6). Brush the top of the pastry with milk or beaten egg to glaze. Don't glaze the scored swirly pattern in order to create the white swirls. Bake on the middle shelf of the oven until well risen and golden brown, about 35–40 minutes. Serve warm or cold.

tip

When glazing, don't brush the pastry edges or the layers will stick together and not rise properly.

Did you know?

An Epiphany cake is traditionally baked with a bean or a trinket hidden inside. The person whose slice of cake contains the bean is made the king or queen of the feast. They are then allowed to instruct others to do whatever they want for the evening.

" *Kings of Orient riding Guided by the starlight Bringing to the baby Gifts of love, this night.* "

Traditional Spanish Carol

Decorative Tree Cookies

Have your children help with these cookies—they look great tied with a thin ribbon and hung from the Christmas tree. But be sure to make plenty, because they're also hard to resist!

Iced Christmas Trees

- 1 stick (4 oz./115 g) butter
- ½ cup (4 oz./115 g) superfine (caster) sugar
- 1 large egg, beaten
- few drops of vanilla extract (essence)
- 2½ cups (11 oz./310 g) all-purpose (plain) flour
- pinch of salt
- Christmas tree cookie cutter
- 1 tube ready-to-use decorating icing
- colored balls
- narrow ribbon

Makes 20

tip

If you are using more than one baking sheet, you may need to move the sheets up or down in the oven, to ensure that all of the cookies cook properly. Cooking times may need to be slightly adjusted when cooking more than one sheet.

1 Preheat the oven to 375°F (190°C/Gas Mark 5). In a bowl, beat the butter until soft. Add the sugar and beat until fluffy, then gradually beat in the egg and vanilla.

2 Sift the flour with the salt and mix into the creamed mixture with a wooden spoon to make a soft dough. Wrap in plastic and chill in the refrigerator for 30 minutes.

3 Roll out the dough thinly on a floured surface and cut out tree shapes, gathering up trimmings and re-rolling them.

4 Lift the shapes onto a greased baking sheet and pierce a hole at the top of each tree with a skewer. Bake for 8–10 minutes, then cool on a wire rack. Decorate with the icing and add colored balls. Thread a ribbon through the hole at the top of each one.

Stained Glass Window Gingerbread Hearts

- 1 quantity of Iced Christmas Trees dough (see previous page, but instead of adding vanilla extract, add 2 tsp. ground ginger to make gingerbread cookies)
- red and green hard candies, broken up
- silver balls
- white confectioners' (icing) sugar

MAKES 18–20

1 Preheat the oven to 375°F (190°C/Gas Mark 5). Line two baking sheets with baking parchment.

2 Roll out the dough and cut out the cookies using a heart-shaped cutter. Using a small sharp knife or a tiny heart-shaped cutter, cut out the center of each cookie and pierce a hole in the top of each with a skewer.

3 Bake for 5 minutes, then remove the cookies from the oven and place a few pieces of hard candy in the center of each one. Return to the oven for a further 3–5 minutes.

4 Cool the cookies on the sheets, then decorate half the cookies with silver balls fixed with confectioners' sugar.

Iced Fun Cookies

- 1 quantity of Iced Christmas Trees dough (see previous page)
- miniature cookie cutters in a variety of shapes
- tubes of ready-to-use decorating icing in white, red, and green
- silver balls

1 Use miniature cutters to cut a variety of shapes from the cookie dough and bake as for Iced Christmas Trees. Allow to cool and decorate using tubes of decorating icing and silver balls.

Celebration Cookies

This selection of cookies are simply irrisistible especially when eaten warm, from the oven—perfect for children and adults alike.

Meringue Nut Cookies

- ½ cup (2 ¼ oz./60 g) walnuts
- ½ cup (2 ¼ oz./60 g) confectioners' (icing) sugar, plus extra for dusting
- 4 tsp. unsweetened cocoa powder
- ½ tsp. cinnamon
- 2 large egg whites

MAKES 36 COOKIES

1 Use two large baking sheets and line with baking parchment. Preheat the oven to 300°F (150°C, Gas Mark 2). Toast the walnuts in a small pan, stirring frequently until crisp, about 7 minutes. Cool briefly, then chop roughly.

2 Sift the confectioners' sugar, cocoa powder and the cinnamon onto a plate.

3 Using an electric mixer, beat the egg whites in a large bowl until stiff peaks form. Gently fold the cocoa mixture into the egg whites with a metal spoon. Fold in the nuts.

4 Drop the batter in generous teaspoons 1 in. (2.5 cm) apart onto the baking sheets. Bake for about 20 minutes, or until set. Turn onto a wire rack to cool. Dust with the extra sugar just before serving.

Cocoa Walnut Cookies

- 1 cup (9 oz./224 g) butter, softened
- 1¼ cups (9¾ oz./252 g) granulated sugar
- 2 cups (9 oz./250 g) all-purpose (plain) flour
- 1 cup (6 oz./168 g) ground walnuts
- 2 tbsp. cocoa powder
- 2 tbsp. ground cinnamon
- 2 tsp. baking powder
- 1 egg white
- 80 walnut halves for decoration

MAKES 80 COOKIES

1 Use large baking sheets and line with baking parchment. Using an electric beater, beat the butter and sugar until the mixture is light and fluffy. Sift the flour and combine with the walnuts, cocoa powder, cinnamon, and baking powder. Add to the butter mixture. Knead with floured hands to form a smooth dough

2 Shape the dough into eight cylinders, each 16 in. (40 cm) long. Wrap the cylinders in plastic; chill overnight in the refrigerator.

3 Preheat the oven to 350°F (180°C/Gas Mark 4). On a floured surface, divide each dough cylinder into 10 balls. Place on the baking sheets. Beat the egg white in a bowl. Dip the undersides of the walnut halves in it. Press a walnut into the top of each cookie. Bake the cookies, a sheet at a time, for 12–15 minutes until golden. Remove from oven, cool slightly, then transfer to a wire rack.

Double Chocolate Chunk and Nut Cookies

- ½ cup (4½ oz./56 g) unsalted butter, softened
- 6 tbsp. packed soft light- brown sugar
- ½ tsp. vanilla extract (essence)
- 1 large egg, beaten
- ⅔ cup (4 oz./75 g) self-rising flour
- ½ cup (2¼ oz./60 g) wholewheat flour
- 3½ tbsp. unsweetened cocoa powder
- 4 oz. (112 g) semisweet chocolate (at least 70% cocoa solids), roughly chopped
- ½ cup (2 oz./55 g) chopped macadamia nuts
- 3 tbsp. low fat (2%) milk

MAKES 12 COOKIES

1 Preheat the oven to 375°F (190°C/Gas Mark 5). Line two cookie sheets with baking parchment.

2 Beat the butter with the sugar and vanilla extract in a bowl until light and fluffy. Gradually add the egg, beating the mixture well after each ingredient is added.

3 Sift the wholewheat and self-rising flours, cocoa powder, and baking powder over the creamed mixture. Add the chocolate, nuts, and milk, mix together.

4 Place tablespoons of the batter on the cookie sheets, arranging the cookies 1½ in. (3.5 cm) apart so there is space for them to spread during baking. Flatten the cookies slightly with the back of a fork. Bake until they feel soft and springy, about 15 minutes.

5 Leave on the cookie sheets for a few minutes, then transfer to a wire rack. These are delicious served while still slightly warm although they will keep in an airtight container for up to five days.

Carrot-Oatmeal-Raisin Cookies

- 1 cup (4½ oz./125 g) all-purpose flour
- 2½ tsp. baking powder
- ½ tsp. salt
- ½ tsp. cinnamon
- ¼ tsp. ground cloves
- 1 cup (4 oz./115 g) rolled oats
- 1 large egg
- ½ cup (4 fl oz./125 ml) vegetable oil
- 1 tsp. vanilla extract (essence)
- 1 cup (8 oz./230 g) packed light-brown sugar
- 1 cup (about 8 oz./225 g) shredded carrots
- ¾ cup (3¼ oz./90 g) dark seedless raisins

MAKES 48 COOKIES

1 Preheat the oven to 375°F (190°C/Gas Mark 5). Coat baking sheets with a nonstick cooking spray.

2 In a medium bowl, stir together the flour, baking powder, salt, cinnamon, and cloves. Stir in the oats.

3 In a large bowl, beat together the egg, oil, and vanilla until blended. Beat in the sugar. Beat in the flour mixture in batches until evenly moistened. Fold in the carrots and raisins. The dough will be stiff.

4 For each cookie, drop one heaped teaspoon of dough onto a baking sheet, spacing about 2 in. (5 cm) apart.

5 Bake until golden brown and slightly darker around the edges, 10–12 minutes. Let the cookies stand on the baking sheets for 2 minutes. With a metal spatula, transfer the cookies to a wire rack to cool. Store in an airtight container for up to a week.

Scrumptious Cookies and Bars

These curly crescents and almond disks are easy to make and taste delicious, too.

Vanilla Crescents

- 2¼ cups (10 oz./280 g) all-purpose (plain) flour
- ¾ cup (6½ oz./185 g) butter, chilled, diced
- ½ cup (4 oz./115 g) granulated sugar
- 1 cup (4 oz./110 g) ground almonds, plus 1 tbsp.
- ¼ cup (2 oz./55 g) superfine (caster) sugar

MAKES 75 CRESCENTS

1 Use large baking sheets and line with baking parchment. Place the flour, butter, sugar, and 1 cup (110 g) almonds in a mixing bowl. Work by hand into a crumbly dough.

2 Place the dough in a sealable freezer bag. Use a rolling pin to shape the dough into a rectangle about 1 in. (2.5 cm) thick. Chill in the refrigerator overnight.

3 Preheat the oven to 350°F (180°C/Gas Mark 4). Remove the dough from the freezer bag and cut into three long strips. Then, cut each strip into 25 pieces, about 4 in. (10 cm) long.

4 Shape the pieces into crescents on a lightly floured work surface. Place on baking sheets about ¾ in. (2 cm) apart.

5 Bake the crescents, one sheet at a time, for 10–12 minutes until pale yellow. Combine the sugar and the remaining ground almonds. Coat the crescents in the mixture while still hot. Place on a wire rack to cool.

tip

If you're in a hurry, chill the dough in the freezer for 1 or 2 hours instead of overnight.

Piped Almond Circles

- 1 cup (9 oz./224 g) butter, softened
- 1 cup (8 oz./230 g) granulated sugar
- 2 egg yolks
- 1 tbsp. rum
- 1½ cups (6 oz./165 g) ground almonds
- 2¾ cups (12 oz./340 g) all-purpose (plain) flour
- 2–3 tbsp. milk
- 1 cup (150 g) good-quality chocolate

MAKES 70 CRESCENTS

1 Use two large baking sheets lined with baking parchment. Preheat oven to 350°F (180°C/Gas Mark 4). Cream the butter, sugar, egg yolks, and rum until fluffy. Combine almonds and flour and stir in alternately with milk.

2 Spoon the dough into a piping bag with a star nozzle. Pipe about 70 circles of dough onto the sheets; place them 1 in. (2.5 cm) apart. The cookies should not be too thin or they are more likely to break later. Bake, one sheet at a time, for 12–15 minutes until golden. Cool on the sheets for a few minutes; transfer to a wire rack.

3 Melt the chocolate in a bowl placed over a pan of simmering water. Dip one half of each cookie into the melted chocolate. Place on sheets of baking parchment and leave to set and dry.

Brownie Thins

- ½ cup (4 oz./112 g) unsalted butter
- ⅓ cup (1½ oz./40 g) cocoa
- pinch of salt
- 1 cup (8 oz./130 g) superfine (caster) sugar
- 2 large eggs
- ⅓ cup (1¼ oz./40 g) self-rising flour
- 1 tsp. vanilla extract (essence)
- 4 tbsp. walnut pieces

MAKES 24

1 Preheat the oven to 350°F (180°C/Gas Mark 4), then line a 12 in. x 8 in. x 1 in. (30 cm x 20 cm x 2.5cm) baking pan with baking parchment.

2 Place the butter in a saucepan, melt gently, then remove from the heat.

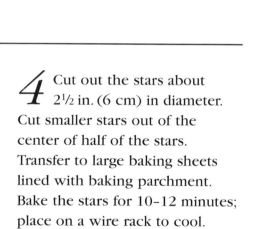

3 Sift the cocoa into the melted butter, add a pinch of salt and the sugar and mix together. Add the eggs into the cocoa mixture and whisk until smoothly blended.

4 Sift the flour into the pan, fold it into the mixture, add the vanilla and the walnuts and stir gently.

5 Pour the brownie mixture into the baking pan. Bake for 18 minutes, or until just set but still soft (it will firm up as it cools).

6 While still warm, turn out onto a large board and cut into square brownies.

Jam Stars

- 3¼ cups (14 oz./400 g) all-purpose (plain) flour
- ½ cup (2 oz./55 g) ground almonds
- ¾ cup (6 oz./170 g) superfine (caster) sugar
- ¾ cup (6½ oz./185 g) butter
- 3 egg yolks
- ⅔ cup (7 oz./200 g) red currant jelly
- 2–3 tbsp. confectioners' (icing) sugar

MAKES 60–80

1 Combine the flour, almonds, and sugar. Dot pieces of butter on top and add the egg yolks. Mix with electric beaters for 1 minute until crumbly, then press the dough together by hand.

2 Divide the dough into three pieces, shape into balls and wrap in plastic. Chill for 30 minutes.

3 Preheat the oven to 400°F (200°C/Gas Mark 6). Roll out the dough thinly on a floured work surface or between two sheets of baking parchment.

4 Cut out the stars about 2½ in. (6 cm) in diameter. Cut smaller stars out of the center of half of the stars. Transfer to large baking sheets lined with baking parchment. Bake the stars for 10–12 minutes; place on a wire rack to cool.

5 Spread the cookies that have not had stars cut out thinly with jelly. Sift the confectioners' sugar thickly over the ones that do have stars cut out. Place a sugar-coated cookie on top of each jelly-covered one. Dip the remaining stars in melted chocolate.

Christmas Tree Stack

A novel and delightful dessert that is less filling than traditional Christmas desserts. Let each guest break off one or more stars for themselves.

For the cookies

- 3 cups (13 oz./375 g) all-purpose (plain) flour
- 1 3/4 cups (8 oz./225 g) confectioners' (icing) sugar
- 1 stick (4 oz./115 g) cold unsalted butter, cut into small pieces
- 1 tbsp. water
- 1 egg, lightly beaten

To Decorate

- confectioners' (icing) sugar

MAKES 12 STAR SHAPES or 1 STACK

tip

The size of the tree is determined by the size of the star shapes. If you can't find graduating cookie cutters, create your own with cardboard cut-outs.

1 Sift together the flour and 1 cup (4 1/4 oz./125 g) confectioners' sugar into a bowl. Rub in the butter with your fingertips until the mixture resembles bread crumbs. Add the water and egg, then mix to form a stiff dough. Wrap it in plastic food wrap and chill in the fridge for 30 minutes.

2 Preheat the oven to 350°F (180°C/Gas Mark 4). Grease two or three large baking sheets. Remove the dough from the fridge and knead lightly until soft enough to roll out.

3 On a floured surface, roll out the dough 1/4 in. (5 mm) thick. Using six star-shaped cookie cutters in graduated sizes, the smallest cutter should be about 1 1/2 in. (3.75 cm) and the biggest about 4 in. (10 cm). You'll need sizes in between these measurements, too (see picture top right). Cut out two shapes of each size. Lift the shapes onto the prepared baking sheets and bake for 10–12 minutes. Remove from the oven and cool for 1 minute before transferring to a wire rack until cold.

4 Make icing by sifting the remaining confectioners' sugar into a bowl. Gradually add 2 tbsp. of water. The icing should be thick enough to coat the back of the spoon thickly.

5 To ice the cookies, first pipe icing around the edge of each one using a pastry bag with a fine nozzle. Allow the icing to set, then fill the center with icing that has been thinned with a few drops of water.

6 When the icing has almost set, assemble the cookies into a tower in order of size, pressing down slightly so the icing holds them together.

Baked Delights

Cranberry, Walnut, and Pumpkin Bread

- 1¼ cups (5½ oz./155 g) all-purpose (plain) flour
- 1 tsp. ground ginger
- 1 tsp. cinnamon
- ¾ tsp. baking soda
- ¼ tsp. salt
- 1 cup (9 oz./250 g) canned solid-pack unsweetened pumpkin
- ⅔ cup (5½ oz./150 g) packed dark-brown sugar
- ¼ cup (2 fl oz./56 ml) walnut oil or vegetable oil
- 2 large eggs, lightly beaten
- 1 tsp. vanilla extract (essence)
- ½ cup (2¼ oz./60 g) walnuts, chopped
- ½ cup (5 oz./140 g) dried cranberries

MAKES 32 PIECES

1 Preheat the oven to 350°F (180°C/Gas Mark 4). Lightly coat a 9-in. x 5-in. (23-cm x 12.5-cm) loaf pan with nonstick cooking spray.

2 In a medium bowl, sift together the flour, ginger, cinnamon, baking soda, and salt. In another medium bowl, stir together the pumpkin, sugar, oil, eggs, and vanilla until smooth. Stir in the flour mixture just until it is evenly moistened. Stir in the walnuts and the cranberries. Spoon into the prepared pan.

3 Bake until a toothpick inserted in the center comes out clean, about 45 minutes. Turn out onto a wire rack and let cool.

Perfect Pralines

- 1½ cups (11½ oz./330 g) granulated sugar
- 1 cup (8 fl oz./225 ml) low-fat (1%) milk
- ¾ cup (6 oz./170 g) firmly packed light-brown sugar
- 3 tbsp. butter or margarine
- 2 tsp. vanilla extract (essence)
- 1 cup (4 oz./125 g) coarsely chopped pecans, toasted (optional)

MAKES 70 CRESCENTS

1 Line a baking sheet with lightly buttered foil. In a large heavy saucepan, combine the granulated sugar, milk, brown sugar, butter, and vanilla. Bring to a boil, stirring constantly with a wooden spoon to dissolve the sugar. (Avoid splashing mixture onto side of the pan.) Boil for 3 minutes. If using a candy thermometer, clip onto the pan. Make sure the bulb is immersed but not touching the bottom.

2 Cook over a moderate heat, stirring occasionally, to 240°F (120°C) on a candy thermometer, soft-ball stage (15–18 minutes). Or, using a spoon, drop a small amount of hot mixture into very cold, but not icy, water. Dip your fingers into the water and form the mixture into a ball. Remove the ball from the water; it should immediately flatten and run between your fingers.

3 Remove the pan from the heat and remove the thermometer from the saucepan. Stir in the pecans (if using). Stir with a wooden spoon until the mixture is slightly thick, and begins to look cloudy, and the pecans stay suspended in the candy mixture (4–5 minutes).

4 Working quickly, drop teaspoons of the mixture onto the prepared foil, spreading each to 1½ in. (4 cm). If the mixture becomes too stiff, stir in a few drops of very hot water, until it is a softer consistency. Cool for 30 minutes or until the candies are firm and have lost their glossy shine.

Festive Delights

Treat your friends and family to this delectable collection of baked goods, ideal for serving with tea or coffee.

Mincemeat Bouchées

- ½ lb. (225 g) store bought puff pastry
- 1 small egg, beaten
- 6 oz. (175 g) mincemeat
- 1 cup (4½ oz./125 g) confectioners' (icing) sugar

MAKES 24

1 Roll out the pastry ¼ in. (5 mm) thick. Using a 2 in. (5 cm) fluted cutter, stamp out 24 circles and place on a baking sheet. Cut part of the way through the pastry in the center of each circle using a 1-in. (2.5-cm) plain cutter. Preheat the oven to 425°F (220°C/ Gas Mark 7).

2 Brush the tops with beaten egg and bake in the oven for 10 minutes or until well risen and golden brown. Lift out the center of each pastry shell and carefully scoop out any soft pastry inside. Cool the shells on a wire rack.

3 Heat the mincemeat in a saucepan over a low heat until thoroughly heated, about 5 minutes. Fill each pastry shell with a spoonful of mincemeat. Sift the confectioners' sugar into a bowl and stir in enough cold water to make a smooth glacé icing. Drizzle the icing over the mincemeat and leave to set.

Chocolate Stars

- 1 stick (4 oz./100 g) unsalted butter, softened
- ½ cup (4 oz./115 g) superfine (caster) sugar
- 1 egg, beaten
- 2 cups (9 oz./250 g) all-purpose (plain) flour
- 1 tsp. ground cinnamon
- 4 oz. (100 g) milk chocolate, melted
- 4 tbsp. finely chopped pistachios
- confectioners' (icing) sugar for dusting

MAKES ABOUT 24

1 In a mixing bowl, beat the butter until creamy. Gradually beat in the superfine sugar until pale and fluffy. Gradually beat in the egg, then sift in the flour and cinnamon. Work the ingredients together with your hands to make a firm but not sticky dough.

2 Roll out the dough about ¼ in. (5 mm) thick and cut out cookies using a star cutter, gathering up and re-rolling the dough trimmings. Divide the cookies between two greased baking sheets and chill for about 30 minutes to firm them up.

3 Preheat the oven to 350°F (180°C/Gas Mark 4) and bake the cookies for about 15 minutes until lightly browned. Transfer to a wire rack to cool.

4 Line the baking sheets with baking parchment. Dip the cookies in the melted chocolate until half coated, place on the baking sheets, and sprinkle the chopped pistachios over the chocolate. Leave to set before removing from the sheets. Dust the undipped sides of the cookies with confectioners' sugar.

Shortbread Shapes

- 3 1/4 cups (14 oz./392 g) all-purpose (plain) flour
- 3/4 cup (7 oz./168 g) butter, chopped
- 3/4 cup (3 1/2 oz./75 g) confectioners' (icing) sugar
- 1 egg plus 1 egg yolk
- pinch of salt
- 2 tsp. cream
- sugar sprinkles, candied (glacé) cherries and blanched almonds, for decoration

MAKES 50

1 Line two baking sheets with baking parchment. Sift the flour onto a work surface; make a well in the center. Add the butter, confectioners' sugar, whole egg, and salt to the well. Starting from the center work the ingredients to a smooth dough. Roll into a ball, wrap in plastic and chill 30 minutes.

2 Preheat the oven to 400°F (200°C/Gas Mark 6). Roll out the dough and use cookie cutters to cut out 50 cookies.

3 Place the shapes 1 in. (2.5 cm) apart on the sheets. Brush with the combined egg yolk and cream. Top with some sugar sprinkles or chopped glacé cherries. Bake the shortbread, one sheet at a time, for 10–15 minutes until golden.

Oatmeal Macaroons

- 1/4 cup (2 1/4 oz./65 g) butter
- 1 1/2 cups (5 1/2 oz./150 g) original rolled oats
- 1 egg
- 1/4 cup (2 oz./56 g) firmly packed light brown sugar
- 1/2 tsp. ground cinnamon
- pinch of ground cloves
- 1/2 cup (4 oz./115 g) dried apricots or dried pitted dates, chopped in small pieces
- 1 tsp. grated lemon zest

MAKES 35

1 Line two baking sheets baking parchment. Preheat the oven to 350°F (180°C/Gas Mark 4). Melt the butter in a pan, add the rolled oats and brown them lightly; stir constantly. Transfer to a large plate and allow to cool.

2 Beat the egg, sugar, and spices with electric beaters until very fluffy. Stir in the oats, dried fruit, and lemon zest.

3 Using a moistened teaspoon, form the mixture into 35 walnut-sized mounds and place on baking sheets about 1 in. (5 cm) apart.

4 Bake the cookies, one sheet at a time, on the top shelf of the oven for 15–18 minutes until they are light brown. Place on a wire rack to cool.

CHAPTER EIGHT

PARTY DRINKS

Whiz up a smoothie, shake up a cocktail, spoon
some cream on a flavored coffee or spice up some
wine—the festive season is the perfect excuse for
serving drinks with flair. Your party selection, both
alcoholic and nonalcoholic, is here.

★ have a merry christmas ★

Winter Warmers

Whether to welcome your guests to your home, or to round off a meal, these delicious and warming beverages will bring festive cheer.

Mulled Wine Punch

- 2 x 25 fl oz. (750 ml) bottles red wine
- 12 fl oz. (370 ml) ruby port
- 12 fl oz. (370 ml) water
- 2 level tbsp. sugar
- 8 tsp. lemon juice
- ½ tsp. nutmeg
- ½ tsp. cinnamon or 1-in. (2.5-cm) cinnamon stick, if preferred
- 4 cloves
- 1 large ripe orange, sliced

SERVES 6

1 Take a large saucepan with a lid and add all of the other ingredients, bar the orange, and stir.

2 Heat the wine gently, but do not allow to boil. When it starts to simmer, turn the heat down a little to keep the wine hot.

3 If serving the mulled wine from a tureen or other heatproof bowl, fill with hot water to warm through. Wipe dry just before adding the wine. Add orange slices just before serving.

4 Use a ladle, or a small jug, with a lip to transfer the hot liquid to the glasses or cups easily. Keep a cloth handy for drips.

Liqueur Coffees

For a Basic Liqueur Coffee

- ½ fl oz. (15 ml) preferred alcohol (see list right)
- 5 fl oz. (150 ml) hot black coffee
- ½ tsp. sugar
- whipping cream
- grated chocolate for topping (optional)

MAKES 1 CUP

1 Pour chosen alcohol into the cup or heatproof glass. Add the coffee. Stir in the sugar, as this helps keep the cream and coffee layers separate.

2 Whip the cream until thick but still of a pouring consistency. Gently pour over the back of a teaspoon to float on the black coffee.

tip

For international variations, replace the alcohol as below:

French: *1 fl oz. (30 ml) Cointreau*
Caribbean: *1 fl oz. (30 ml) dark rum*
German: *½ fl oz. (15 ml) kirsch*
Irish: *1 fl oz. (30 ml) Irish whisky*
Italian: *½ fl oz. (15 ml) amaretto*
Jamaican: *½ fl oz. (15 ml) white rum*
Mexican: *½ fl oz. (15 ml) Gold Tequila*
Russian: *1 fl oz. (30 ml) vodka*

For a slightly sweeter coffee flavor, also add ½ measure Kahlua or Tia Maria to the above versions.

Nonalcoholic Drinks

Make sure that you can offer wonderful drinks for friends and family who don't like alcohol or who have to drive home.

Mocha Magic

- 1¼ cups (½ pint/300 ml) freshly made strong black coffee
- 4 tbsp. chocolate-flavored syrup
- light brown sugar, to taste
- ⅝ cup (¼ pint/150 ml) heavy cream, lightly whipped
- mini chocolate flake bar and coffee beans, to garnish

SERVES 2

1 Pour the coffee into two heatproof glasses and stir in the liqueur. Add sugar to taste, stirring until it has dissolved.

2 Top each coffee with large spoonfuls of whipped cream. Sprinkle over the chocolate flake and add a coffee bean to each glass. Serve at once.

tip

Drink the hot coffee through the whipped cream topping because if you stir the cream into the coffee it will cool it down too much.

Hot Wassail

- 4 cups (1¾ pint/1 liter) unsweetened apple juice
- 4 cups (1¾ pint/1 liter) unsweetened pineapple juice
- 2 cups (¾ pint/500 ml) cranberry juice
- ¼ tsp. ground nutmeg
- 1 cinnamon stick
- 3 whole cloves
- 10 lemon slices

SERVES 10

1 Place all the ingredients into a large saucepan and heat until simmering. On a low heat, simmer for at least 10 minutes before serving in a heat-proof glass with a slice of lemon.

❄ ***Did you know?***

The word "wassail" comes from an Anglo-Saxon toast for good health—"waes hael". To wassail is to drink someone's health at Christmas time.

Mango, Peach, and Apricot Fizz

- 1 ripe mango
- 1 ripe peach
- 2 large ripe apricots
- 2¼ cups (18 fl oz./500 ml) ginger ale
- fresh mint or lemon balm leaves, to garnish (optional)

SERVES 4

1 Peel the mango and cut the flesh away from the central seed. Roughly chop the flesh and put it into a blender or food processor. (Alternatively, if you are using a stick blender, put the mango in a large tall jug).

2 Cover the peach and apricots with boiling water and leave for about 30 seconds, then drain and cool under cold water. Slip off the skins and roughly chop the flesh, discarding the pits. Add the flesh to the mango in the blender or food processor.

3 Pour enough of the ginger ale over just to cover the fruit, then process until smooth. Pour in the remaining ginger ale and process again.

4 Quickly pour into tall glasses, preferably over crushed ice. Decorate with fresh mint or lemon balm leaves, if you like. Serve immediately with wide straws or swizzle sticks.

Banana and Lime Smoothie

- 1 banana
- ¾ cup (6 fl oz./180 ml) pineapple juice
- juice of ½ lime
- finely grated zest of 1 lime (optional)

SERVES 2

1 Peel the banana and cut it into small chunks. Place it in a blender or food processor.

2 Add the pineapple and lime juices. For a stronger citrus flavour, also add lime zest to taste. Whizz until the mixture is smooth, but do not overblend.

3 Pour into a tall glass. Sprinkle with additional lime zest, if desired.

Classy Cocktails

Exotic drinks, stylishly presented, will make your party seem special—just remember to have plenty of ice, mixers, and cocktail glasses available.

Berry Martini

- 9 oz. (250 g) mixed berries
- 1½ tbsp. confectioners' (icing) sugar
- juice of ½ lemon
- 5 fl oz. (150 ml) water
- 8 fl oz. (240 ml) vodka
- 3 fl oz. (90 ml) crème de cassis
- 6 bay leaves

SERVES 6

1 Blend the fruit in a food processor, then push it through a sieve to remove any seeds.

2 Mix the purée with the rest of the ingredients, stirring to create a smooth mixture.

3 Chill the mixture. Make a slit in each bay leaf from the edge to the center vein. Pour out the berry martinis, then adorn each glass with a single leaf before serving.

Bourbon Triple Sour

- 1 fl oz. (30 ml) bourbon
- 1 fl oz. (30 ml) triple sec
- 1 fl oz. (30 ml) lemon juice
- 1 tsp. sugar syrup
- ice
- 1 slice of apple
- 1 green olive

MAKES 1 DRINK

1 Place the liquid ingredients into a cocktail shaker with some ice. Shake to blend the ingredients. Strain into a glass and add apple slice and olive to garnish.

Rose Sparkle

- 1 fl oz. (30 ml) Southern Comfort
- ½ fl oz. (15 ml) strawberry liqueur
- 3 fl oz. (90 ml) Champagne
- 1 fl oz. (30 ml) tonic
- 4 strawberry chunks
- 3 orange chunks

MAKES 1 DRINK

1 Mix the Southern Comfort and strawberry liqueur together. Pour into a flute. Add the Champagne and tonic and stir. Finally, add the fruit chunks with a spoon to avoid spills.

Champagne Cocktails

- ¼ pint (150 ml) brandy
- 6 sugar cubes
- 9 oz. (250 g) raspberries (frozen are fine if fresh not available)
- 1 x 25 fl oz. (750 ml) bottle Champagne or sparkling wine
- ¼ cup (55 g) superfine (caster) sugar

SERVES 6

1 Pour in 1 fl oz. (30 ml) brandy into each of six Champagne flutes, then pop in the sugar cube. Add a generous amount of raspberries to each flute, then top up with Champagne or sparkling wine.

Bloody Caesar

- 1 fl oz. (30 ml) vodka
- 5 fl oz. (150 ml) clamato juice
- 1 dash Worcestershire sauce
- 1 dash Tabasco® sauce
- pinch salt and pepper
- celery salt
- 1 celery stick
- 1 lime wedge

MAKES 1 DRINK

1 Rim a tall glass with celery salt and fill with ice. Pour the vodka, clamato juice, Worcestershire sauce, Tabasco® sauce, and salt and pepper over the ice. Garnish with the celery stick and lime wedge. Alternatively you could make a Bloody Mary, simply by replacing clamato juice with tomato juice and follow the recipe above.

Did you know?

The Bloody Caesar cocktail was invented in 1969 by Walter Chell, a bartender, to commemorate the opening of Marco's Italian restaurant in Calgary, Alberta. It rapidly became Canada's favorite cocktail.

TEMPLATES & CHARTS

Pages 18-19 Pretty Pink Angel

Template for Standing Angel

Enlarge templates by 150 percent

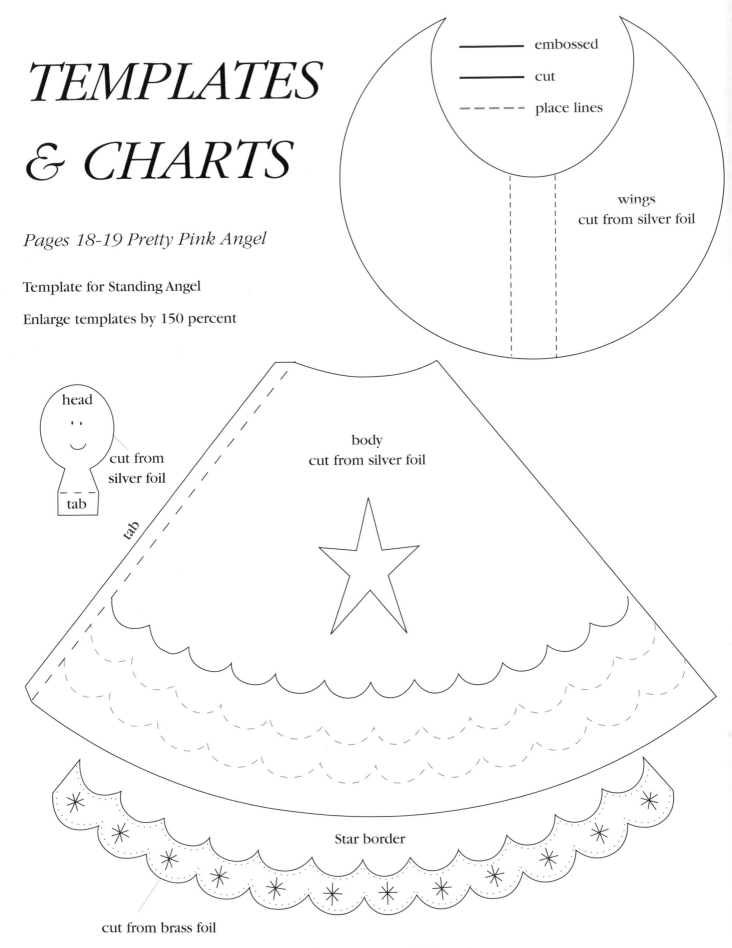

embossed

cut

place lines

wings
cut from silver foil

head

cut from
silver foil

tab

tab

body
cut from silver foil

Star border

cut from brass foil

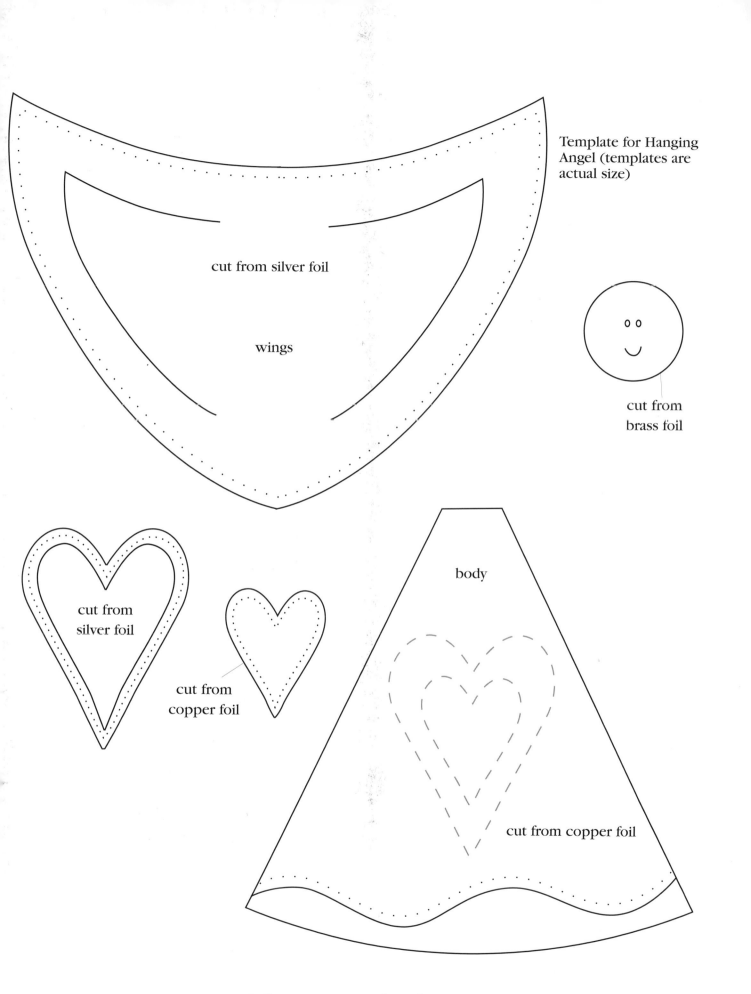

Template for Hanging
Angel (templates are
actual size)

cut from silver foil

wings

cut from
brass foil

cut from
silver foil

cut from
copper foil

body

cut from copper foil

t e m p l a t e s   a n d   c h a r t s

Page 22 Country-Style Heart

Enlarge template by 150 percent

Enlarge templates on a Xerox machine by just selecting or keying in the stated multiplier.

Trace over the outlines and detail lines of the template using a sharp hard pencil onto a sheet of tracing paper. Remove the tracing paper and, with a soft pencil, shade over the lines on the reverse side. Now place the rubbed side down, onto the surface where you wish to transfer the template. Draw firmly over the lines again with the hard pencil; this will transfer the pencil marks. Check that all the lines have been transferred before taking off the tracing paper.

Alternatively, place a sheet of carbon paper (or dressmaker's carbon paper if working on fabric), ink-side down under the tracing of the outlines (do not shade over the lines on the reverse side). Draw firmly over the outlines again to transfer the lines.

Page 26 Tin Tree Decorations

Templates actual size

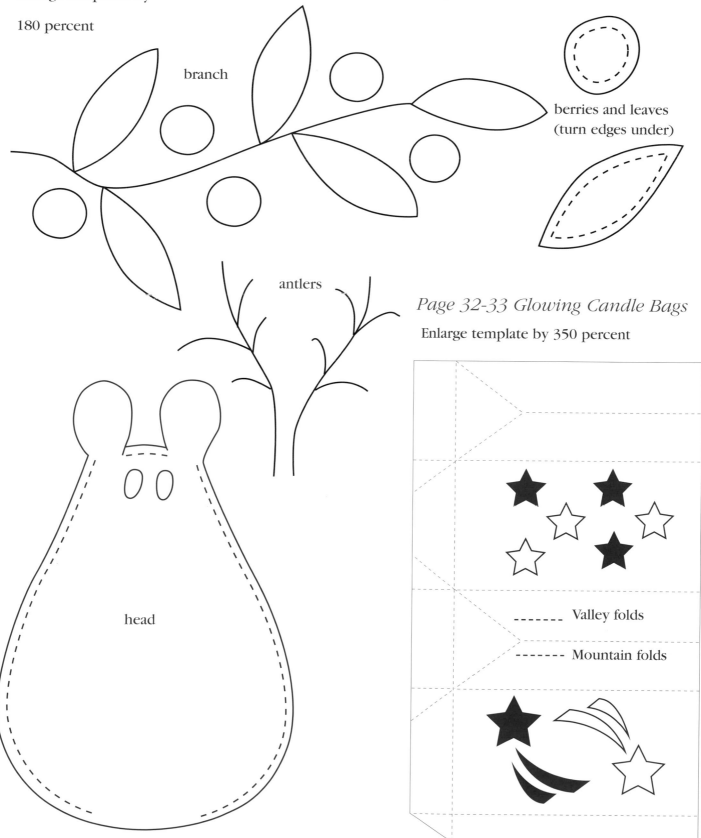

Pages 28-29 Reindeer Fun

Enlarge templates by

180 percent

branch

berries and leaves
(turn edges under)

antlers

head

Page 32-33 Glowing Candle Bags

Enlarge template by 350 percent

- - - - - Valley folds

- - - - - Mountain folds

Pages 44-45 Gift-laden Coronet

Actual size

fold

tab

tab

tab

Pages 46-47 Swag of Gift Bags
Actual size

petal
cut 120

gathering thread

Pages 48-49 Rose and Ivy Panel

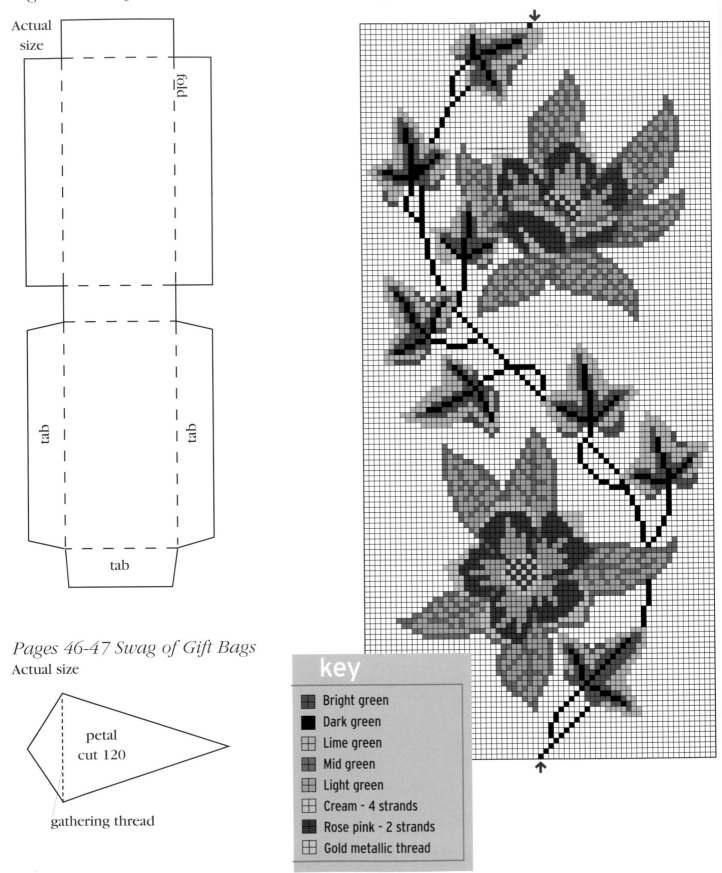

key

▦	Bright green
■	Dark green
⊞	Lime green
▦	Mid green
⊞	Light green
⊞	Cream - 4 strands
▦	Rose pink - 2 strands
⊞	Gold metallic thread

Page 50-51 Holly Berry Base

key
- ■ Purple
- ⊡ Light green
- ■ Red
- ⊞ Dark green

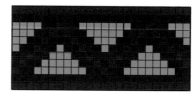

For the Table Centerpiece

Repeat to fill each strip (check the number of repeats will fit. You may need to work extra stitches to fill the plastic canvas.)

For the Serving Dish

Repeat to fill each strip

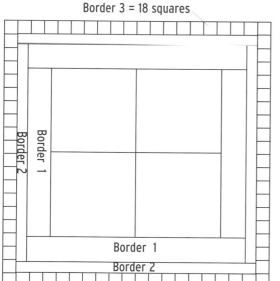

Border 3 = 18 squares

Border 3
Border 2
Border 1
Border 1
Border 2

Cutting the border strips

Border 1 red floral:
2 strips 4 in. x 26 in. (10.5 cm x 66 cm);
2 strips 4 in. x 33 in. (10.5 cm x 84 cm)

Border 2 gold:
2 strips $1^1/_2$ in. x 33 in. (4 cm x 84 cm);
2 strips $1^1/_2$ in. x 36 in. (4 cm x 92 cm)

Border 3 red and green squares:
38 squares $2^1/_2$ in. x $2^1/_2$ in. (6.5 cm x 6.5 cm) in each of red and green—76 in total. Join 2 lengths of 18 squares and 2 lengths of 20 squares.

Page 54-55 Patchwork Tablecloth

Numbers given for each of 4 central blocks

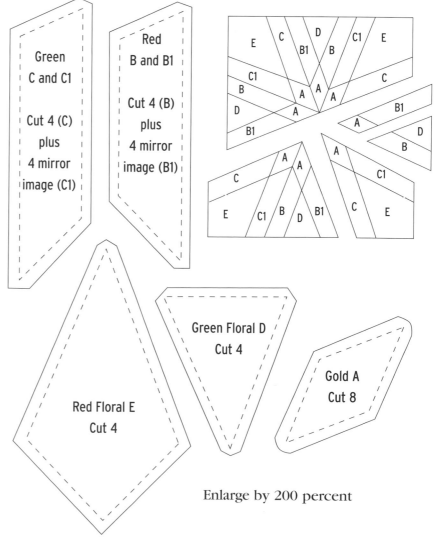

Green
C and C1

Cut 4 (C)
plus
4 mirror
image (C1)

Red
B and B1

Cut 4 (B)
plus
4 mirror
image (B1)

Red Floral E
Cut 4

Green Floral D
Cut 4

Gold A
Cut 8

Enlarge by 200 percent

Page 56-57 Silk Table Runner

Enlarge to 160 percent

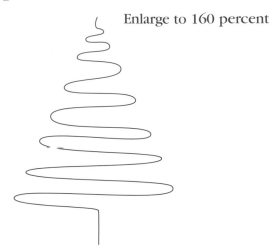

Page 60-61 Festive Floral Linen

For the napkins

Page 58-59 Beaded Napkin Rings

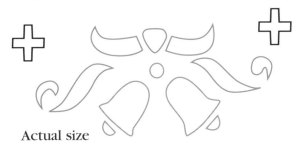

Actual size

key

White	
Medium pink	
Pale orange	
Dark pink	
Beige/gray	
Pale beige/gray	
Burgundy	
Deep coral	
Dark green	
Medium green	
Pale green	
Buttermilk	
Pale pink	

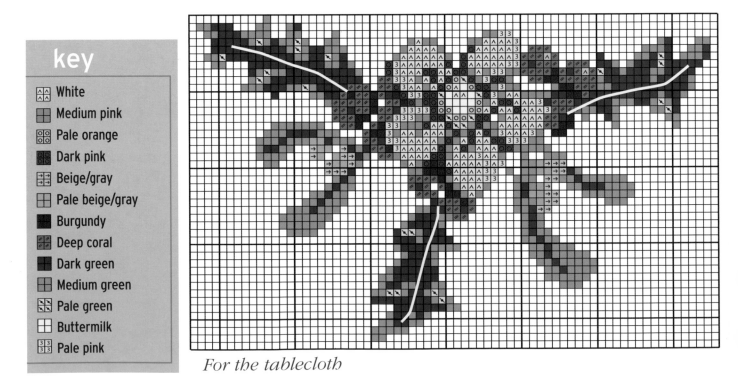

For the tablecloth

t e m p l a t e s   a n d   c h a r t s

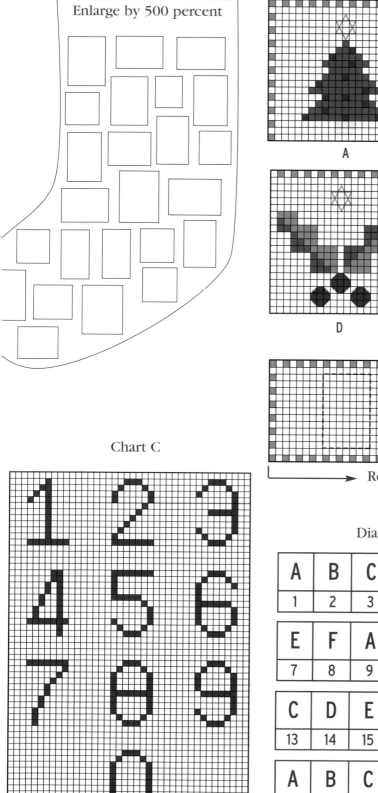

Page 65 Advent Stocking

Enlarge by 500 percent

Chart C

Pages 70-71 Picture Advent Calendar

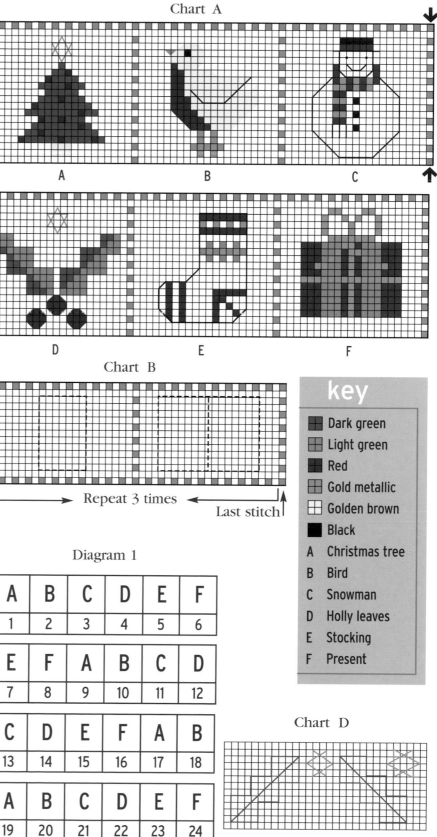

Chart A

A   B   C

D   E   F

Chart B

Repeat 3 times ← Last stitch

key

- ■ Dark green
- ▦ Light green
- ■ Red
- ▦ Gold metallic
- □ Golden brown
- ■ Black
- A Christmas tree
- B Bird
- C Snowman
- D Holly leaves
- E Stocking
- F Present

Diagram 1

A	B	C	D	E	F
1	2	3	4	5	6

E	F	A	B	C	D
7	8	9	10	11	12

C	D	E	F	A	B
13	14	15	16	17	18

A	B	C	D	E	F
19	20	21	22	23	24

Chart D

t e m p l a t e s   a n d   c h a r t s

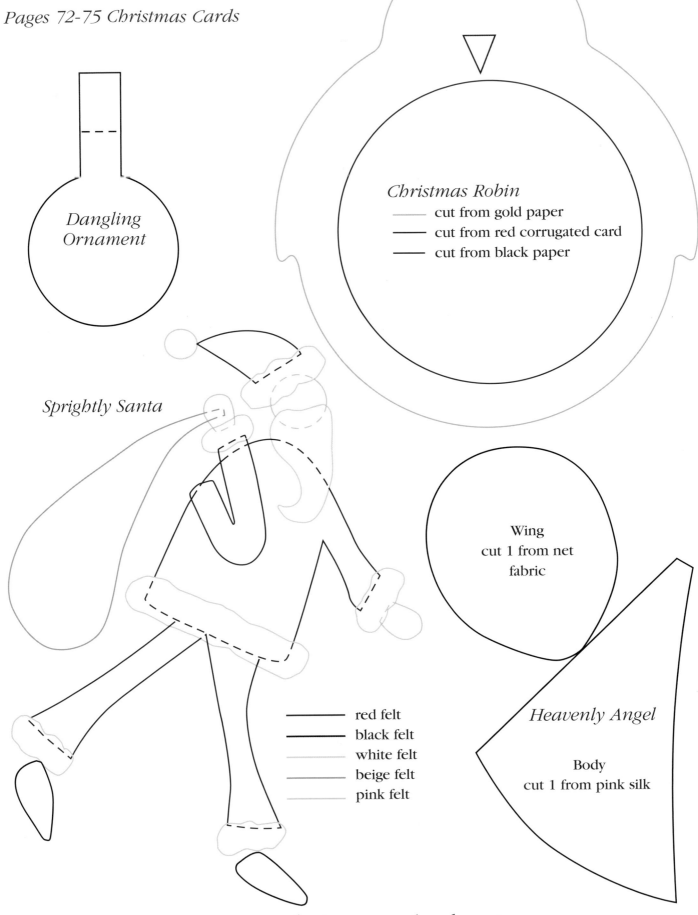

*Dangling
Ornament*

Christmas Robin

— cut from gold paper
— cut from red corrugated card
— cut from black paper

Sprightly Santa

Wing
cut 1 from net
fabric

— red felt
— black felt
— white felt
— beige felt
— pink felt

Heavenly Angel

Body
cut 1 from pink silk

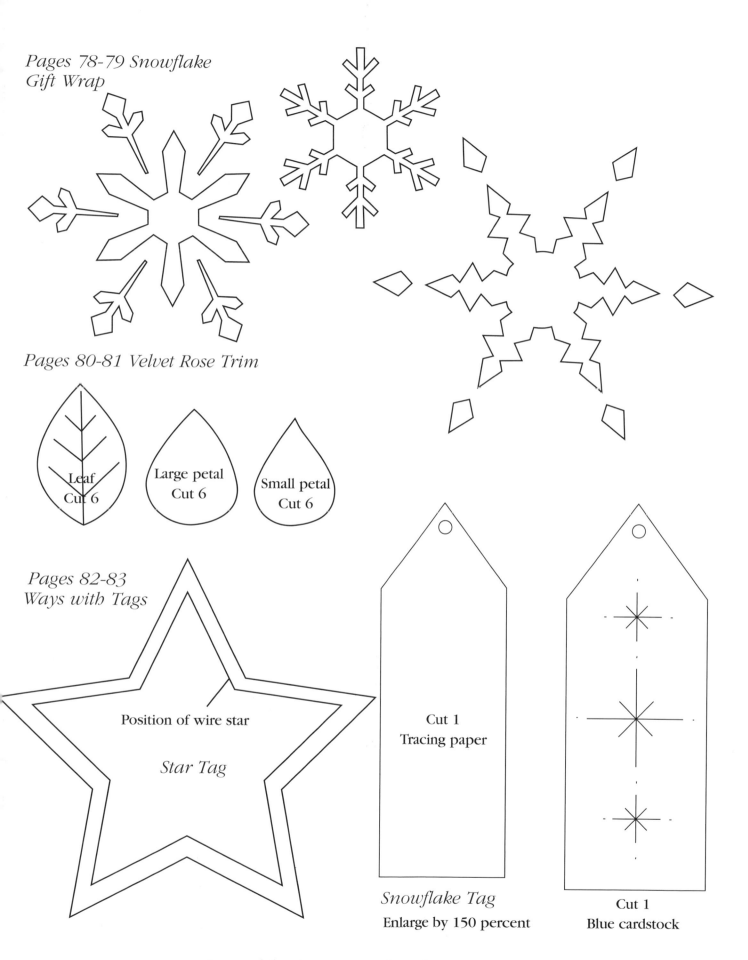

*Pages 78-79 Snowflake
Gift Wrap*

Pages 80-81 Velvet Rose Trim

Leaf
Cut 6

Large petal
Cut 6

Small petal
Cut 6

*Pages 82-83
Ways with Tags*

Position of wire star

Star Tag

Cut 1
Tracing paper

Snowflake Tag
Enlarge by 150 percent

Cut 1
Blue cardstock

t e m p l a t e s   a n d   c h a r t s

Cut along black lines to make stencil

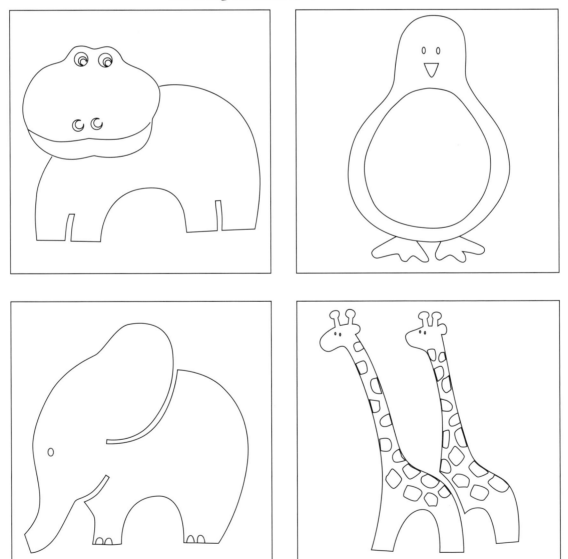

Pages 90-91 Pretty Padded Hangers

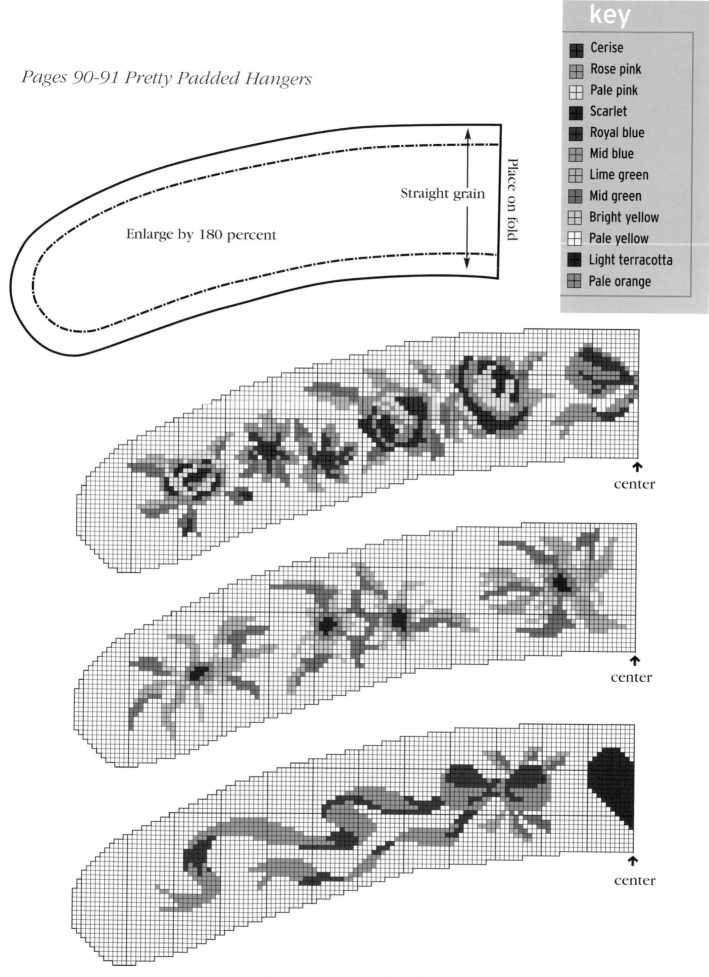

Straight grain

Place on fold

Enlarge by 180 percent

key

Cerise	
Rose pink	
Pale pink	
Scarlet	
Royal blue	
Mid blue	
Lime green	
Mid green	
Bright yellow	
Pale yellow	
Light terracotta	
Pale orange	

center

center

center

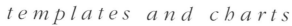

t e m p l a t e s   a n d   c h a r t s

Page 94 Filigree Jewelry

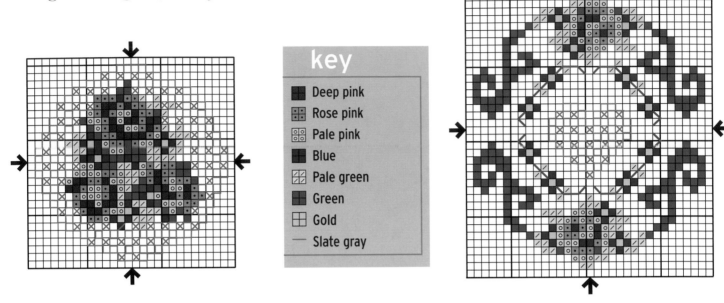

key

- Deep pink
- Rose pink
- Pale pink
- Blue
- Pale green
- Green
- Gold
- — Slate gray

Pages 96-97 Snowflake Frosted Vase

key

■	Black	■	Bright pink	⊞	Yellow	■ Orange
■	Christmas green	▨	Gray green	▨	Green	⊞ Pale pink
⊞	Pale green	⦂⦂	Light Christmas green	▨	Bright Christmas green	⊞ Pink
⊞	Olive green	⊞	Light green	■	Gray	▦ Dark pink
■	Dark red	⊞	Pale peach	⊞	Light gray	— Backstitch
▨	Red	⊞	Pale yellow	⊞	White	

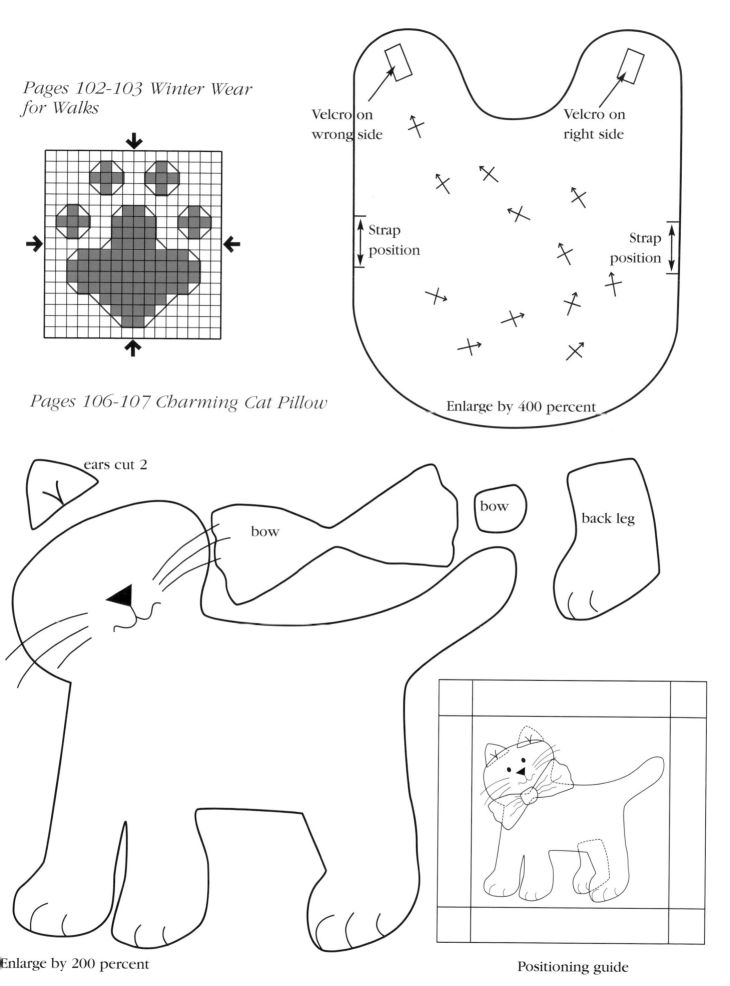

Pages 102-103 Winter Wear for Walks

Velcro on wrong side

Velcro on right side

Strap position

Strap position

Enlarge by 400 percent

Pages 106-107 Charming Cat Pillow

ears cut 2

bow

bow

back leg

Enlarge by 200 percent

Positioning guide

t e m p l a t e s   a n d   c h a r t s

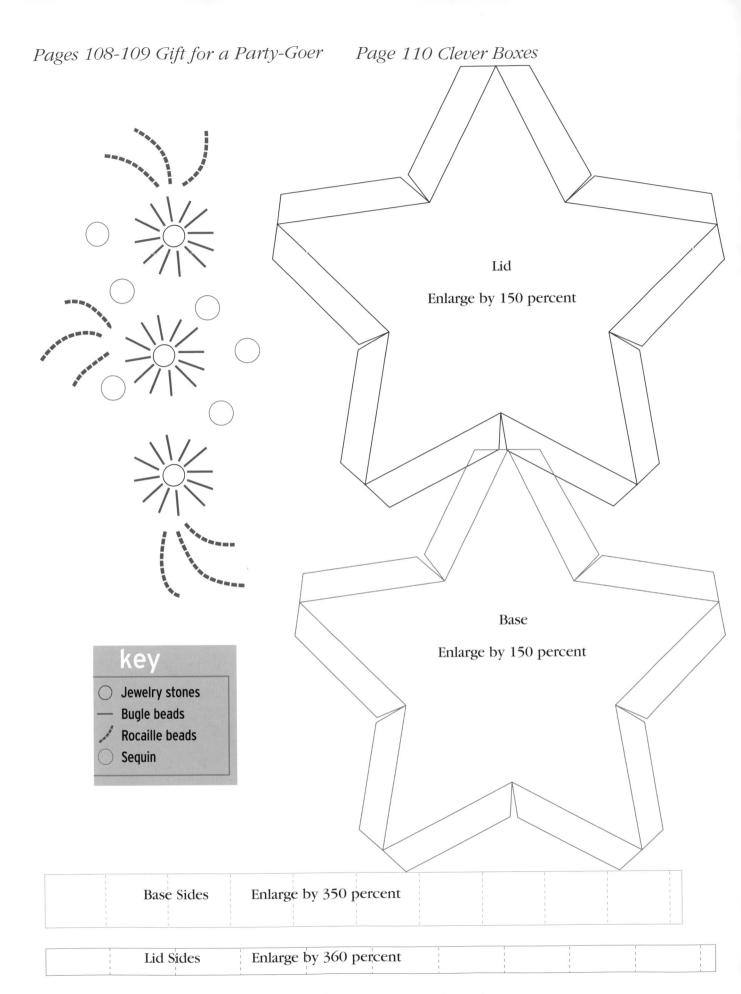

Lid

Enlarge by 150 percent

Base

Enlarge by 150 percent

key

○ Jewelry stones
— Bugle beads
╱ Rocaille beads
○ Sequin

Base Sides   Enlarge by 350 percent

Lid Sides   Enlarge by 360 percent

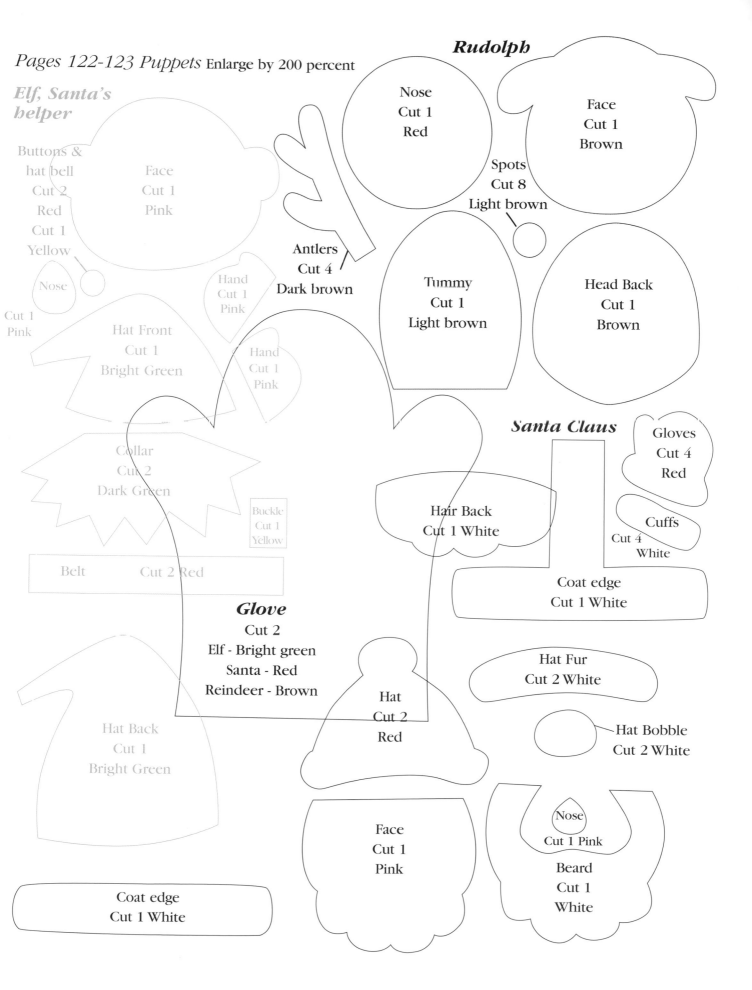

Pages 122-123 Puppets Enlarge by 200 percent

Rudolph

Elf, Santa's helper

Buttons & hat bell
Cut 2
Red
Cut 1
Yellow

Face
Cut 1
Pink

Nose
Cut 1
Red

Face
Cut 1
Brown

Spots
Cut 8
Light brown

Nose
Cut 1
Pink

Hand
Cut 1
Pink

Antlers
Cut 4
Dark brown

Tummy
Cut 1
Light brown

Head Back
Cut 1
Brown

Hat Front
Cut 1
Bright Green

Hand
Cut 1
Pink

Santa Claus

Gloves
Cut 4
Red

Collar
Cut 2
Dark Green

Buckle
Cut 1
Yellow

Hair Back
Cut 1 White

Cuffs
Cut 4
White

Belt   Cut 2 Red

Coat edge
Cut 1 White

Glove
Cut 2
Elf - Bright green
Santa - Red
Reindeer - Brown

Hat Fur
Cut 2 White

Hat
Cut 2
Red

Hat Bobble
Cut 2 White

Hat Back
Cut 1
Bright Green

Nose
Cut 1 Pink

Face
Cut 1
Pink

Beard
Cut 1
White

Coat edge
Cut 1 White

templates and charts

281

Page 123 Tiny Reindeer

Actual size

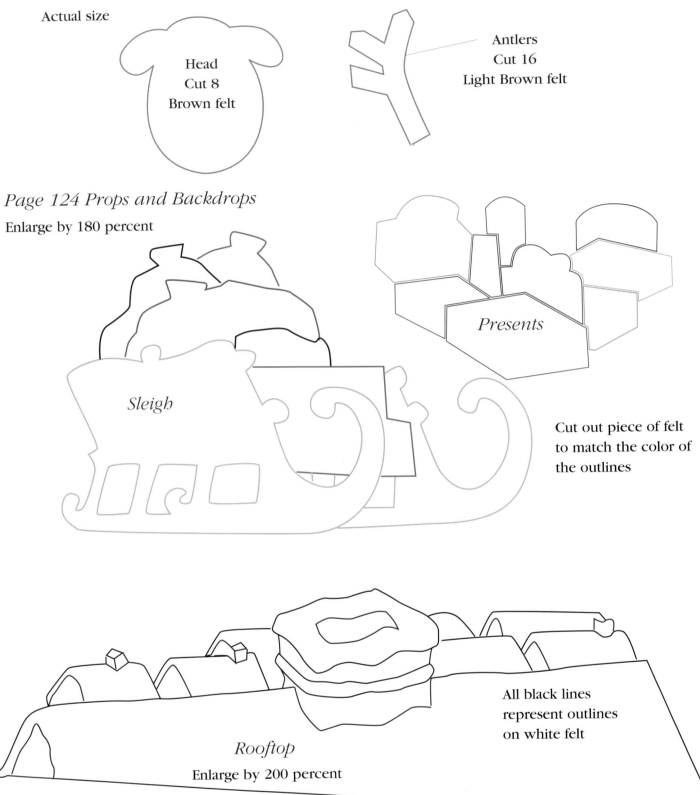

Head
Cut 8
Brown felt

Antlers
Cut 16
Light Brown felt

Page 124 Props and Backdrops

Enlarge by 180 percent

Sleigh

Presents

Cut out piece of felt
to match the color of
the outlines

All black lines
represent outlines
on white felt

Rooftop

Enlarge by 200 percent

t e m p l a t e s   a n d   c h a r t s

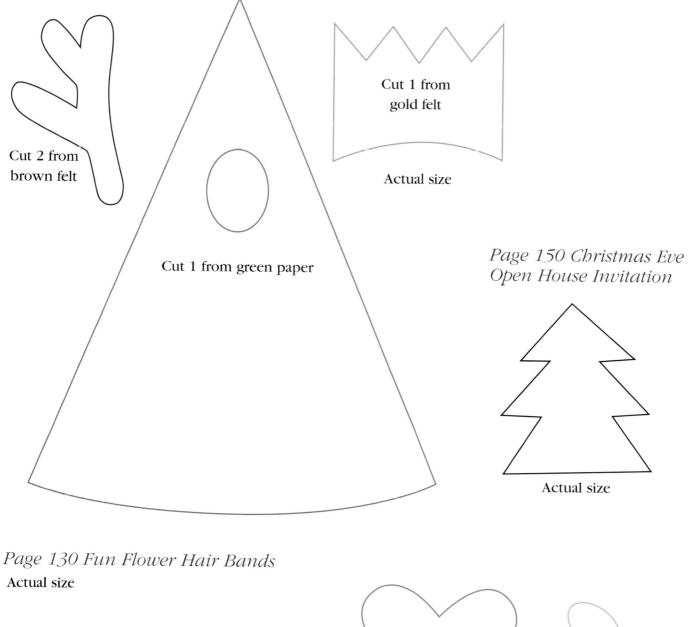

Page 127 Photo Christmas Cards

Cut 2 from
brown felt

Cut 1 from green paper

Cut 1 from
gold felt

Actual size

*Page 150 Christmas Eve
Open House Invitation*

Actual size

Page 130 Fun Flower Hair Bands

Actual size

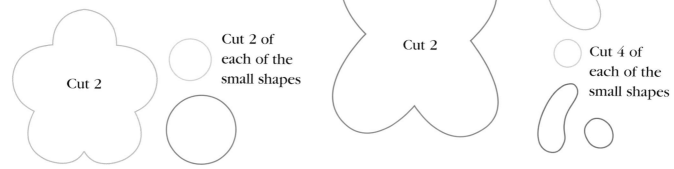

Cut 2

Cut 2 of
each of the
small shapes

Cut 2

Cut 4 of
each of the
small shapes

Use the colored felt that matches the outline of the shape

Index

index

For Reader's Digest
Canadian Project Editor Pamela Chichinskas-Johnson
U.S. Project Editor Dolores York
Senior Designer Andrée Payette
Cover Design Anik Belliveau
Contributing Editor Anita Winterberg
Production Manager Gordon Howlett

Reader's Digest Association (Canada) Ltd.
Vice President, Book Editorial Robert Goyette

For Reader's Digest Association, Inc.
Editor-in-Chief Neil Wertheimer
President Eric W. Schrier

Creative Plus Publishing Limited
2nd Floor, 151 High Street, Billericay, Essex, CM12 9AB, England
www.creative-plus.co.uk

Project Manager Corrine Ochiltree

The Creative Plus Team plus additional contributions from:
Writer Wendy Sweetser
Indexer Gisela Roberts
Editors Sue Churchill, Gisela Roberts, Patsy North, Margaret Maino
Projects by Gina Read, Venita Kidwai, Lianne South, Cheryl Owen, Katharine Gurney, Diane Baistow, Sharon Blackman
Art Direction Venita Kidwai
Photography by Alan Roberts, Richard Jackson
Illustrations Gina Read, Venita Kidwai
Authentication Jan Senn, Judith Ferguson
Layout designers Gina Read, Venita Kidwai

Ingredient Substitutions

Every attempt has been made to use recipe ingredients that are available throughout the world. In some cases, however, some may be known by another name or may require the substitution of a different ingredient altogether. Use the chart below as a handy reference when in doubt about a particular ingredient.

In this book we use...	...but where you live, it may be called by another name or you may need to substitute or make your own.
Amaretti	Almond-flavored macaroons
Apple butter	Apple puree
Baking soda	Bicarbonate of soda
Chocolate, semi-sweet, bittersweet	Dark, semi-sweet, and bittersweet chocolate are interchangeable in recipes; use any good-quality cooking chocolate
Chocolate-mint candy	After-dinner mints
Cocoa powder, unsweetened	Pure cocoa powder
Coconut flakes	Shredded coconut
Cornstarch	Cornflour
Cranberries, dried, sweetened	Use dried (unsweetened) cranberries
Flour, all-purpose	Plain household flour or white flour
Granola	Muesli
Half and half	Equal parts cream and milk
Heavy cream	Double cream
Jelly	Jam
Maple extract	Maple syrup
Piecrust mix	Ready prepared or frozen pastry
Raisins, golden	Sultanas
Ratafia biscuits	Almond-flavored macaroons
Sugar, confectioners'	Icing sugar
Sugar, granulated	Ordinary white sugar
Sugar, superfine	Caster sugar
Vanilla extract	Vanilla essence